D1066420

Adventures of
the Dialectic

Northwestern University
STUDIES IN *Phenomenology &*
Existential Philosophy

GENERAL EDITOR
John Wild

ASSOCIATE EDITOR
James M. Edie

CONSULTING EDITORS
Hubert L. Dreyfus
William Earle
J. N. Findlay
Dagfinn Føllesdal
Marjorie Grene
Aron Gurwitsch
Emmanuel Levinas
Alphonso Lingis
Maurice Natanson
Paul Ricoeur
George Schrader
Calvin O. Schrag
Herbert Spiegelberg
Charles Taylor

Maurice Merleau-Ponty

Translated by

Adventures of the Dialectic

JOSEPH BIEN

NORTHWESTERN UNIVERSITY PRESS

EVANSTON   1973

Copyright © 1973 by Northwestern University Press
All rights reserved
Library of Congress Card Catalog Number: 72–96697
ISBN 0–8101–0404–0
Printed in the United States of America

Originally published in French under the title *Les Aventures de la dialectique,* copyright © 1955 by Editions Gallimard, Paris.

Joseph Bien is Associate Professor of Philosophy at the University of Missouri at Columbia.

Contents

Translator's Introduction

MERLEAU-PONTY AND THE CRISIS IN MARXISM

A LARGE NUMBER OF WORKS have been devoted to various aspects of Merleau-Ponty's phenomenology and to his contributions to theories of perception and language. By contrast, his political philosophy has, at least in English-speaking countries, passed almost unnoticed.[1] This is especially surprising, for Merleau-Ponty constantly confronted his thought with Marxism and wrote both *Humanism and Terror* and *Adventures of the Dialectic* for this purpose. Almost all his writings contain references to politics and political theory, and extensive treatment is accorded to political subjects in several books.[2]

Since it would be impossible in the following short essay to present Merleau-Ponty's political philosophy in its totality, I have limited myself to one of the central problems in Marxism that Merleau-Ponty tried to resolve, namely, the realization of the potentially universal class, the proletariat. After a presentation

1. Even such a book-length treatment as Albert Rabil's *Merleau-Ponty: Existentialist of the Social World* (New York and London, 1967) devotes rather limited space to his political philosophy.
2. One immediately thinks of the last chapter on freedom and the long footnote on historical materialism in *Phenomenology of Perception,* of the two essays dealing with Marxism in *Sense and Non-Sense,* of his essays on Machiavelli and Montaigne and most of the essays in Part III of *Signs,* and of his reference to Marx in *In Praise of Philosophy.* Claude Lefort has informed us that another of Merleau-Ponty's soon-to-be-published posthumous works deals in part with the political.

of the background out of which this problem arose for Merleau-Ponty, I will (1) show the origins of this problem in Hegel's philosophy and its development from Marx's critique of capitalist society; (2) explain why Merleau-Ponty found unsatisfactory the different interpretations of the proletariat class in Lukács, Lenin, Sartre, and Trotsky; and (3) briefly criticize Merleau-Ponty's conclusions.

I

IN POSTWAR FRANCE many new influences were at work in the intellectual community. On the one hand, much of the French Right had been discredited by its collaboration with the German occupation forces, and, at the same time, the Communist Party had been elevated to a place of prestige for its participation in the underground movement; on the other hand, the recently discovered *Economic and Philosophic Manuscripts of 1844* laid new stress on the humanistic aspects of Marxism, and Hyppolite's and Kojève's interpretations of Hegel tended to reinforce this reading of Marx. Alain's "politics of understanding," by which social problems were to be resolved one by one through discussion by reasonable men, had been discredited by the force of Nazism and the occupation of France by the German armies. "Violence beyond reason" had brought about the situation, and it was only again by violence that it had been overcome. In a period of historical calm, during which one perfects the established regime and adjusts its laws, one might hope for a history without extreme violence.

Merleau-Ponty, however, saw the postwar period not as one of calm but as one in which society was crumbling, and he saw its traditional grounds as no longer sufficient for constructing human relations. It was one in which each man's liberty threatened all the others, one in which violence was once more the daily topic; and the only solution lay with man, who had to reconstruct human relations. Starting from his own historical situation and following Marx's critique, Merleau-Ponty found the appeal to "rationalism" in the Western liberal countries only an excuse for not examining their own situation of violence. While through reflection a man may consider himself simply as man and thus join all other men, as soon as he returns to his everyday life he finds himself again to be a worker, a university professor, a banker, a doctor, and so forth. The attempt to speak beyond one's particular situation and class, to speak before ideology, is itself seen to be an ideology when the actual relations of man with man are examined—not in the constitutions and anthems of Western liberal countries but in their actual imperialism, race relations, and distribution of wealth. One then finds the appeal to "man in the abstract" or to the "reasonable man" to be but another way of defending whatever the established violence may be. The situation in communist countries was also found wanting, inasmuch as the balance between the objective and subjective factors of the revolution had been ruptured. This had supposedly resulted from the fact that the revolution took place in a single backward country—Russia—rather than on an international scale. The emphasis had been laid on building the economic infrastructure of Russian society and on the "clairvoyance of the Party" rather than on the world proletariat. Whether this emphasis on one aspect of Marxism would lead to a change in its nature in Russia was not yet clear. At best one could say that the revolution had passed into a period of Thermidor from which it might or might not return. In the meantime, there remained the question of how violence was to be justified, for "it takes a long time for [the Revolution] to extend its economic and legal infrastructures into the lived relations of men—a long time, therefore, before it can be indisputable and guaranteed against harmful reversals to the old world." [3]

One might question this limited choice that we appear to have between communism and Western liberalism. It should not be seen simply as some new either/or situation but rather should be understood as deriving from a basic premise in Merleau-Ponty's political philosophy—that politics is an order of the real world and therefore that any theory that claims to be political philosophy must also provide for its own realization. [4] Anything else, no matter how interestingly or forcefully argued, turns out to be another utopian exercise. Both communism and liberalism were in some form instantiated in the world. Any new or different description of man's relations would also have to include

3. *Humanism and Terror*, trans. John O'Neill (Boston, 1969), pp. 104–5.
4. *Ibid.*, pp. xxxii–vi.

the real possibility of its instantiation in order to merit serious examination.[5]

In *Humanism and Terror* and *Adventures of the Dialectic* Merleau-Ponty confronted not only the particular question of the intellectual's position in relationship to Marxism but, through a discussion of proletarian consciousness, the question whether Marxism could ever overcome the barriers of violence that are always with us and arrive at a universal conception of man in which man and the world penetrate each other, thus giving birth to a richer intersubjectivity.

Merleau-Ponty points us toward the origins of Marx in Hegel's philosophy:

> It has been remarked without paradox that *Capital* is a concrete *Phenomenology of Mind,* that is to say, that it is inseparably concerned with the working of the economy and the realization of man. The point of connection between these two problem areas lies in the Hegelian idea that every system of production and property implies a system of relations between men such that their social relations become imprinted upon their relations to nature, and these in turn imprint upon their social relations. There can be no definitive understanding of the whole import of Marxist politics without going back to Hegel's description of the fundamental relations between men.[6]

Before going on, let us pause to give a brief account of the development of these relations in Hegel and Marx.

5. Until the 1950s Merleau-Ponty was the unofficial political editor of *Les Temps modernes,* a journal organized after the war to present a "clear enough course of action" between the dogmatism of both the Right and the communists. In its first issue Merleau-Ponty and Sartre stated their position: "[We propose] to fight against that pathetic and prophetic spirit which is becoming more widespread every day and demands of our contemporaries blind decisions and painful commitments. It is not true that the world is divided into two empires of good and evil. It is not true that we cannot think without weakening nor be strong without talking nonsense. It is not true that good intentions justify everything, nor that we have the right to the opposite of what we want. The comedy of history, the switching of roles and the frivolity of the actors do not prevent us from discerning a clear enough course of action, provided only that we take pains to know what is going on rather than nourish phantasms, and provided that we distinguish anguish from anxiety and commitments from fanaticism" (quoted by Michel-Antoine Burnier, *Choice of Action: The French Existentialists on the Political Front Line,* trans. Bernard Murchland [New York, 1969], pp. 26–27).

6. *Humanism and Terror,* pp. 101–2.

II

HEGEL'S WORK might be read as the conception of historical movement which culminates in the realization that truth is the unity of thought and being.[7] This is accomplished through the dialectical relationship of subject and object in which the subject continually encounters the object as one thing, finds it to be another, and adjusts its new view of the object that it has now taken in. This in turn leads to another view of the object, setting the stage for a new conception of the object by the subject. In the end one finds that the subject has appropriated all otherness to the conception that it holds of it and has arrived at absolute knowledge. For Hegel, the culmination of this movement, the movement of subject-object realization, is to be found in the State.[8]

In the *Philosophy of Right* Hegel takes up the three stages of man's social existence—the family, civil society, and the State. He is attempting to arrive at that final stage in which there is a collapse of the "ought" into the "is." Civil society is the stage of many particular individuals brought together through need. In an earlier moment property was seen as the mediating factor between the subject and the external object; through it social relations became possible. Now within the system of needs there is a division of labor which results in a division of classes. The highest of these classes is the class of civil servants, which Hegel refers to as a universal class. It is the class which, while being in society, is somehow above it and is thus able to mediate between the various particular interests one finds in civil society.

7. Merleau-Ponty's interpretation of Hegel's philosophy owes much to Jean Hyppolite's writings and refers to Hegel's *The Phenomenology of Mind*. See especially Merleau-Ponty's essay "Hegel's Existentialism" in *Sense and Non-Sense*, trans. Hubert and Patricia Dreyfus (Evanston, 1964), pp. 63–70.

8. This is not to deny the further progression in the *Encyclopedia* on the level of "Absolute Spirit." But on this level both subject and object are explicitly constituted by Spirit (*Geist*), and one can no longer speak of a "realization" in the sense of a structure proper to the world of temporal-spatial objectivity. The State can be regarded as the culmination of the movement of subject-object realization precisely because it is construed by Hegel as the most perfect structure in the realm of "Objective Spirit."

It is in the State that Hegel believes that the "is" and the "ought" are finally united. Man's end is to live the universal life. Man is only in part able to find this realization in the family and civil society. The State allows him to live this life universally. Opposition to the State is unthinkable, for man would be opposing the very essence of his life. Not only ought he to live in this unity of particulars in the universal, but in fact he does do so. Reason has finally worked itself out in the Hegelian State, the subject has appropriated all otherness in its conception of the other, and man has realized his universalization through the collapsing of the "ought" into the "is." As Merleau-Ponty and others have suggested, historical movement had come to an end in the 1827 Prussian State.

Denying that the end of history had already been realized, Marx saw the class of civil servants not as a universal class but as a new bureaucracy. For the very reasons that Hegel thought it rose above particular class interests, Marx believed it only reflected civil society with all its particularities. Rather than freeing this universal class from particular interests, the very dependence for its livelihood on government-provided pensions would at least indirectly make it interested in the economy and attuned to those groups which controlled the economy. Far from being a universal class, it would be a new class which needed to perpetuate itself and which, in doing so, would need to rely on whatever class was dominant in civil society.

In the *Economic and Philosophic Manuscripts of 1844* Marx distinguished two modes of man's existence, "species being" and "natural being." [9] Man is first a natural being, a being of needs. He never transcends this aspect of himself; but once he has both realized his place in nature and distinguished himself from nature and has overcome his basic state of dependence on nature and satisfied his strivings at this level, he is more fully capable of realizing the second aspect of his nature, which is species being, a term that for the moment we will describe as his social existence. On the natural level man already differs from the animals inasmuch as he is already producing and projecting himself, that is to say, already seeing himself in his future. Why, then, the need for this second mode of existence, which Marx calls

9. *The Economic and Philosophic Manuscripts of 1844*, trans. Martin Milligan (New York, 1964), especially pp. 106–19, 132–64, 170–93.

species being? Marx thought that Feuerbach had already pointed toward species being when, by means of his philosophical anthropology, he attempted to show how man had attributed his own qualities to an uncontrolled nature outside himself which he called God. The problem with Feuerbach is that he leaves man in a vacuum. No longer is there a God, but neither is man able to realize himself in the vacuum that has been left.

To solve this problem, Marx turns to man's labor relationship with his fellow men in order to witness man's striving for his second level of existence. Hegel had been correct in describing the alienation process but confusedly took the alienation of consciousness to be man's only alienation. Marx, rather than pointing to man's relationship to nature, finds alienation in man's estrangement from nature. Through the production process the worker in a highly industrialized capitalist society is reduced to the role of an instrument in the production of goods which are external to him. His labor becomes a part of an external product which is both alien to and independent of his control. The worker's value is seen strictly in terms of the contribution he makes to these external goods; and, as more and more goods are produced and their value decreases, so also his value as an instrument in producing them decreases. In other words, the more he produces, the poorer he becomes. The more the worker appropriates from nature for the satisfaction of his needs, the less return there is from it; and so this labor, which was supposed to liberate man, now deprives him of his very humanity. He becomes completely alienated from the very source that was to fulfill him as man. Man depends on the other for his own realization; but this realization is now denied him, and the other is made his enemy. Man, who is supposed to realize his true nature both through his objectivation in nature and his recognition of and by others, finds himself instead alienated from his nature and at the mercy of private property and capital.

The very reduction of man as worker to misery through alienation implies the second level of man's existence, and it is the very state of extreme misery found in capitalism which will lead to an overthrow of this deprived state of man and to a fulfillment of his nature. Marx makes this very clear when he says:

Communism is for us not a *state of affairs* which is to be established, an ideal to which reality [will] have to adjust itself. We call communism the *real* movement which abolishes the present state

of things. The conditions of this movement result from the premises now in existence.[10]

The vehicle by which this union of natural and species being will
take place is the proletariat. Until now revolution has been seen
as a means of gaining control of the State and perpetuating a
given class's control over the other classes in civil society. With
the communist revolution, however, a potentially universal class
will arise to put an end to revolution and to finally join the "is"
and the "ought" beyond class struggle in a recognition of man by
man. In *Contribution to the Critique of Hegel's Philosophy of
Right* Marx describes this class for us:

> [It is a class] . . . which has RADICAL CHAINS, a class in civil
> society which is *not a class of civil society,* a class which is the
> *dissolution of all classes,* a sphere of society which has a *universal
> character* because its *sufferings are universal,* and which does not
> claim a PARTICULAR REDRESS because the wrong which is done
> to it is not a PARTICULAR WRONG BUT *WRONG IN GENERAL.*
> *There must be formed* a sphere of society which claims no TRADI-
> TIONAL status but only a human status, . . . a sphere, finally,
> which cannot emancipate itself without emancipating itself from
> all other spheres of society, without, therefore, emancipating all
> these other spheres, which is, in short, a TOTAL LOSS of humanity
> and which can only redeem itself by a TOTAL REDEMPTION OF
> HUMANITY. This dissolution of society, as a particular class, is the
> *PROLETARIAT.*
> . . . what constitutes the proletariat is not NATURALLY
> EXISTING poverty, but poverty ARTIFICIALLY PRODUCED, is not
> the mass of people mechanically oppressed by the weight of society,
> but the mass resulting from the DISINTEGRATION of society.[11]

It is not, therefore, simply a class of the poor, although it too will
be poor, not only in material goods, but also in its deprivation
of species being. Its emancipation will be the emancipation of
man. The proletariat has been brought into existence through
the production process in this particular historical moment, and
only through the proletariat can man overcome his one-sided
existence as object and arrive at the fulfillment of his nature.
    Accepting that Marxism is the only philosophy which pro-

10. *The German Ideology,* trans. S. Ryazanskaya (Moscow,
1968), p. 48.
11. *Karl Marx: Early Writings,* trans. T. B. Bottomore (New
York, Toronto, and London, 1964), p. 58. Italics added.

poses a real unification of men in a universal class of man, Merleau-Ponty believed Marxism to have a special moral claim for our examination, for history is a series, not of juxtaposed self-consciousnesses, but rather of situated consciousnesses opening onto one another:

> When one says that there is a history, one means precisely that each person committing an act does so not only in his own name, engages not only himself, but also others whom he makes use of, so that as soon as we begin to live, we lose the alibi of good intentions; we are what we do to others, we yield the right to be respected as noble souls.[12]

History is to be seen not as a mere plurality of subjects but rather as an intersubjectivity wherein men have common situations. It is from the particular situation of workers under capitalism that proletarian class consciousness will arise to liberate man in his present historical situation. The proletarian experiences both the objective and subjective elements of dependence, and thus the class of the proletariat comes closer than any other class to experiencing a continuing sense of community. Objectively the proletarian experiences this through his total dependency on the whims of the production process and through the inadequacy of his wages. This objective element leads to the subjective one, namely, his becoming conscious of his alienation. These two dependencies are not independent elements that can somehow be tied together but, rather, naturally grow out of each other and are mutually influential. Once the worker has realized himself as a member of the proletariat class, he is, at least in part, aware of the need for the overthrow of capitalism and of the historical mission of realizing a universal class. But between the proletariat and the bourgeoisie there are many gradations of class: semiproletarians, petty bourgeois, and so on. There are, additionally, potential confusions of nationality, race, religion, territory, and so forth. Because these potential impediments to class consciousness exist, there is the need for a "Party which clarifies the proletariat to itself."[13] The Party and the proletariat regulate each other through the proletariat's communication with its Party and by the interaction of the particular historical situation with the Marxist idea of history. The problem

12. *Humanism and Terror*, p. 109.
13. *Ibid.*, p. 117.

here is evident. The leaders of the Party could come to practice a subjective politics by which the proletariat would be turned into objects, and universality would disappear into the Hegelian conception of the civil servants (now seen as the leaders of the Party), acting as the only subjects of history. In no way would the subject-object duality have been overcome. The Party must regulate and hasten the advancement of the proletariat toward the communist society and, in so doing, must recognize the proletariat as the vehicle by which the communist society is realized. Not to do this would be to ignore the spontaneous tendency of the workers to become class conscious and to accomplish their mission as proletariat.

III

THE ANSWER TO THIS PROBLEM must lie in a discussion of class consciousness. Let us grant at the beginning that, in some manner or form, the proletariat is at least potentially the universal class which will bring about the collapse of the "ought" into the "is," heralded since Hegel's attempt to overcome the subject-object dichotomy. Merleau-Ponty begins by stating the fact that this union has not taken place, for today in the Soviet Union one sees a situation much like those Trotsky described in *The Revolution Betrayed:*

> [We find] . . . historical tasks which can only be accomplished by forsaking generalizations; there are periods in which generalizations and predictions are incompatible with immediate success. . . . The very experience and endowments which qualified the October generation for its historical task now disqualify it for the period we have entered.[14]

Russia has moved from revolution to Thermidor. Revolution has been put aside, either because it was impossible to continue or for reasons of consolidation. The Party which was to bring the proletariat to consciousness and thus free history from class struggle has instead become a new ruling elite. Something has gone wrong with the relationship between Party and proletariat.

In *Adventures of the Dialectic* Merleau-Ponty examines the question of class consciousness and the Party through a critical

14. *Ibid.*, p. 75.

presentation of three major commentators and historical actors
—Lukács, Lenin, and Trotsky.

Merleau-Ponty found much in the early writings of Georg
Lukács that could more fully elaborate his own conception of
man as not being realized simply as consciousness or as objectivity but rather as defined in relationship with objects and
things in history. Such a relationship would not be simply
thought but would engage in the world in such a manner that
it would have an external side as well as be, at the same time,
subjective. For Lukács there is a proletarian praxis present for
class existence before it is actually known, but such an existence
is not sufficient unto itself and demands a further critical elaboration. The Party is the instrument in history that does this by
degrees through a dual mediation: there is a first mediation—the
Party, mediating between the proletariat and history—and a second mediation—the Party, consulting the proletariat or, in other
words, the proletariat mediating between the Party and history.
The two form a dual mediation in which the speaking, thinking
workers are capable of making the views proposed to them by
the Party their own, and the Party, which is also composed of
living men, is capable, therefore, of "collecting in their theses
that which other men are in the process of living." [15] Thus the
Party and the proletariat together bring about the proletarian
consciousness and lead it to action.

Although Merleau-Ponty did not point to it directly, one might
here ask whether the second mediation—that of the proletariat
between the Party and history—is to be considered anything
more than the Party's consulting the proletariat on such tactical
questions as whether to strike against General Motors tomorrow,
next week, or never. If it is to be considered anything more than
this—in other words, if it is a true mediation—why is the first
mediation—that between proletariat and history by the Party—
necessary? The proletariat would then seem to need only such
practical aids as experts at making bombs, doctors, organizers,
and so forth. Nowhere does Lukács say that it will be the Party
that makes the revolution, for this would be in direct contradiction to Marx. Rather, he says that only through consultation,
through the awakening of the proletariat, will the Party aid in
leading the proletariat to victory. But if this is the case, why
glorify these experts with the title of revolutionary Party when

15. See below, p. 50.

they are only trained specialists in the proletariat? If such a view of the consequences of Lukács' description of mediation is true, then the proletariat not only can, but will, go it alone. The proletariat is the force in and of itself that will change history.

Such a view brings up the question whether Marx saw history as so determined that the proletariat will automatically bring about this change in history, or at least the question whether it is possible to predict in some scientific form how history will take place. Either of these views would be quite different from those advanced earlier, and certainly neither determinism nor scientism would conform to Merleau-Ponty's view of man as the central agent making and transcending himself in history; nor would it conform to the young Marx's view of man as "the human world, the State, society." According to the young Marx, man is that animal which can go beyond his immediate activity, can transcend himself, and, in so doing, can look to a future in which the "is" and the "ought" are united in natural and species being. Whether or not such an interpretation of Lukács' conception of the roles of the Party and proletariat is true can be seen only in praxis itself. Only there, Merleau-Ponty suggests, can it be seen whether, as Lukács says, the Party, when it places itself in relationship to the proletariat, "focuses on a principle of universal strife and intensifies human questioning instead of ending it" [16] or whether, when it does, it shows itself to be unnecessary.

One can understand easily enough why Lenin objected to Lukács' interpretation, which allowed for a possible collapse of the first mediation into the second and presented one with an indefinite period of waiting for history to complete itself in a spontaneous proletarian revolution.[17] This, at least, was the way the Party under Lenin read Lukács' effort, in *History and Class Consciousness*,[18] to "falsely" unite Party and proletariat. To paraphrase Lenin, history shows that in no country has working-class

16. See below, p. 57.

17. A major factor in Lenin's disputes with both Karl Kautsky and Rosa Luxemburg was the fact that the revolution had taken place in the backward country of Russia rather than in England or Germany. For Lenin this excluded the possibility of an evolutionary or democratic move to the dictatorship of the proletariat and necessitated a strong central Party.

18. In 1924 Lukács was so strongly criticized for his views that he wrote an essay on Lenin as a sort of peace offering to the Party and later allowed *History and Class Consciousness* to reappear in a slightly "corrected" form. It is interesting to note that more recently

consciousness spontaneously developed beyond a trade-union or syndical consciousness. It stops at this point and needs some initially external agent to push it further. Lenin was to advance a form of scientific socialism in which the proletariat, while being able to generally sense a new rational order, was nevertheless unable to advance to it until this order had first been made particular by a particular agent, the Party. Lenin here certainly differs from Marx. Lenin does not ignore consciousness but rather develops the idea that on its own the proletariat can maintain only a trade-union consciousness. It can get beyond this only by participating in and identifying with the Party organization. The divided working class will be led to final victory by a unified Party acting as the very personification of socialist consciousness. Capitalism would not be what it is if the proletariat were not surrounded by various intermediate groups between the proletariat and the potential members of the proletariat, as well as between them and various other classes. For this very reason, "a Party which clarifies the proletariat to itself" is needed; and because of the many and continual divisions and illusionary allies, this Party must be a Party of iron. As Merleau-Ponty comments,

> We began with abstract alternatives: either history is made spontaneously or else it is the leaders who make it through cunning and strategy—either one respects the freedom of the proletarians and the revolution is a chimera or else one judges for them what they want and Revolution becomes Terror.[19]

With Lenin we find a Party that mediates between proletariat and history, a proletariat which, without the Party, could not complete its mission, in short, a proletariat that is brought from the worker state to the proletarian state of consciousness by the Party. The proletariat depends on the Party for its existence and finds its means through the end of the Party, which interprets history for it and tells it what it is and what it must do—all of this while supposedly being only "a step in advance" of the proletariat.

---

he has again somewhat "revised" his views. See, for example, the Preface to the 1967 German edition of *History and Class Consciousness* and his interview in the July/August, 1971, issue of *New Left Review*.

19. *Humanism and Terror*, p. 117.

So far we are left with these alternatives: either history is determined, and we are sooner or later to witness the coming-to-power of the proletariat as the potentially universal class, or, with Lenin, the proletariat is only the means used by the Party intelligentsia to lead unreason (the workers) to reason in their life as species beings.

This was much the situation in which Merleau-Ponty saw himself and all intellectuals who wished to understand the movement of history in the present historical epoch. The revolution had been betrayed. Trotsky's analysis was correct. Stalinism in one country had so twisted the original view of Marx that it was no longer recognizable there. How, then, was one to choose an institution in the hope of change or of remaining beyond institutions when institutions necessarily compromise their best intentions? Associating oneself with a political institution and thus compromising one's thought signified the abandoning of any hope of influencing the course of intersubjective history.

Jean-Paul Sartre, Merleau-Ponty's closest associate and former political student, attempted to show in his book *The Communists and Peace* how the only hope for the working class was its adherence to the Communist Party. In a capitalist country such as France, where roughly 25 per cent of the electorate voted Communist, the Party was the only group that spoke for the workers. The question for Sartre, as Merleau-Ponty saw it, was

> to know whether there are only *men* and *things* [subjects and objects] or whether there is also the interworld, which we call history, symbolism, truth-to-be-made. If one sticks to the dichotomy, men, as the place where all meaning arises, are condemned to an incredible tension. . . . To feel responsible for everything in the eyes of everyone and present to all situations—if this leads to approving an action which, like any action, refuses to acknowledge these principles, then one must confess that one is imprisoned in words.[20]

To call the workers to the Communist Party when the Soviet Union has shown itself to be primarily interested in preserving its own position—and, according to Merleau-Ponty, since the Korean War, having even shown itself to be an imperialist power —is to ask for an act of faith that is unwarranted even by scientific prediction, much less by any hope for a reconciliation of man

20. See below, p. 200.

with man. Furthermore, Sartre's description of the Party very clearly recalls his earlier problem in *Being and Nothingness,* namely, the subject-object dichotomy. According to Sartre, the Party is the only group in France that can give the workers meaning, can give them a sense of community, can supposedly overcome their particularity and object-existence under capitalism. But if it is the only group that can do so, is it not, by the very fact that it holds the workers together in their consciousness of community as proletariat, holding them in existence itself? By his presentation of the Party as the meeting place of the proletarian community, Sartre treats the Party as an individual, and the workers end up having one will, that which is expressed by the source of their community, the Party. The Party must then be seen as the subject which gives meaning to its object, the proletariat. The result is that we have now framed the Party and the proletariat in Sartre's familiar conception of the gaze of the other. We are very near to Lenin's view of the Party but are without (since Stalin) even the hope of a realization of the historical mission of the proletariat. Sartre's presentation leaves the proletariat held in existence by the Party's gaze in the present, which, as Merleau-Ponty points out, is always eternal or always new (which, in this case, amounts to the same thing).

After Marx, the political writer most often referred to by Merleau-Ponty is Leon Trotsky. One might even say, after a study of the texts, that Merleau-Ponty uses Trotsky's situation more than that of any other political theorist to express his own dilemma. Trotsky spoke to two points, the first being that of spontaneous revolution. By this he meant that, under certain extreme conditions, the proletariat would recognize its consciousness and identify itself with the Party at the moment of revolution. In Russia, a backward country, the proletariat would be a small minority of the total population and would necessarily have free discourse with the Party members. This first part of Trotsky's analysis, the concept of proletarian spontaneity, was to reappear after Trotsky found himself in exile. What most interested Merleau-Ponty was the second aspect of his analysis of the relationship between the proletariat and the Party. Trotsky spoke of a critical relationship between the proletariat and the Party and even of a critical group within the Party, a sort of inner democracy which allowed for the expression of all points of view up to the point of action. For Merleau-Ponty this relationship was best seen in Trotsky's personal career, which came as close as that of any revolutionary to a union of theory and practice.

Following Lenin's death, Trotsky refused to enter into the struggle which was developing for control of the Party. This is not to say that he did not oppose Stalin, but rather that he did not do so openly. As the leader of a changing minority group within the Party, he hoped to re-establish the Party's revolutionary movement. If the Party was still at least potentially the Party of the proletariat, even though in reality, at the present moment, it was not, then it was the only place from which and in which to act, even though, like Trotsky, one was certain of defeat. Deviation would be only secondary if the revolutionary dictatorship the Party exercised were valid. But if one were in the minority and believed that at present the Party was not the revolutionary dictatorship, how was one to assent or to give qualified agreement? The only alternative to the rule of discipline in Lenin's Party was to proclaim Thermidor. A minority group within the Party could work only as long as a certain degree of tension was present. Trotsky chose to speak for the proletariat from outside the Party. From exile he attempted to speak to the Russian workers by pointing to the deviations within the Bolshevik Party under Stalin, falling back on the thesis of the spontaneity of the proletariat. In short, he founded one of many splinter groups that lost their grip on reality because they placed their faith in the false hope of mass spontaneity that could no longer seriously point to a Marxism of scientific predictability as a crutch; at best, they fell back on some form of historical determinism.

But if proletarian truth is not to be found in Trotsky, where, then, is the Party that is mediator for the proletariat with history? Is it a Party composed of "reasonable men" who, somehow, may (or may not) read history better than anyone else? We have seen a move, from man to proletariat as liberator of man, to Party as mediator, to Party leaders as subjective actors. We have a group of intellectuals leading the uneducated or less-enlightened. And one need not look far to imagine the infinite interpretations of history (or of anything else) that might issue from them. If this is not the conclusion to be drawn, agreeing with Merleau-Ponty, one might say that Thermidor also follows revolution and may or may not consolidate what has been gained during the revolution, but it never of itself pushes it forward. In the moment of revolution, truth is being discovered; during Thermidor, truth is given.

If an attempt is made to establish revolution as a permanent order of things, the result may well be to accept the truth of the revolutionary moment as the entire view of man's history. By trying to speak of a permanent revolution, something escapes. What it is is what Marx spoke of so long ago: the very course of historical development of man toward species being.

IV

LET US NOW SUMMARIZE. Merleau-Ponty has presented three views or interpretations of the roles the proletariat and Party play in history. The first, Lenin's view, refuses the proletariat the possibility of arriving at revolution on its own and requires that the Party lead it there. Such a position at least hints at an elitist theory of revolution which allows a subjectivist politics to control the role of the proletariat. Sartre's variation on this allows the workers to overcome their alienation only through identifying with the Party, and it results in the Party's holding the proletariat in existence. We seem to have returned to Hegel, where the subject (the Party) is holding its object (the proletariat) in existence through its conception of it.

The second position is Lukács' dual mediation. On the one hand, the Party mediates between the proletariat and history, and, on the other, the proletariat mediates between the Party and history. The basis for this dual mediation is the free exchange among thinking, speaking men. But just as it had silenced Trotsky, the Party silenced Lukács and collapsed the second mediation into the first, leaving an all-knowing Party to be the final interpreter of history for everyone.

The third position is Trotsky's. Here, on the one hand, we have the spontaneity of the proletariat, with the Party playing only an incidental role; this position leaves change aside and reduces the proletariat to a foreordained agent which will move history to its next stage. Trotsky's second position or dilemma asks the question: if the Party is the Party of Lenin and, as under Stalin, it has gone wrong, how can one speak of changing it, since the Party is the spokesman for the potentially universal class of the proletariat?

We appear to be torn between elitism, on the one hand, and either historical determinism or scientific predictability, on the other. Scientific predictability has been proved wrong by actual history (nearly one hundred years after Marx's death, revolution has turned into Thermidor in the Soviet Union), and elitism and determinism have undercut the view of the young Marx, which pointed to a union of the "is" and the "ought" worked out by *men* in the totality of their historical situation. We no longer have the picture of a Marx fighting both the idealism of Hegel and positivism but, as Merleau-Ponty points out, a Marx of *Capital*, where the dialectics of history are already determined in the relationship of things. Through an examination of our present situation, we see that such a position ends up, not with the universal recognition of men by men in a classless society, but with the Party speaking for all history and claiming present knowledge of the supposed end of history in order to continue to practice a subjectivist politics while holding the rest of mankind in an object-like existence. In stressing the social, Marx, like many other revolutionaries, failed to realize the important fact that the political cannot be divorced from man's total existence.[21] While Marx accepted the possibility of a new bureaucracy, he denied its irreversibility, for "This would have amounted to admitting that the revolution could betray itself and to renouncing the immanence of truth." [22] But as Merleau-Ponty has shown, this is just what did take place with the Party's attempt to make the negative dialectic positive.

Marx had based his model on the highly industrialized countries of western Europe and America, and it was from these countries that revolution was to come. In fact, the "proletarian revolutions" have taken place in backward countries, with the result that we hear talk of jumping from precapitalism to socialism, bypassing the bourgeois stage of development. It may well be that Marx, plus the Marxists, has given a model which will allow underdeveloped countries to "leap" into the modern age; but there is no reason for saying that they will arrive at the society promised by Marx, in which object-like existence has been overcome and man acts as a union of species and natural being. If Marxism is, rather, destined for backward countries, it is likely that we will see the same, or variations of the same, problems of Party-proletariat relations appear. Marx from his perspective in the nineteenth century could only present a critique of the existing capitalist society and posit its overcoming

21. Hannah Arendt, *On Revolution*, (New York, 1965), p. 262.
22. See below, p. 83.

or sublation in a classless society. But, Merleau-Ponty says, we who have seen the revolution and its turn to Thermidor, and know its weight in history, should not be asked to continue the idea of a "homogeneous society" indefinitely. History has shown us otherwise. The conclusion that should rather be drawn is that "revolutions are true as movements and false as regimes." [23] The Marxist attempt to unite species being and natural being fails in praxis.

This, of course, is not to fall back on the capitalist model of society. Marx has already shown that the universality of the reasonable man, spoken of under capitalism, is nothing more than an illusion of a class-structured society. The conclusion that Merleau-Ponty draws for the philosopher is similar to that of Socrates. The philosopher is seen as gadfly to his society, pointing out its injustices and keeping in mind the critique of capitalism already made by Marx, while working through the ambiguity of the world that is man's relationship with his fellow men. To be a revolutionary today is not to call for permanent revolution, which has been discredited for the Western world, but rather to look to the possibility of changing the social relations within one's own lived situation. To call for revolution today may well amount to another form of illusion or an excuse for not trying to overcome the contradictions one finds at home.

One direction in which Merleau-Ponty may have been pointing throughout his analysis of Marx and Marxism is to a new definition of man. A central element in such a conception would be not only history but, for lack of a more specific word, culture. For example, when one speaks of Lukács' double or dual mediation, this third term, culture, is at least hinted at. It is not merely a two-way mediation, which in both cases is between subject and object, but a mediation among men for a totality which is man. This totality we might call culture. Nowhere does Merleau-Ponty call for the economic to be *the* determining factor; rather, he says that it is *a* factor in man's total relationship with the world.[24] The emphasis may well be to see man not only realized by his labor but engaged in work and culture, using his total human character to transform nature and social relationships. Such a task would call for a new critique of society rather than

23. See below, p. 207.
24. Joseph Bien, "Man and the Economic: Merleau-Ponty's Interpretation of Historical Materialism," *Southwestern Journal of Philosophy*, III (1972), 121–27.

merely a criticism of the old critique. Through his analysis of the Marxist critique, Merleau-Ponty may well have cleared the way for a critique of society in the twentieth century much as Marx did in the nineteenth.

Marxism represented itself as a realization of theory and praxis, of critique and practice. It failed in practice in its attempt to present a potentially universal class, the proletariat, which would bring about a reconciliation of all men. Instead, it led to a subjective politics in which the leaders were deluded into believing that they spoke and acted universally. Rather than a class which is the suppression of classes, one finds in communist countries a new variation on the subject-object dichotomy. Hegel spoke of the collapsing of the "ought" into the "is," Marx of a realization of species being and natural being, and the Marxists of an overcoming of the subject-object dichotomy. In each case one is left with an unrealized utopian vision that demands that leaders claim a present knowledge of the end of history so that they may continue in their attempts to achieve it. In each case man's ambiguous situation in history is either overlooked or denied. History comes to be judged in its own name; and man, in his particular situation and in the situations he shares with other men, is lost in the process. This is not to suggest that we do away with discussion of the proletariat, for any society that produces a proletariat is to that extent unjustifiable; but we must renounce the proletariat as the necessary vehicle by which man will overcome the barriers that exist between himself and his fellow men. It may well be that Marx's emphasis on changing the production process is no longer the central question for the working classes in Western liberal democracies. (It seems odd, at best, to expect the American workingman to identify his material situation with that of the proletariat in communist countries.) Instead of looking at man's relationship to the production process, one might look at his social relations in order to get beyond the sterile subject-object discussion.

Merleau-Ponty points us this way when he speaks of situated consciousnesses. The "human condition" is to be a historical being in situation and to find that one's situation is not unique but opens onto and demands others for its own definition. One has a shared knowledge of the past (history) and a shared experience and tradition. This commonality in which man participates is his human condition, and his representation of it to his fellow men in all ages is his cultural tradition, which, just because it encompasses the totality of his existence, is necessarily ambiguous and never fully realizable. Language, work, law, and art all participate in it and represent various but incomplete pictures of it. This appeal to culture as the expression of man's historical situation with respect to all mankind is certainly not to be interpreted as an attempt at a new critique of society, but it may hint at the direction for a groundwork of such a critique; and, at least initially, it could prevent us from taking only one aspect of social existence as *the* determining factor of human totality. Such a move could recognize man's intersubjective relationship, not only to his present lived reality, but also to his past, to other men in other ages, with whom present man has a common bond. Through such a study, new meaning might emerge, and man's present situation might be structured without denying that truth is always in the process of being understood through the agency of man in the present.[25]

JOSEPH BIEN

*The University of
Texas at Austin*

25. In his later work Merleau-Ponty examined the concept of culture, laying particular stress on Max Weber's contribution to the question. Besides his discussion of Weber in *Adventures of the Dialectic,* Merleau-Ponty relates culture and man's role as historian to the discussion of historical institutions. See *Themes from the Lectures at the Collège de France 1952–1960,* trans. John O'Neill (Evanston, 1970), pp. 27–45.

Acknowledgments

I would like to thank Kirk Augustine, James Edie, Craig Goodrum, Oscar Haac, Florence Haywood, Flore Nève, Terry Pinkard, and Paul Ricoeur for advice and help of various sorts, Robert Audi and Richard Zaner for their suggestions concerning the Introduction, and the University of Texas at Austin for supporting the work with a research grant.

Most important I wish to thank my wife, Françoise Bien, not only for her patience and encouragement, but for her many helpful suggestions in resolving the ambiguities of the original text.

J. B.

Adventures of
the Dialectic

Preface

WE NEED A PHILOSOPHY of both history and spirit to deal with the problems we touch upon here. Yet we would be unduly rigorous if we were to wait for perfectly elaborated principles before speaking philosophically of politics. In the crucible of events we become aware of what is not acceptable to us, and it is this experience as interpreted that becomes both thesis and philosophy. We are thus allowed to report our experience frankly with all its false starts, its omissions, its disparities, and with the possibility of revisions at a later date. By doing so we manage to avoid the pretense of systematic works, which, just like all others, are born of our experience but claim to spring from nothing and therefore appear, at the very moment when they catch up with current problems, to display a superhuman understanding when, in reality, they are only returning to their origins in a learned manner. From this, and before treatises can appear, comes the idea of one or several small works, wherein one will find samplings, probings, philosophical anecdotes, the beginnings of analyses, in short, the continual rumination which goes on in the course of reading, personal meetings, and current events.

But one must tie all this together, and that is the object of this preface.

ALAIN SPOKE of a politics of reason which totalizes history, ties all the problems together, orients itself on a future that is already written in the present and where all problems will be solved; having realized a tactical strategy, it considers mankind's history as prehistory, it postulates a new beginning through an

[3]

overthrow of existing relationships enabling humanity to recreate itself capable, this time, of living. To this grand politics Alain opposed a politics of understanding, which, unlike the other, does not flatter itself with having embraced all of history but rather takes man as he is, at work in an obscure world, resolves problems one at a time, attempting in each instance to infuse in things something of the values which man when he is alone discerns without hesitation. Such a politics knows no strategy other than the sum of these random assaults. Alain thought that all our misfortunes come from a failure to practice the politics of understanding. He has been answered, with reason, that there is only one politics, that of understanding and reason.[1] Politics is never the encounter between conscience and individual happenings, nor is it ever the simple application of a philosophy of history. Politics is never able to see the whole directly. It is always aiming at the incomplete synthesis, a given cycle of time, or a group of problems. It is not pure morality, nor is it a chapter in a universal history which has already been written. Rather it is an action in the process of self-invention.

He who espouses the politics of understanding is not able to judge from the event alone. If the decision he makes, which is just in itself, should tomorrow, because of its consequences, compromise the values he recognizes, no one will absolve him for having bought his momentary tranquillity at this price. He is not quit with history for acting in the moment according to what seemed just to him. One does not simply ask him to go through events without compromising himself; one also wants him, according to the occasion, to change the terms of the problem. It is necessary for him to enter into things, to be responsible for them, and not separate himself from what he does. In other words, there are no *just decisions*, there is only a *just politics*. It is fine to do all that is possible step by step and to leave the rest to the gods, but how is one to know where the possible stops? Let us take, for example, a general strike. The man of understanding either swears not to abandon the oppressed—because the oppressed are always in the right—and so perhaps finds himself a revolutionary; or he follows the oppressed only to the point where

1. Raymond Aron, *Introduction à la philosophie de l'histoire* (Paris, 1938). English translation by George Irwin, *Introduction to the Philosophy of History* (New York, 1961).

property and the State apparatus are put into question, and since, when one is uncommitted, one is continually reassuring the rights of property and the State, he soon finds himself more conservative than anyone. Whether its attitude be one of respect or contempt, the understanding decides everything. When closely looking at this open and even candid politics, which wishes in every case to judge without ulterior motives, one finds it to be unable to decide between "accommodation" and revolt. By its inflexible manner of leaving a pure value and a factual situation face to face, this politics must give in, sometimes to one side, sometimes to the other; and this patient action, which was little by little to construct the world, can only keep the world as it is or destroy it— and always unwillingly.

Must one therefore be conservative, or rather, since to keep things as they are is the surest way of losing everything at the moment when everything is put in question, must one then be revolutionary and, in order to get out of this bind, remake this poorly made world, staking everything on a new future that one believes one sees dawning in the perplexity of things? But what is that *end of history* on which some people make everything depend? One supposes a certain boundary beyond which mankind stops being a senseless confusion and comes back to the immobility of nature. This idea of an absolute purification of history, of an inertialess regime without chance or risk, is the inverse reflection of our own anxiety and solitude. There is a "revolutionary" spirit that is nothing more than a way of disguising the state of one's soul. One speaks of universal history, of efficacy, and of a movement of the whole. But the real wherein one places oneself has been prepared according to one's own wishes and is nothing more than a landscape against which one develops one's personal dreams. It is nothing more than a masquerade for one's personal inclinations. The important revolutionaries, and first of all Marx, are not revolutionaries in that sense. They lived their time rather than looked to it in the hope of forgetting their own obsessions, as the minor figures did. They well understood that universal history is not to be contemplated but to be made, and what they put of themselves into the revolution is an acute understanding of events and not a vague strain of millenarianism. Marx did not speak of an end of history but of an end to prehistory. This means that after, just as before, the revolution the true revolutionary, each day confronting each new problem, rediscovers what is to be done. He navigates without a map and with a limited view of the present. The knowledge of history's secret does not give knowledge of its paths. In its own way, the politics of reason also oscillates between values and facts. The only difference is that, here, values are disguised in *perspectives*, and personal decisions in *historical processes*. In 1917, when Bukharin wanted to continue the war against Germany, which he said had become a revolutionary war, Trotsky advised "neither war nor peace" and Lenin favored an immediate peace. Their agreement on the ultimate ends left aside the question of the path to follow, and the way this path was traced by each of them expressed the total relation of each to the world. He who makes a mistake about the path to take betrays the ultimate ends, and in a decisive moment he may be more dangerous for the revolution than a bourgeois. There is, therefore, no revolutionary fraternity. Revolution tears itself apart; the future which was going to guide it withholds itself in consciences, becomes opinion and point of view—a point of view one tries to impose. Politics, whether of understanding or of reason, oscillates between the world of reality and that of values, between individual judgment and common action, between the present and the future. Even if one thinks, as Marx did, that these poles are united in a historical factor—the proletariat—which is at one and the same time power and value, yet, as there may well be disagreement on the manner of making the proletariat enter history and take possession of it, Marxist politics is, just like all the others, undemonstrable. The difference is that Marxist politics understands this and that it has, more than any other politics, explored the labyrinth.

Such, then, are the acquirements of this half-century: the false modesty of understanding does not get around the problem of the whole, nor does the self-confidence of reason avoid the problem of events. Understanding is drawn toward the revolutionary problem, and revolution does not remove the difficulties of understanding but rather finds them once again, and in an even more complicated form than before. Each political act engages the whole of history, but this totality does not give us a rule on which we can rely, because it is nothing more than opinion. We now know that subject and object, conscience and history, present and future, judgment and discipline, all these opposites, decay without one another, that the attempt at a revolutionary resolution destroys one of the two series, and that we must look for something else.

THIS BOOK is an attempt to stake out experience, not on the ground of politics, but on the ground of political philosophy. It begins at the moment when, with Max Weber, the politics of understanding recognizes its limits, when liberalism stops believing in eternal harmony, legitimizes its adversaries, and conceives itself as a task (Chapter 1). Cannot the contraries held together by Max Weber with a heroic effort be reconciled? The communist generation of 1917 thought so. We find witness for this in the penetrating work published by Georg Lukács in 1923, which was for a while the bible of what was called Western communism (Chapter 2). Revolutionary politics proclaimed synthesis as its immediate goal. The dialectic was going to appear in concrete facts. Revolution was the *sublime moment* in which reality and values, subject and object, judgment and discipline, individual and totality, present and future, instead of colliding, would little by little enter into complicity. The power of the proletariat was the complete novelty of a society which was self-critical and which eliminated its own contradictions by a historically infinite work. The prefiguration of this was to be found in the life of the proletarian vanguard in its party. What is left of these hopes? It is not so much that they were deceived or that the revolution was betrayed; rather it is that the revolution found itself loaded down with other tasks that Marxism thought had been accomplished and that, whereas a mature and powerful proletariat could have exercised power, it did not take it, or it quickly lost it. Whatever the case, from 1917 on, in Russia a Marxism of antitheses, of which Lenin's philosophical books (Chapter 3) are the model, appeared in opposition to the German-language Marxist synthetic philosophy.[2] This persistence of antinomies in communist philosophy reflects their persistence in action (Chapter 4). It is significant that Sartre now bases his defense of communist philosophy (Chapter 5) on the antinomies that the revolution eliminated, and in a relativist manner justifies communism as a completely voluntary effort to go beyond, to destroy and to recreate history, whereas Marx himself understood it also as the realization of history.

In concluding our work, we try to bring this liquidation of the revolutionary dialectic to its conclusion.

2. Lukács, Revai, Fogarasi, and Korsch.

1 / The Crisis
of Understanding

MAX WEBER'S FEELING toward freedom and truth was extremely exacting and distrustful. But he also knew that they appear only in certain cultures, provided that certain historical choices are made, that they are not fully realized there, and that they never assimilate the confused world from which they sprang. They have, therefore, no claim to divine right and no other justifications than those which they effectively bring to man, no other titles than those acquired in a struggle where they are in principle at a disadvantage, since they are unable to exhaust all possible means. Truth and freedom are of another order than strife and cannot subsist without strife. It is equally essential to them to legitimize their adversaries and to confront them. Because he remains faithful to knowledge and to the spirit of investigation, Weber is a liberal. His liberalism is brand new, because he admits that truth always leaves a margin of doubt, that it does not exhaust the reality of the past and still less that of the present, and that history is the natural seat of violence. Contrary to previous liberalism, it does not ingenuously consider itself to be the law of things; rather it perseveres in becoming such a law, through a history in which it is not predestined.

In the first place, Weber thinks it possible to juxtapose the order of truth and that of violence. We know history in the same way that Kant says we know nature, which is to say that the historian's understanding, like that of the physicist's, forms an "objective" truth to the degree that it constructs, and to the degree that the object is only an element in a coherent representation, which can be indefinitely corrected and made more precise but which never merges with the thing in itself. The historian cannot look at the past without giving it a meaning, without putting into perspective the important and the subordinate, the essential and the accidental, plans and accomplishments, preparations and declines. And already these vectors which are traced through the dense whole of the facts distort the original reality, in which everything is equally real, and cause our own interests to crystallize on its surface. One cannot avoid the invasion of the historian into history; but one can see to it that, like the Kantian subject, the historical understanding constructs according to certain rules which assure an intersubjective value to its representation of the past. The meanings, or, as Weber says, the ideal types, which it introduces into facts must not be taken as keys to history. They are only fixed guideposts for determining the difference between what we think and what has been and for making evident what has been left out by any interpretation. Each perspective is there only to prepare for others. It is well founded only if we understand that it is partial and that the real is still beyond it. Knowledge is never categorical; it is always open to revision. Nothing can make us be the past: it is only a spectacle before us which is there for us to question. As the questions come from us, the answers in principle cannot exhaust historical reality, since it does not depend on them for existence.

The present, on the contrary, is us: it depends on our consent or our refusal. Suspension of judgment, which is the rule with respect to the past, is here impossible; to wait for things to take shape before deciding is to decide to let them go their own way. But the proximity of the present, which makes us responsible for it, nevertheless does not give us access to the thing itself. This time it is lack of distance which allows us to see only one side of it. Knowledge and practice confront the same infinity of historical reality, but they respond to it in opposite ways: knowledge, by multiplying views, confronts it through conclusions that are provisional, open, and justifiable (that is to say, conditional), while practice confronts it through decisions which are absolute, partial, and not subject to justification.

But how can we hold to this dualism of past and present, which is evidently not absolute? Tomorrow I will have to construct an image of that which I am now living; and I cannot, at the time when I live it, ignore it. The past that I contemplate has been lived; and as soon as I want to enter into its genesis, I cannot be unaware that it has been a present. Because of the fact that the order of knowledge is not the only order, because it is not closed in on itself, and because it contains at least the gaping blank of the present, the whole of history is still action, and action is already history. History is one, whether we contemplate it as spectacle or assume it as responsibility. The historian's condition is not so different from that of the man of action. He puts himself in the place of those whose action has been decisive, reconstitutes the horizon of their decisions, and does again what they have done, with this difference: he knows the context better than they, and he is already aware of the consequences. This is not to say that history consists in penetrating the state of mind of great men. Even the search for motives, says Weber, involves ideal types. It is not a question of coinciding with what has been lived but rather of deciphering the total meaning of what has been done. To understand an action, it is necessary to restore the horizon, which is to say, not only the perspective of the agent but also the "objective" content. One could thus say that history is action in the realm of the imaginary, or even the spectacle that one gives oneself of an action. Conversely, action consults history, which teaches us, says Weber, certainly not what must be willed, but the true meaning of our volitions. Knowledge and action are two poles of a single existence. Our relationship to history is not only one of understanding—a relationship of the spectator to the spectacle. We would not be spectators if we were not involved in the past, and action would not be serious if it did not conclude the whole enterprise of the past and did not give the drama its last act. History is a strange object, an object which is ourselves. Our irreplaceable life, our fierce freedom, find themselves already prefigured, already compromised, already played out in other freedoms, which today are past. Weber is obliged to go beyond the domain of the double truth, the dualism of the objectivity of understanding and of moral feeling, to look beyond it for the formula of this singular situation.

HE HAS NOWHERE GIVEN this formula. His methodological writings postdate his scientific applications. We must look in his historical works to see how he comes to terms with this object which adheres to the subject, how he forges a method out of this difficulty, and how he tries, by going beyond the past as spectacle, to understand the past itself by making it enter into our own lives. We cannot be content with the past as it saw itself; and it is understood that the very attempt to discover the past as it actually was always implies a spectator, and there is a danger that we will discover the past only as it is for us. But is it perhaps in the nature of history to be undefined so long as it remains in the present and to become completely real only when it has once been given as a spectacle to a posterity which passes judgment upon it? Is it perhaps the case that only successive generations ("générations appélantes," as Péguy called them) are in a position to see whether what has been brought about really deserved to be, to correct the deceptions of recorded history, and to reinstate other possibilities? Is our image of the past preceded only by sequences of events, which form neither a system nor even perspectives and whose truth is held in abeyance? Is it perhaps a definition of history to exist fully only through that which comes after, to be in this sense suspended into the future? If this is true, the historian's intervention is not a defect of historical understanding. That facts interest the historian, that they speak to the man of culture, that they may be taken up again in his own intentions as a historical subject—all this threatens historical knowledge with subjectivity but also promises it a superior objectivity, if only one succeeds in distinguishing between "comprehension" and arbitrariness and in determining the close relationship which our "metamorphoses" violate but without which they would be impossible.

Let us, for example, attempt to understand the relationship between Protestantism and the capitalistic spirit. The historian intervenes initially by abstracting these two historical identities. Weber does not consider speculative or venture capitalism, which depends upon venture politics. He takes as his object an economic system within which one can expect continuous return from a durable and profitable enterprise, a system which therefore involves a minimum of accountancy and organization, encourages free labor, and tends toward a market economy. In the same way he limits his discussion of the Protestant ethic to Calvinism, and more especially to the Calvinism of the sixteenth and seventeenth centuries, considered more as collective fact than in its original form as set forth by Calvin. These facts are chosen as interesting and historically important because they reveal a certain logical structure which is the key to a whole series of other facts. How does the historian know this when he begins? Strictly speaking, he does not know. His abstraction anticipates certain results that he has an inkling of, and it will be justified to the degree that it brings to light facts which had not contributed to the initial definitions. He is therefore not sure that they designate essences;

they are not developed by proximate genus and specific difference
and do not represent, as geometric definitions do, the genesis of
an ideal being. They give only, as Weber says, a provisional il-
lustration of the point of view chosen, and the historian chooses
this point of view in the same way that one remembers a word of
an author, or someone's gesture: in one's first encounter with it,
one becomes aware of a certain style. It was a passage from one of
Franklin's works that gave Weber this initial view of the relationship between Calvinism and capitalism. Dating from the age of
the maturity of Puritanism and preceding the adult age of capitalism, Franklin's text shows the transition from one to the other.
These famous words are striking and illuminating because they
express a work ethic. We have a duty to augment our capital, to
earn always more, without enjoying what we have earned. Production and accumulation are in themselves holy. One would
miss the essential point if one thought that Franklin attempts
here to disguise interest as virtue. On the contrary, he goes so far
as to say that God uses interest to bring him back to faith. If he
writes that time is money, it is first of all because he has learned
from the Puritan tradition that time is spiritually precious and
that we are in the world to bear witness to the glory of God at
each moment. The useful could become a value only after having
been sanctified. What inspired the pioneers of capitalism was not
the philosophy of enlightenment and immanence, the joy of life,
which will come later. The "righteous, strict, and formalistic"
character that brought them success can be understood only in
terms of their sense of a worldly calling and in terms of the economic ethic of Puritanism. Many of the elements of capitalism
exist here and there in history; but if it is only in western Europe
that one finds the rational capitalistic enterprise in the sense that
Weber defines it, this is perhaps because no other civilization has
a theology which sanctifies daily labor, organizes a worldly asceticism, and joins the glory of God to the transformation of nature. Franklin's text presents us with a vital choice in its pure
state, a mode of *Lebensführung* which relates Puritanism to the
capitalistic spirit and enables Calvinism to be defined as worldly
asceticism and capitalism to be defined as "rationalization"; and
finally, if the initial intuition is confirmed, it enables us to discover an intelligible transition from one to the other. If, in extending the work ethic back to its Calvinistic origins and toward
its capitalistic consequences, Weber succeeds in understanding
the basic structure of the facts, it is because he has discovered

an objective meaning in them, has pierced the appearances in which reason is enclosed, and has gone beyond provisional and partial perspectives by restoring the anonymous intention, the dialectic of a whole.

Tracing worldly asceticism back to its premises, Weber finds in Calvinism the feeling of an infinite distance between God and his creatures. In themselves they merit only eternal death; they can do nothing and are worth nothing and have no control over their destiny: God decides who is to be among the elect and who is not. They do not even know that they truly are: God alone, seeing the hidden side of things, knows whether they are lost or saved. The Calvinist conscience oscillates between culpability and justification, both equally unmerited, between an anguish without limits and a security without conditions. This relationship to God is also a relationship to others and to the world. Because there is an infinite distance between God and man, no third party can intervene in the relationship. The ties which man has with others and with the world are of a different order from those he has with God. In essential matters he cannot expect any help from a church where sinners are as numerous as the righteous or any aid from sermons and sacraments which can do nothing to alter the *decretum horribile*. The church is not a place where man can find a sort of other natural life. It is an institution created by will and attached to predetermined ends. The Catholic lives in his church as if a running account were open to him, and it is not until the end of his life that the balance is struck between what he has and what he owes. The solitude of the Calvinist means that he confronts the absolute continually and that he does so futilely because he knows nothing of his destiny. At each instant he poses in full the whole question of his salvation or damnation, and this question remains unanswered. There is no gain in the Christian life; it can never be self-sufficient. "The glory of God and personal salvation remain always above the threshold of consciousness." [1] Summoned to break the vital alliance that we have with time, with others, and with the world, the Calvinist pushes to its limits

1. Max Weber, "Die Protestantische Ethik und der Geist des Kapitalismus," *Archiv für Sozialwissenschaft und Sozialpolitik, neue Folge des Archivs für soziale Gesetzgebung und Statistik*, III (1905), 13. English translation by Talcott Parsons, *The Protestant Ethic and the Spirit of Capitalism* (New York, 1958), p. 223. [The English translation will be referred to as "ET."]

a demystification that is also a depoetization or a disenchantment (*Entzauberung*). The sacraments, the church as the place of salvation, human friendships, which are always on the point of deifying creatures, are rejected as magic. This absolute anguish finds no relaxation in brotherly relations with created things. The created is the material upon which one works, the matter which one transforms and organizes to manifest the glory of God. The conscious control which is useless for salvation is transferred to a worldly enterprise that takes on the value of duty. Plans, methods, balance sheets are useless in dealing with God, since, from his perspective, everything is done, and we can know nothing. All that is left to us is to put the world in order, to change its natural aspect, and to rationalize life, this being the only means we have of bringing God's reign to earth. We are not able to make God save us. But the same anguish that we feel before that which we do not control, the same energy that we would expend to implement our salvation, even though we cannot do so, is expended in a worldly enterprise which depends on us and is under our control and which will become, even in Puritanism, a presumption of salvation. The terror of man in the face of a supernatural destiny over which he has no control weighs heavily upon the Puritan's activity in the world. By an apparent paradox, because he wishes to respect the infinite distance between God and man, he endows the useful and even the comfortable with dignity and religious meaning. He discredits leisure and even poverty and brings the rigors of asceticism into his dealings with the world. In the Calvinist's estimation, the relation to being and to the absolute is precipitated by and perpetuated in the goods of this world.

Let us now move forward from the Calvinist ethic to the spirit of capitalism. Weber cites one of Wesley's phrases that marks this transition: "Religion necessarily produces the spirit of industry and frugality, and these cannot but produce riches. But as wealth increases, so will pride, passion, and the love of worldly things. . . . So although the form of religion remains, the spirit gradually declines." Franklin's generation leaves to its successors the possibility of becoming rich in good conscience. They will forget the motive and concentrate on gaining the best of this world and the next. Once crystallized in the world by the Protestant ethic, capitalism will develop according to its own logic. Weber does not believe that it is sustained by the motive that brought it into existence, or that it is the truth of Calvinism:

The capitalistic economy of the present day is an immense cosmos into which the individual is born, and which presents itself to him, at least as an individual, as an unalterable order of things in which he must live. It forces the individual, insofar as he is involved in the system of market relationships, to conform to capitalistic rules of action. . . . Thus the capitalism of today, which has come to dominate economic life, educates and selects the economic subjects which it needs through a process of economic survival of the fittest. But here one can easily see the limits of the concept of selection as a means of historical explanation. In order that a manner of life [*Lebensführung*] so well adapted to the peculiarities of capitalism could be selected at all, i.e., should come to dominate others, it had to originate somewhere, and not in isolated individuals alone, but as a way of life common to whole groups of men. This origin is what really needs explanation.[2]

There is thus a religious efficacy and an economic efficacy. Weber describes them as interwoven, exchanging positions so that now one, now the other, plays the role of tutor. The effect turns back on its cause, carrying and transforming it in its turn. Furthermore, Weber does not simply integrate spiritual motives and material causes; he renews the concept of historical matter itself. An economic system is, as he says, a cosmos, a human choice become a situation; and that is what allows it to rise from worldly asceticism to religious motives, as well as to descend toward its capitalistic decay: everything is woven into the same fabric. History has meaning, but there is no pure development of ideas. Its meaning arises in contact with contingency, at the moment when human initiative founds a system of life by taking up anew scattered givens. And the historical understanding which reveals an interior to history still leaves us in the presence of empirical history, with its density and its haphazardness, and does not subordinate it to any hidden reason. Such is the philosophy without dogmatism which one discerns all through Weber's studies. To go beyond this, we must interpret freely. Let us do this without imputing to Weber more than he would have wished to say.

THESE INTELLIGIBLE NUCLEI of history are typical ways of treating natural being, of responding to others and to death. They appear at the point where man and the givens of nature or of the past meet, arising as symbolic matrices which have no pre-

2. *Ibid.*, II (1904), 17–18; ET, pp. 54–55.

existence and which can, for a longer or a shorter time, influence history itself and then disappear, not by external forces but through an internal disintegration or because one of their secondary elements becomes predominant and changes their nature. The "rationalization" by which Weber defines capitalism is one of these seminal structures that can also be used to explain art, science, the organization of the State, mysticism, or Western economy. It emerges here and there in history and, like historical types, is confirmed only through the encounter of these givens, when, each confirming the other, they organize themselves into a system. For Weber, capitalism presupposes a certain technology of production and therefore presupposes science in the Western sense. But it also presupposes a certain sort of law, a government based on certain rules, without which bourgeois enterprise cannot exist, though venture or speculative capitalism may. To these conditions Weber adds a "rational conduct of life," which has been the historical contribution of Protestantism. In law, science, technology, and Western religion we see prime examples of this "rationalizing" tendency. But only after the fact. Each of these elements acquires its historical meaning only through its encounter with the others. History has often produced one of them in isolation (Roman law; the fundamental principles of calculus in India), without its being developed to the degree that it would have to be in capitalism. The encounter of these elements confirms in each one of them the outline of rationality which it bore. As interactions accumulate, the development of the system in its own sense becomes more likely. Capitalistic production pushes more and more in the direction of a development of technology and the applied sciences. At the start, however, it is not an all-powerful idea; it is a sort of *historical imagination* which sows here and there elements capable one day of being integrated. The meaning of a system in its beginnings is like the pictorial meaning of a painting, which not so much directs the painter's movements but is the result of them and progresses with them. Or again, it can be compared to the meaning of a spoken language which is not transmitted in conceptual terms in the minds of those who speak, or in some ideal model of language, but which is, rather, the focal point of a series of verbal operations which converge almost by chance. Historians come to talk of "rationalization" or "capitalism" when the affinity of these products of the historical imagination becomes clear. But history does not work according to a model; it is, in fact, the advent of meaning. To say that the elements of rationality were related to one another before crystallizing into a system is only a manner of saying that, taken up and developed by human intentions, they ought to confirm one another and form a whole. Just as, before the coming of the bourgeois enterprise, the elements which it joins did not belong to the same world, each must be said to be drawn by the others to develop in a way which is common to them all but which no one of them embodies. Worldly asceticism, whose principles have been established by Calvinism, is finished by capitalism, finished in both senses of the word: it is realized because, as activity in the world, capitalism surpasses it; it is destroyed as asceticism because capitalism strives to eliminate its own transcendent motives. There is, Weber says, an *elective affinity* between the elements of a historical totality:

> In view of the tremendous confusion of interdependent influences between the material basis, the forms of social and political organization, and the ideas current in the time of the Reformation, we can only proceed by investigating whether and at what points certain correlations (*Wahlverwandtschaften*) between forms of religious belief and practical ethics can be worked out. At the same time, we shall as far as possible clarify the manner and the general *direction* in which, by virtue of those relationships, the religious movements have influenced the development of material culture. Only when this has been determined with reasonable accuracy can the attempt be made to estimate to what extent the historical development of modern culture can be attributed to those religious forces and to what extent to others.[3]

This relationship is supple and reversible. If the Protestant ethic and capitalism are two institutional ways of stating the relationship of man to man, there is no reason why the Protestant ethic should not for a time carry within itself incipient capitalism. Nor is there anything to prevent capitalism from perpetuating certain typically Protestant modes of behavior in history or even from displacing Protestantism as the driving force of history and substituting itself for it, allowing certain motives to perish and asserting others as its exclusive theme. The ambiguity of historical facts, their *Vielseitigkeit*, the plurality of their aspects, far from condemning historical knowledge to the realm of the provisional (as Weber said at first), is the very thing that agglomerates the dust of facts, which allows us to read in a religious fact the first

3. *Ibid.*, p. 54; ET, pp. 91–92.

draft of an economic system or read, in an economic system, positions taken with regard to the absolute. Religion, law, and economy make up a single history because any fact in any one of the three orders arises, in a sense, from the other two. This is due to the fact that they are all embedded in the unitary web of human choices.

This is a difficult position to hold and one which is threatened on two sides. Since Weber tries to preserve the individuality of the past while still situating it in a developmental process, perhaps even in a hierarchy, he will be reproached, sometimes for concluding too little and at other times for presuming too much. Does he not leave us without means for criticizing the past? Does he not in principle give the same degree of reality and the same value to all civilizations, since the system of real and imaginary methods by which man has organized his relations with the world and with other men has always managed, somehow or other, to function? If one wishes to go so far as to understand the past even in its phantasms, is one not inevitably led to justify it and thus be rendered unable to judge it? On the other hand, when Weber presents us with a logic of history, one can always object that, as Malraux has shown, the decision to investigate and understand all civilizations is the act of a civilization which is different from them, which transforms them. It transforms the crucifix into a work of art, so that what had been a means of capturing the holy becomes an object of knowledge. Finally, the objection can be made that historical consciousness lives off this indefensible paradox: fragments of human life, each of which has been lived as absolute, and whose meaning thus in principle eludes the disinterested onlooker, are brought together in the imagination in a single act of attention, are compared and considered as moments in a single developmental process. It is necessary, therefore, to choose between a history which judges, situates, and organizes—at the risk of finding in the past only a reflection of the troubles and problems of the present—and an indifferent, agnostic history which lines up civilizations one after another like unique individuals who cannot be compared. Weber is not unaware of these difficulties; indeed, it is these difficulties which have set his thought in action. The path which he seeks lies precisely between history considered as a succession of isolated facts and the arrogance of a philosophy which lays claim to have grasped the past in its categories and which reduces it to our thoughts about it. What he opposes to both of them is our *interest* in the past: it is ours, and we are its. The dramas which have been lived inevitably remind us of our own, and of ourselves; we must view them from a single perspective, either because our own acts present us with the same problems in a clearer manner or, on the contrary, because our own difficulties have been more accurately defined in the past. We have just as much right to judge the past as the present. The past, moreover, comes forward to meet the judgments we pass upon it. It has judged itself; having been lived by men, it has introduced values into history. This judgment and these values are part of it, and we cannot describe it without either confirming or annulling them. In most past mystifications those involved were to a certain extent aware of the deception. Objectivity asks only that one approach the past with the past's own criteria. Weber reconciles evaluative history with objective history by calling upon the past to testify concerning itself. Wesley enables him to discern the moment when religion becomes mystification. Ideology is never mystification completely unawares; it requires a great deal of complacency to justify the capitalistic world by means of Calvinistic principles; if these principles are fully articulated, they will expose the ruse of attempting to turn them to one's own purposes. The men of the past could not completely hide the truth of their era from themselves; they did not need us in order to catch a glimpse of it. It is there, ready to appear; we have only to make an effort to reveal it. Thus the very attempt to understand the past completely would oblige us to order the facts, to place them in a hierarchy, in a progression or a regression. In so doing we recapture the very movement of the past. It is true that the *Kulturmensch* is a modern type. History appears as a spectacle only to those who have decided to consider all the solutions and who place themselves before the solutions, freely disposed toward all. History thus stands in contrast to both the narrow and the profound passions which it considers. Truth, says Weber, "is that which *seeks* to be recognized by all those who *seek* the truth." [4] The decision to question each epoch concerning a fundamental choice that is diffused in its thoughts, its desires, and its actions, and of which it has perhaps never made an accounting, is the result of living in an epoch that has tasted of the tree of knowledge. Scientific history is in principle the exact opposite of naïve history, which it

4. Max Weber, *Gesammelte Aufsätze zur Wissenschaftslehre* (Tübingen, 1922), p. 184.

would, however, like to recapture. It presupposes itself in what it constructs. But this is not a vicious circle of thought; it is the postulate of all historical thought. And Weber consciously enters into it. As Karl Löwith shows, Weber well knows that scientific history is itself a product of history, a moment of "rationalization," a moment of the history of capitalism.[5] It is history turning back upon itself, presuming that we are theoretically and practically able to take possession of our life and that clarification is possible. This presumption cannot be demonstrated. It will be justified or not according to whether it will or will not give us a coherent image of "the universal history of culture"; and nothing guarantees in advance that the attempt will be successful. In order to try, it is enough to know that to make any other hypothesis is to choose chaos and that the truth which is sought is not, in principle, beyond our grasp. Of that we are certain. We discover that we possess a power of radical choice by which we give meaning to our lives, and through this power we become sensitive to all the uses that humanity has made of it. Through it other cultures are opened up to us and made understandable. All that we postulate in our attempt to understand history is that freedom comprehends all the uses of freedom. What we contribute ourselves is only the prejudice of not having any prejudices, the fact that we belong to a cultural order where our own choices, even those which are opposed to each other, tend to be complementary:

> Culture is a closed segment abstracted from the infinity of events which is endowed with meaning and signification only for man. . . . The transcendental condition of all cultural science is not that we find this or that culture valuable but the fact that we are "cultural men," endowed with the capacity consciously to take a position with regard to the world and to give meaning to it. Whatever this meaning might be, its consequence is that in living we abstract certain phenomena of human coexistence and in order to judge them we take a position (positive or negative) with regard to their significance.[6]

Historical understanding thus does not introduce a system of categories arbitrarily chosen; it only presupposes the possibility that we have a past which is ours and that we can recapture in

5. Karl Löwith, "Max Weber und Karl Marx," *Archiv für Sozialwissenschaft und Sozialpolitik*, LVII (1932).
6. Weber, *Gesammelte Aufsätze*, pp. 180–81.

our freedom the work of so many other freedoms. It assumes that we can clarify the choices of others through our own and ours through theirs, that we can rectify one by the other and finally arrive at the truth. There is no attitude more respectful, no objectivity more profound, than this claim of going to the very source of history. History is not an external god, a hidden reason of which we have only to record the conclusions. It is the metaphysical fact that the same life, our own, is played out both within us and outside us, in our present and in our past, and that the world is a system with several points of access, or, one might say, that we have fellow men.

Because a given economy, a given type of knowledge, a given law, and a given religion all arise from the same fundamental choice and are historical accomplices, we can expect, circumstances permitting, that the facts will allow themselves to be ordered. Their development will manifest the logic of an initial choice, and history will become an experience of mankind. Even if the Calvinistic choice has transcendent motives which capitalism is unaware of, we can still say that in tolerating certain ambiguities capitalism assumed responsibility for what followed, and thus we can treat this sequence as a logical development. Calvinism confronted and juxtaposed the finite and the infinite, carried to the extreme the consciousness we have of not being the source of our own being, and organized the obsession with the beyond at the same time that it closed the routes of access to it. In so doing it paved the way for the fanaticism of the bourgeois enterprise, authorized the work ethic, and eliminated the transcendent. Thus the course of history clarifies the errors and the contradictions of the fundamental choice, and its historical failure bears witness against Calvinism. But in factual sciences there is no proof by absurdity, no crucial experiment. We know, then, that certain solutions are impossible. We do not gain from the working operations of history that comprehensive understanding which would reveal the true solution. At best we rectify errors which occur along the way, but the new scheme is not immune to errors which will have to be rectified anew. History eliminates the irrational; but the rational remains to be created and to be imagined, and it does not have the power of replacing the false with the true. A historical solution of the human problem, an end of history, could be conceived only if humanity were a thing to be known—if, in it, knowledge were able to exhaust being and could come to a state that really contained all that humanity had been and all that it could ever be. Since, on the contrary, in the density of social reality each decision brings unexpected consequences, and since, moreover, man responds to these surprises by inventions which transform the problem, there is no situation without hope; but there is no choice which terminates these deviations or which can exhaust man's inventive power and put an end to his history. There are only advances. The capitalist rationalization is one of them, since it is the resolve to take our given condition in hand through knowledge and action. It can be demonstrated that the appropriation of the world by man, the demystification, is better because it faces difficulties that other regimes have avoided. But this progress is bought by regressions, and there is no guarantee that the progressive elements of history will be separated out from experience and be added back in later. Demystification is also depoetization and disenchantment. We must keep the capitalistic refusal of the sacred as external but renew within it the demands of the absolute that it has abolished. We have no grounds for affirming that this redress will be made. Capitalism is like a shell that the religious animal has secreted for his domicile, and it survives him:

> No one knows who will live in this cage [shell] in the future, or whether at the end of this tremendous development entirely new prophets will arise, or there will be a great rebirth of old ideas and ideals, or, if neither, mechanized petrification, embellished with a sort of convulsive self-importance. For of the last stage of this cultural development, it might well be truly said: "Specialists without spirit, sensualists without heart; this nullity imagines that it has attained a level of civilization never before achieved." [7]

If the system comes to life again, it will be through the intervention of new prophets or by a resurrection of past culture, by an invention or reinvention which does not come from something in that system. Perhaps history will eliminate, together with false solutions to the human problem, certain valid acquisitions as well. It does not locate its errors precisely in a total system. It does not accumulate truths; it works on a question that is confusedly posed and is not sheltered from regressions and setbacks. Projects change so much in the course of things that the lessons taught

7. *Ibid.*, p. 240. [The passage Merleau-Ponty here refers to also appears in "Die Protestantische Ethik," *Archiv für Sozialwissenschaft und Sozialpolitik*, III (1905), 109; ET, p. 182.—Trans.]

by events are not reaped, since the generations of men who make the accounting are not those who began the experiment. Weber's phenomenology is not systematic like Hegel's. It does not lead to an absolute knowledge. Man's freedom and the contingency of history exclude, definitively,

> the idea that the goal of the cultural sciences, even their remote goal, is to construct a closed system of concepts in which reality will be confined according to a definitive order . . . and from which it can be deduced. The course of unforeseeable events is transformed endlessly, stretching to eternity. The cultural problems that move men are constantly posed anew and from other aspects. That which becomes meaningful and significant in the infinite flow of individual data constantly changes the field, and it becomes a historical concept, just as the relations of thought are variable under which it is considered and posited as an object of science. The principles of the cultural sciences will keep changing in a future without limits as long as a sclerosis of life and of spirit does not disaccustom humanity, as in China, to posing new questions to an inexhaustible life. A system of the cultural sciences, even if confined to an area which is systematic and objectively valid for questions and for the domains which these questions are called upon to treat, will be nonsense in itself. An attempt of this type could only reassemble pell-mell the multiple, specific, heterogeneous, disparate points of view under which reality is presented to us each time as "culture," i.e., each time it is made significant in its specificity.[8]

The intelligible wholes of history never break their ties with contingency, and the movement by which history turns back on itself in an attempt to grasp itself, to dominate itself, to justify itself, is also without guarantee. History includes dialectical facts and adumbrative significations; it is not a coherent system. Like a distracted interlocutor, it allows the debate to become sidetracked; it forgets the data of the problem along the way. Historical epochs become ordered around a questioning of human possibility, of which each has its formula, rather than around an immanent solution, of which history would be the manifestation.

BECAUSE ITS AIM is to recover the fundamental choices of the past, Weber's science is a methodical extension of his experience of the present. But have this experience and its practical options benefited in turn from historical understanding? For only

8. Weber, *Gesammelte Aufsätze*, p. 185.

if they have would Weber have reconciled theory and practice.

Weber is not a revolutionary. It is true that he writes that Marxism is "the most important instance of the construction of ideal types" and that all those who have employed its concepts know how fruitful they are—on condition that they take as *meanings* what Marx describes as *forces*. But for him this transposition is incompatible with both Marxist theory and practice. As historical materialism, Marxism is a causal explanation through economics; and in its revolutionary practices Weber never sees the fundamental choice of the proletariat appear. It thus happens that, as has been said, this great mind judges the revolutionary movements which he witnessed in Germany after 1918 as if he were a provincial, bourgeois German. The Munich riot had placed at the head of the revolutionary government the most moralistic of his students ("God, in his wrath, has made him a politician," Weber will say when defending him before the tribunal at the time of the repression).[9] Weber confines himself to these minor facts and never sees a new historical significance in the revolutions after 1917. He is against the revolution because he does not consider it to be revolution—that is to say, the creation of a historical whole. He describes it as essentially a military dictatorship and, for the rest, as a carnival of intellectuals dressed up as politicians.

Weber is a liberal. But, as we said at the beginning, his is a different kind of liberalism from those which preceded him. Raymond Aron writes that his politics is, like that of Alain, a "politics of the understanding." Only, from Alain to Weber, the understanding has learned to doubt itself. Alain recommended a policy which is not quite adequate: do each day what is just, and do not worry about the consequences. However, this maxim is inoperative every time we approach a critical situation, and understanding is then, against its principles, sometimes revolutionary, sometimes submissive. Weber himself well knows that understanding functions easily only within certain critical limits, and he consciously gives it the task of keeping history within the region where history is free from antinomies. He does not make an isolated instance of it. Since we cannot even be sure that the history within which we find ourselves is, in the end, rational, those who choose truth and freedom cannot convince those who

9. Marianne Weber, *Max Weber, ein Lebensbild* (Tübingen, 1926).

make other choices that they are guilty of absurdity, nor can they even flatter themselves with having "gone beyond" them:

> It is the destiny of a cultural epoch which has tasted of the tree of knowledge to know that we cannot decipher the meaning of world events, regardless of how completely we may study them. We must, rather, be prepared to create them ourselves and to know that world-views can never be the product of factual knowledge. Thus the highest ideals, those which move us most powerfully, can become valid only by being in combat with the ideals of other men, which are as sacred to them as ours are to us.[10]

Weber's liberalism does not demand a political empyrean, it does not consider the formal universe of democracy to be an absolute; he admits all politics is violence—even, in its own fashion, democratic politics. His liberalism is militant, even suffering, heroic. It recognizes the rights of its adversaries, refuses to hate them, does not try to avoid confronting them, and, in order to refute them, relies only upon their own contradictions and upon discussions which expose these. Though he rejects nationalism, communism, and pacifism, he does not want to outlaw them; he does not renounce the attempt to understand them. Weber, who under the Empire decided against submarine warfare and in favor of a white peace, declared himself jointly responsible with the patriot who had killed the first Pole to enter Danzig. He opposed the pacifist left, which made Germany alone responsible for the war and which exonerated in advance the foreign occupation, because he thought that these abuses of self-accusation paved the way for a violent nationalism in the future. Still, he testified in favor of his students who were involved in pacifist propaganda. Though he did not believe in revolution, he made public his esteem for Liebknecht and Rosa Luxemburg. Weber is against political discrimination within the university. Perhaps, he says, anarchist opinions might allow a scholar to see an aspect of history of which he would otherwise have been unaware. Though he scrupulously left out of his teaching anything which might have favored some cause or have exhibited his personal beliefs, he is in favor of professors who become engaged in politics. However, they should do this outside the classroom—in essays, which are open to discussion, and in public gatherings,

10. Max Weber, *Gesammelte Aufsätze*, p. 154.

where the adversary can respond. The academic soliloquy should
not be fraudulently used for the purposes of propaganda. Thus he
holds both ends of the chain. Thus he makes truth work together
with decision, knowledge with struggle. Thus he makes sure that
repression is never justified in the name of freedom.[11]

Is this better than a compromise? Has he succeeded in
uniting, except in his own person, the meanings of force and
freedom? Is there any other way of satisfying them both except
through alternation? When he wished to found a political party
on these bases, Weber was so easily expelled and returned so
quickly to his studies that it was thought that he did not adhere
to these ideas too strongly, that he felt there was an insurmountable obstacle in them, and that a party which did not play according to the rules of the game would be a utopia. However, this
failure is perhaps only of Weber the man. Perhaps it leaves intact
the political wisdom which he at least sketched out once, even if
he did not know how to put this wisdom into practice. For he did
not content himself with setting values and efficacy, feelings and
responsibility, in opposition to each other. He tried to show how
one must go beyond these alternatives. The taste for violence, he
says, is a hidden weakness; the ostentation of virtuous feelings is
a secret violence. These are two sorts of histrionics or neurosis,
but there is a *force,* that of the true politician, which is beyond
these. The true politician's secret is to not try to form an image
of himself and of his life. Because he has put a certain distance
between himself and his success, he does not take pleasure in his
intentions alone, nor does he accept the judgment of others as
final. Because his action is a "work," a devotedness to a "thing"
(*Sache*) which grows outside him, it has a rallying power which
is always lacking in undertakings which are done out of vanity.
"Lack of distance" from oneself, from things, and from others is
the professional disease of academic circles and of intellectuals.
With them, action is only a flight from oneself, a decadent mode
of self-love. By contrast, having once and for all decided to "bear
the irrationality of the world," the politician is patient or in-
tractable when he must be—that is to say, when he has
compromised as much as he will allow himself and when the very
sense of what he is doing is involved. Precisely because he is not
a man of the ethics of ultimate ends [*la morale du coeur*], when

11. On all these points see Marianne Weber, *op. cit.*

he says no to others and to things, even this is an action, and it is
he who gratifies the sterile wishes of the politics of ultimate ends
[*la politique du coeur*]:

> If in these times, which, in your opinion, are not times of "sterile"
> excitation—excitation is not, after all, genuine passion—if now
> suddenly the *Weltanschauungs*-politicians crop up *en masse* and
> pass the watchword, "The world is stupid and base, not I," "The
> responsibility for the consequences does not fall upon me but upon
> the others whom I serve and whose stupidity or baseness I shall
> eradicate," then I declare frankly that I would first inquire into
> the degree of inner poise backing this ethic of ultimate ends. I am
> under the impression that in nine out of ten cases I deal with wind-
> bags who do not fully realize what they take upon themselves but
> who intoxicate themselves with romantic sensations. From a
> human point of view this is not very interesting to me, nor does it
> move me profoundly. However, it is immensely moving when a
> *mature* man—no matter whether old or young in years—is aware
> of a responsibility for the consequences of his conduct and really
> feels such responsibility with heart and soul. He then acts by fol-
> lowing an ethic of responsibility, and somewhere he reaches the
> point where he says: "Here I stand; I can do no other." That is
> something genuinely human and moving. And every one of us who
> is not spiritually dead must realize the possibility of finding him-
> self at some time in that position. Insofar as this is true, an ethic
> of ultimate ends and an ethic of responsibility are not absolute con-
> trasts but rather supplements, which only in unison constitute a
> genuine man—a man who *can* have the calling for politics.[12]

It will be said that this talisman is a small thing, that it is
only a question of ethics, that a major political viewpoint prolongs
the history of a time, and that it should therefore give it its
formula. But this objection perhaps ignores the most certain conclusion Weber establishes. If history does not have a direction,
like a river, but has a meaning, if it teaches us, not a truth, but
errors to avoid, if its practice is not deduced from a dogmatic
philosophy of history, then it is not superficial to base a politics
on the analysis of the political man. After all, once the official
legends have been put aside, what makes a politics important is
not the philosophy of history which inspires it and which in other
hands would produce only upheavals. What makes it important is

12. Max Weber, *Politik als Beruf* (Munich, 1919), p. 66. English
translation, "Politics as a Vocation," by H. H. Gerth and C. Wright
Mills, in *From Max Weber: Essays in Sociology* (New York, 1958),
p. 127.

the human quality that causes the leaders truly to animate the political apparatus and makes their most personal acts everyone's affair. It is this rare quality that elevates Lenin and Trotsky above the other authors of the 1917 revolution. The course of things is meaningful only to those who know how to read it, and the principles of a philosophy of history are dead letters if they are not recreated in contact with the present. To succeed in this, one must possess the capacity of which Weber speaks, the capacity to live history. In politics, truth is perhaps only this art of inventing what will later appear to have been required by the time. Certainly Weber's politics will have to be elaborated. It is not by chance that the art of politics is found in some places and not in others. One can think of it more as a symptom of the "intentions" of history than as a cause. One can seek to read the present more attentively than Weber did, to perceive "elective affinities" that escaped him. But what he has shown definitively is that a philosophy of history that is not a historical novel does not break the circle of knowledge and reality but is rather a meditation upon that circle.

We wanted to begin this study with Weber because, at a time when events were about to bring the Marxist dialectic to the fore, Weber's effort demonstrates under what conditions a historical dialectic is serious. There were Marxists who understood this, and they were the best. There developed a rigorous and consistent Marxism which, like Weber's approach, was a theory of historical comprehension, of *Vielseitigkeit,* and of creative choice, and was a philosophy that questioned history. It is only by beginning with Weber, and with this Weberian Marxism, that the adventures of the dialectic of the past thirty-five years can be understood.

2 / "Western" Marxism

AT THE BEGINNING of the twentieth century, Marxists found themselves confronted by a problem which had been hidden from Marx by the remnants of Hegelian dogmatism: can one overcome relativism, not by ignoring it, but by truly going beyond it, by going further in the same direction? Weber had glimpsed the road to follow, namely, ideal types, significations that we introduce into our representation of the past that would cut us from it only if they were arbitrary. But they themselves are part of history: history as a science, with its methods and its idealizations, is an aspect of history as reality, of the capitalistic rationalization. Our ideas, our significations, precisely because they are relative to our time, have an intrinsic truth that they will teach to us if we succeed in placing them in their proper context, in understanding them rather than merely suffering them. We are able to speak of the metamorphosis of the past through knowledge only because we measure the distance there is between the past and this knowledge. History is not only an object in front of us, far from us, beyond our reach; it is also our awakening as subjects. Itself a historical fact, the true or false consciousness that we have of our history cannot be simple illusion. There is a mineral there to be refined, a truth to be extracted, if only we go to the limits of relativism and put it, in turn, back into history. We give a form to history according to our categories; but our categories, in contact with history, are themselves freed from their partiality. The old problem of the relations between subject and object is transformed, and relativism is surpassed as soon as one puts it in historical terms, since here the

[30]

object is the vestige left by other subjects, and the subject—
historical understanding—held in the fabric of history, is by this
very fact capable of self-criticism. There is an oscillation from one
to the other which, as much as we could hope for, reduces the
distance between knowledge and history. It is along this road that
Weber stops. He does not pursue the relativization of relativism to
its limits. He always considers the circle of the present and the
past, of our representation and real history, as a vicious circle.
He remains dominated by the idea of a truth without condition
and without point of view. By comparison with this absolute
knowledge, with this pure theory, our progressive knowledge is
degraded to the rank of opinion, of simple appearance. Would not
a more radical criticism, the unrestricted recognition of history
as the unique milieu of our errors and our verifications, lead us to
recover an absolute in the relative?

This is the question that Georg Lukács asks of his teacher,
Weber.[1] He does not reproach him for having been too relativistic
but rather for not having been relativistic enough and for not
having gone so far as to "relativize the notions of subject and object." For, by so doing, one regains a sort of totality. Certainly
nothing can change the fact that our knowledge is partial in both
senses of the word. It will never be confused with the historical
in-itself (if this word has a meaning). We are never able to refer
to completed totality, to universal history, as if we were not within
it, as if it were spread out in front of us. The totality of which
Lukács speaks is, in his own terms, "the totality of observed
facts," not of all possible and actual beings but of our coherent
arrangement of all the known facts. When the subject recognizes
himself in history and history in himself, he does not dominate
the whole, as the Hegelian philosopher does, but at least he is
engaged in a work of totalization. He knows that no historical fact
will ever have its whole meaning for us unless it has been linked
to all the facts we are able to know, unless it has been referred to
as a particular moment in a single enterprise which unites them,
unless it has been placed in a vertical history which is the record
of attempts which had a meaning, of their implications and of
their conceivable continuations. If one takes on the responsibility
of deciphering fundamental choices in history, there is no reason

1. We are especially thinking of his 1923 book, *Geschichte und
Klassenbewusstsein* (History and Class Consciousness). It will be
seen in the next chapter how something of this remains in even his
most recent essays.

to limit oneself to partial and discontinuous intuitions. Lukács completely accepts the analysis sketched by Weber of the Calvinistic choice and of the capitalistic spirit; he only wishes to continue it. The Calvinistic choice needs to be confronted with all the others; and all choices must together form a single action if each of them is to be understood. The dialectic is this continued intuition, a consistent reading of actual history, the re-establishment of the tormented relations, of the interminable exchanges, between subject and object.[2] There is only one knowledge, which is the knowledge of our world in a state of becoming, and this becoming embraces knowledge itself. But it is knowledge that teaches us this. Thus, there is that moment in which knowledge looks back on its origins, recaptures its own genesis, equals as knowledge what it was as event, gathers itself together in order to totalize itself, and tends toward consciousness. The same whole is, in the first relationship, history; in the second, philosophy. History is philosophy realized, as philosophy is history formalized, reduced to its internal articulations, to its intelligible structure.

For Lukács, Marxism is, or should be, this integral philosophy without dogma. Weber understood materialism as an attempt to deduce all culture from economics. For Lukács, it is a way of saying that the relations among men are not the sum of personal acts or personal decisions, but pass through things, the anonymous roles, the common situations, and the institutions where men have projected so much of themselves that their fate is now played out outside them. "As . . . the personal interests become self-contained in class interests, the personal conduct of the individual reobjectifies itself (*sich versachlichen*), necessarily alienates itself (*entfremden*), and at the same time exists without him as an . . . independent force." [3] In the nineteenth century, especially through the development of production, "the material forces become saturated with spiritual life (*mit gei-*

2. Thus, despite Engels, Lukács refuses to admit the prime importance of the dialectic of nature—nature is unaware of the subject. But the passage of the subject into the object and of the object into the subject is the driving force of dialectic. Only in a secondary or derivative sense is there a dialectic of nature. The nature that *we* observe offers data of reciprocal action and quantitative leaps, but, as in the case of movement in Zeno, this dialectic fails. It is a destruction of opposites. They are resolved only in history and man.

3. Karl Marx and Friedrich Engels, *The German Ideology*, ed. S. Ryazanskaya (Moscow, 1964).

stigem Leben ausgestattet werden) and human existence is dulled (to the point that it becomes) a material force (*zu einer materiellen Kraft verdummt*)." [4] This exchange, by which things become persons and persons things, lays the foundation for the unity of history and philosophy. It makes all problems historical but also all history philosophical, since forces are human projects become institutions. Capital, says Marx in a famous passage, is "not a thing, but a social relationship between persons mediated by things (*nicht eine Sache, sondern ein durch Sachen vermitteltes gesellschaftliches Verhältnis zwischen Personen*)." [5] Historical materialism is not the reduction of history to one of its sectors. It states a kinship between the person and the exterior, between the subject and the object, which is at the bottom of the alienation of the subject in the object and, if the movement is reversed, will be the basis for the reintegration of the world with man.

Marx's innovation is that he takes this fact as fundamental, whereas, for Hegel, alienation is still an operation of the spirit on itself and thus is already overcome when it manifests itself. When Marx says that he has put the dialectic back on its feet or that his dialectic is the "contrary" of Hegel's, this cannot be simply a matter of exchanging the roles of the spirit and the "matter" of history, giving to the "matter" of history the very functions Hegel accorded to the spirit. As it becomes material, the dialectic must grow heavy. In Marx spirit becomes a thing, while things become saturated with spirit. History's course is a becoming of meanings transformed into forces or institutions. This is why there is an inertia of history in Marx and also an appeal to human invention in order to complete the dialectic. Marx cannot therefore transfer to, and lay to the account of, matter the *same* rationality which Hegel ascribed to spirit. The meaning of history appears in which he calls "human matter," an ambiguous setting where ideas and rationality do not find the *de jure* existence which in Hegel they owed to the dogma of totality as completed system and to the dogma of philosophy as the intellectual pos-

4. Karl Marx, *The Class Struggles in France, 1848 to 1850* (Moscow, 1952).

5. In German the complete sentence reads, "Er entdeckte, dass das Kapital nicht eine Sache ist, sondern ein durch Sachen vermitteltes gesellschaftliches Verhältniss zwischen Personen" (Karl Marx, *Das Kapital* [Hamburg, 1890], I, 731; *Capital*, trans. Samuel Moore and Edward Aveling [New York, 1906], p. 839).

session of this system. It is true that Marx often seems to claim the very authority of Hegel's absolute knowledge for his own antidogmatic criticism when, for example, he says that reason "has always existed though not always in a rational form." [6] But what is a reason which does not yet have the form of reason? Unless he claimed as his own the all-encompassing philosophical consciousness which he reproaches in Hegel, how could Marx affirm that reason pre-existed its manifestations and itself organized the coincidence of events from which its history benefited? Lukács thinks that Marxism cannot claim as its own this rationalistic dogma:

> But it must not be forgotten that "the ruse of reason" can only claim to be more than a myth if authentic reason can be discovered and demonstrated in a truly concrete manner. In that case it becomes a brilliant explanation for stages in history that have not yet become conscious. But these can only be understood and evaluated as stages from a standpoint already achieved by a reason that has discovered itself.[7]

In considering his past, man finds its meaning retrospectively in the coming-about of a rationality, the absence of which was not at first a simple privation but truly a state of nonreason, and which, at the moment this rationality appears, has the right to subordinate what precedes it only in the exact measure to which rationality comprehends this as its own preparation. Thus, Marxism disassociates the rationality of history from any idea of necessity. Rationality is necessary neither in the sense of physical causality, in wihch the antecedents determine the consequents, nor even in the sense of the necessity of a system, in which the whole precedes and brings to existence what happens. If human society does not become aware of the meaning of its history and of its contradictions, all one can say is that the contradictions will occur again, always more violently, by a sort of "dialectical mechanics." [8] In other words, the dialectic of things only makes the problems more urgent. It is the total

6. ". . . nur nicht immer in der vernünftigen Form," "Nachlass," I, 381, cited by Lukács in *Geschichte und Klassenbewusstsein* (Berlin, 1923), p. 32. English translation by Rodney Livingstone, *History and Class Consciousness* (Cambridge, Mass.: M.I.T. Press, 1971), p. 18. [In subsequent footnotes the German edition will be cited as *GK*, the translation as ET.]

7. *GK*, p. 162; ET, p. 146.

8. *GK*, p. 216; ET, p. 198.

dialectic, in which the subject interposes its authority, which can find a solution to the problems.[9] Marxism cannot hide the *Weltgeist* in matter. It must justify in another way the meaning of history, and it can do so only by conceiving a historical selection which eliminates the antinomistic realities from the course of history but does not have, in itself and without men's initiative, the power to create a coherent and homogeneous system.

Marxism understood in such a way had to be a revolutionary philosophy precisely because it refused to be a dogmatic philosophy of history. Two moments which succeed each other perpetually in it, but each time at a higher level, composed its spiral movement—a reading of history which allows its philosophical meaning to appear, and a return to the present which lets philosophy appear as history.

IF THE MAN of a capitalist society looks back to its origins, he gets the impression that he is witnessing the "realization of society (*Vergesellschaftung der Gesellschaft*)." A precapitalistic society, for example a caste society, divides itself into sectors which scarcely belong to the same social world. The canals and roads created by the process of production to join these sectors are at each moment blocked by relationships of prestige and by the brute facts of tradition. The economic function is never without its religious, legal, or moral components, which do not have exact equivalents in economic language. We must not merely say that these societies are unaware of their economic substructure, as if it were there and they only failed to see it—in Lukács' terms, as if falling bodies were there before Galileo. We must say that these societies are not economically based, as if what we call the imagination of history had established them in a fantastic order (where misery, of course, is very real). The economic analysis would miss criteria essential to the distribution of privileges; and if relationships between castes are religiously observed by the exploited as well as by the exploiter, it

9. Lukács sketches here a Marxist criticism of the idea of progress which would be full of lessons for contemporary Marxists who are so far removed from the dialectic that they often confuse it with the bourgeois optimism of progress. He says that the ideology of progress is an expedient which consists in placing a contradiction which has already been reduced to a minimum against the backdrop of an unlimited time and in supposing that it will there resolve itself. Progress dissolves the beginning and the end, in the historical sense, into a limitless natural process and hides from man his own role.

is because these relationships cannot be challenged as long as men do not think of themselves as partners in a common work of production. Lukács says that between the fragments of social life which admit of an economic interpretation are inserted "interworlds" which are dominated by relationships of blood, sex, or mythical kinship. This society, he continues, has not cut the "umbilical cord" which binds it to prehistory or nature. It has not yet defined itself as a relationship of man with man. Capitalist society, on the contrary, places all who live in it under the common denominator of work and in this sense is homogeneous. Even the wage system, that is to say, exploitation, places all those who participate in it within a single market. Here the phantasms and ideologies can in principle be recognized for what they are. There is in the system itself, whether it is made explicit or not, a distinction between appearance and reality, because there is truly, both within the boundaries of a single State and in the entire capitalistic world, a unity beneath local phenomena. Because there is a truly common ground, destinies can be compared. A balance sheet, or a calculation of the social whole, is conceivable because the system is deliberately rational, is designed to refund more than it costs, and translates everything it consumes and produces into the universal language of money. In saying that capitalism is a "socialization of society," [10] one states, therefore, an observable property. It is not that all other societies are nothing but a sketch of this one: for themselves, as we have said, they are something completely different. The notion of precapitalism under which we are grouping them pell-mell is obviously egocentric. A true knowledge of "precapitalism" will demand that one rediscover it as it has been lived—as it was in its own eyes. What we have just said about it is rather the point of view of capitalism on what preceded it; and to get to the integral truth, one will have to go beyond the limits of the capitalistic present. But even if it is partial, this point of view about precapitalism is well founded. The comparison is not false, even if it is not exhaustive. The direction of development marked out in this way is not a fiction. The capitalistic structure has displaced the precapitalistic ones. One is witness to the historical work through which the currents of production break open new cleavages or dismantle and destroy the traditional partitions. The movement is accelerated by violence when established capitalism

10. [In the French: "devenir-société de la société."—Trans.]

tries to take over and control backward societies. Nothing permits one to say that this transition is necessary, that capitalism is contained within precapitalism as its inevitable future, or that it contains to any great degree all that has preceded it, or, finally, that any society, to go beyond capitalism, must inevitably pass through a capitalistic phase. All these conceptions of development are mechanical. A dialectical conception demands only that, between capitalism, where it exists, and its antecedents, the relationship be one of an integrated society to a less integrated one. The formula *Vergesellschaftung der Gesellschaft* says nothing more.

This formula makes immediately evident a philosophical meaning of social development which, however, is not transcendent to it. To say that there is a "socialization of society" is to say that men begin to exist for one another, that the social whole retraces its dispersion in order to totalize itself, that it goes beyond various partitions and taboos, toward transparency, that it arranges itself as a center or an interior from which it is possible to think it, that it gathers itself around an anonymous project in relation to which various attempts, errors, progress, and a history would be possible, and, finally, that brute existence is transformed into its truth and tends toward meaning. The question is not, of course, to derive a collective consciousness from the social whole. Consciousness is presupposed in this description. Society would never become conscious of itself if it were not already made up of conscious subjects. What one wants to say is that the consciousness of principle which is at the outset granted to men finds a complicity in the structuration realized by history. This complicity allows consciousness to become knowledge of the social. Thus, in the eyes of consciousness, its "object," society, comes to meet consciousness and, so to speak, prepares itself to be known by establishing a decisive relationship with itself. There are different relationships of society with itself, and it is this that prevents us from placing them all at an equal distance from consciousness on the pretext that they are all its "objects." As a living body, given its behavior, is, so to speak, closer to consciousness than a stone, so certain social structures are the cradle of the knowledge of society. Pure consciousness finds its "origin" in them. Even if the notion of interiority, when applied to a society, should be understood in the figurative sense, we find, all the same, that this metaphor is possible with regard to capitalistic society but not so with regard to precapitalistic ones. This is enough for us to say that the history which produced capitalism symbolizes the emergence of a subjectivity. There are subjects, objects, there are men and things, but there is also a third order, that of relationships between men inscribed in tools or social symbols. These relationships have their development, their advances, and their regressions. Just as in the life of the individual, so in this generalized life there are tentative aims, failure or success, reaction of the result on the aim, repetition or variation, and this is what one calls history.

When one says that Marxism finds a meaning in history, it should not be understood by this that there is an irresistible orientation toward certain ends but rather that there is, immanent in history, a problem or a question in relation to which what happens at each moment can be classified, situated, understood as progress or regression, compared with what happens at other moments, can be expressed in the same language, understood as a contribution to the same endeavor, and can in principle furnish a lesson. In short it *accrues* with the other results of the past to form a single significant whole. The principle of the logic of history is not that all problems posed are solved in advance,[11] that the solution precedes the problem, or that there would be no question if the answer did not pre-exist somewhere, as if history were built on exact ideas. One should rather formulate it negatively: there is no event which does not bring further precision to the permanent problem of knowing what man and his society are, which does not make this problem a present concern, which does not bring back the paradox of a society of exploitation that is nonetheless based on the recognition of man by man. The "socialization of society" does not mean that the development of history is subordinated to an eternal essence of society. Rather, it means only that the moments of this development are interconnected, complement one another, step by step constitute a single event, and that the negative conditions of a solution are thus brought together. This sober principle requires neither that backward civilizations be completely surpassed by our own (it

11. Marx did say that humanity does not ask questions which it cannot resolve. But this possibility is certainly not, in his eyes, a pre-existence of the solution in the problem since elsewhere he has admitted that history can fail. The solution is possible in the sense that no destiny opposes it or since, as Max Weber has said, there is no irrational reality. But indeterminate adversity without intention or law can cause it to miscarry.

can, on the contrary, be, as Lukács says, that, in a time when the capitalistic apparatus with its constraints was not yet formed, culture attained expressions of the world which have an "eternal charm") nor that the progress achieved in later civilizations be regarded as absolute progress. First of all, it is only in the structure of the whole that there is progress. The balance sheet of history shows that, taken as a whole, there is a growing relationship of man to man. This does not alter the fact that, right now, the piece of furniture built by the craftsman speaks more eloquently of man than furniture made by the machine. But there is more to be said. Even in considering the whole of a civilization, its progress is secure only when followed by further progress. It cannot stand still. Historical accumulation or "sedimentation" is not a deposit or a residue. The very fact that an advance has occurred changes the situation; and to remain equal to itself, progress has to face the changes that it instigated. If, on the contrary, the progress that has been achieved becomes immobilized, it is already lost. All progress is then relative in the profound sense that the very historical movement which inscribes it in things brings to the fore the problem of decadence. Revolution become institution is already decadent if it believes itself to be accomplished. In other words, in a concrete conception of history, where ideas are nothing more than stages of the social dynamic, all progress is ambiguous because, acquired in a crisis situation, it creates a condition [12] from which emerge problems that go beyond it.

The sense of history is then threatened at every step with going astray and constantly needs to be reinterpreted. The main current is never without countercurrents or whirlpools. It is never even given as a fact. It reveals itself only through asymmetries, vestiges, diversions, and regressions. It is comparable to the sense of perceived things, to those reliefs which take form only from a certain point of view and never absolutely exclude other modes of perception. There is less a sense of history than an elimination of non-sense. No sooner does the direction of becoming indicate itself than it is already compromised. It is always in retrospect that an advance can be affirmed: it was not implied in the past, and all that one can say is that, if it is real progress, it takes up problems immanent in the past. The bourgeoisie established itself as ruling class, but the very development of its power,

12. [In the French: "une phase d'état."—Trans.]

by isolating in the midst of the new society another class which is not integrated into this society and by accentuating the conflict between the demands immanent in production and the forms to which the bourgeois society subjects its production, shows that it is not a universal class. "The limit of capitalism is capital itself" (Marx). While they may be termed "progressist" when compared with what preceded them, the capitalist forms are soon regressive or decadent when compared to the productive forces which capitalism itself has created. These forms were at first a projection of human freedom. With decadence, the product becomes detached from productive activity and even takes possession of it. Objectification becomes reification (*Verdinglichung*). In the period of transition, doubt is possible concerning the historical function of this or that form, and, moreover, the passage to decadence is not made in all sectors of history at the same moment. A difficult analysis will always be necessary to determine at a given moment what has kept, and what has lost, historical actuality. In a sense, everything is justified, everything is or has been true; in another sense, everything is false, unreal, and the world will begin when one has changed it. Revolution is the moment when these two perspectives are united, when a radical negation frees the truth of the entire past and allows the attempt to recover it. But when can one think that the moment of negation has passed, when must one begin the recovery? Within the revolution itself the scintillation of truth and falsity continues. The development which is outlined in things is so incomplete that it is left to consciousness to complete it. In rediscovering its birth certificate and its origins in history, consciousness perhaps thought it had found a guide to rely on, but now it is consciousness which must guide the guide. The two relationships—consciousness as a product of history, history as a product of consciousness—must be maintained together. Marx unites them in making consciousness, not the source of social being, not the reflection of an external social being, but a singular sphere where all is false and all is true, where the false is true as false and the true is false as true.

This is how Lukács sees the meaning of the theory of ideologies. This mixture of truth and falsity is already inextricable in the ideologies of science. The bourgeois conception of science taught us to think of the social as a second nature and inaugurated its objective study, just as capitalist production opened up a vast field of work. But, just as the capitalistic forms of production end by paralyzing the productive forces out of which they were born, the "natural laws of the social order," detached from the historical structure of which they are the expression and considered as the features of an eternal countenance of the universe, conceal the profound dynamic of the whole. A difficult critique is necessary if we are to go beyond scientism without sliding back to prescience, if we are to maintain the relative right of objective thought against objectivism, if we are to articulate the universe of the dialectic with the universe of science. The difficulty is even greater when one turns to literature. One must insist on this, for with his theory of ideologies and of literature, not changed in thirty years, Lukács is trying to preserve—and his enemies are trying to attack—a Marxism which incorporates subjectivity into history without making it an epiphenomenon. He is trying to preserve the philosophical marrow of Marxism, its cultural value, and finally its revolutionary meaning, which, as we shall see, is an integral part of Marxism. Many Marxists are satisfied to say that consciousness is in principle mystified and therefore that literature is suspect. They do not see that, if consciousness were ever absolutely cut off from truth, they themselves would be reduced to silence, and no thought, not even Marxism, would ever be able to lay a claim to truth. There is no point in answering that Marxism is true, and alone true, as the ideology of the rising class, because, as Lenin says, Marxism and the theory of the social are initially brought to the working class from outside. This means that there can be truth outside the proletariat and that, inversely, not everything that comes from the proletariat is true, since the proletariat, in a society where it is powerless, is contaminated by its bourgeoisie. Thus Marxism needs a theory of consciousness which accounts for its mystification without denying it participation in truth. It is toward this theory that Lukács was leaning in his book of 1923. We cannot, he said, establish "an inflexible confrontation of true and false." [13] Hegel was able to integrate falsity into the logic of history only as partial truth, that is to say, only after having subtracted precisely what makes it false. Thus for him synthesis is transcendent with regard to the moments which prepare it. In Marx, on the contrary, since the dialectic is history itself, it is the whole experience of the past, without philosophical preparation, without transposition or suppression, which must pass into the present

13. *GK,* p. 61; ET, p. 50.

and into the future. ". . . in so far as the 'false' is an aspect of the 'true,' it is both 'false' and 'non-false.'"[14] Even illusions have some sort of sense and call for deciphering because they always present themselves against the background of a lived relationship with the social whole and because they are thus not like something mental, opaque, and isolated; instead, like the expressions of faces or of speeches, they bring with them an underlying meaning that unmasks them, and they hide something only by exposing it. Lukács still holds today[15] that, because literature is the expression of the lived world, it never expresses the postulates of a single class but rather the class's meeting and eventual collison with other classes. Literature is then always the reflection of the whole, even if the class perspective distorts this reflection. Balzac's very prejudices helped him to see certain aspects of his time to which a more "advanced" mind, such as Stendhal, remained indifferent. As long as the writer still has a writer's integrity, that is to say, as long as he gives a picture of the world in which he lives, his work, through interpretation, always touches truth. Because the artist gives himself the strange task of objectifying a life, with all its ramifications in its surroundings, literature cannot simply be false. Consciousness, the relation of the self to itself, is "*subjectively* justified in the social and historical situation, as something which can and should be understood, i.e. as 'right.' At the same time, *objectively*, it bypasses the essence of the evolution of society as a 'false consciousness.'"[16] To say that it is "false consciousness" is not to state the thesis of an essential "falsity of consciousness." It is, on the contrary, to say that something within warns it that it is not altogether correct and invites it to rectify itself. This fundamental relationship with truth allows past literature to furnish models for the present. Literature is mystification only in decadence. This is when consciousness becomes ideology, mask, diversion, because it gives up domination of the social whole and can only be used for hiding it. In the rising period of capitalism, literature remained a sufficient expression of the human whole. It must perhaps even be said that the great bourgeois literature is the only model we have at our disposal. In the other camp, the society in which the proletariat tries its best to suppress itself as a class,

14. *GK*, p. 12; *ET*, p. xlvii.
15. Georg Lukács, *Karl Marx und Friedrich Engels als Literaturhistoriker* (Berlin, 1947); see, e.g., pp. 141, 150.
16. *GK*, p. 62; *ET*, p. 50.

writers, as Gorki said, necessarily lag behind the workers and can only be the unfaithful heirs of bourgeois culture. If, on the other hand, one considers a classless society, finally realized, it is not a "proletarian" culture which it produces but one which is beyond classes. One can therefore ask oneself whether for the moment a culture other than bourgeois culture is possible. In any case, we have no other example of ruling-class literature, where an energetic attempt to express the world has been made, than that of capitalism in its organic phase. This is why, after the war, Lukács still proposed Goethe, Balzac, and Stendhal as models for revolutionary writers. Now, as soon as one admits that man is open to truth through his lived relationship with totality, one defines an order of expression which does not conform to that of everyday action. The demands of discipline could not possibly be the same for militants, who act at the level of the immediate, and for the writer, who prepares instruments of knowledge, valid, in principle, at least for some time and perhaps forever. There would be a political action and a cultural action which are not always parallel. To transfer the rules of the first to those of the second would be to make culture a form of propaganda. That is why, a few years ago, Lukács was still defending the writers who were fellow travelers of the Party and were called "snipers." It is not that he ever excluded litera-ture from history but rather that he distinguished between the "center" and the "periphery" of historical dialectic, between the rhythm of political action and that of culture. The two develop-ments are convergent, but truth does not march with the same step in both cases. This results from a double relationship that an integral philosophy admits of between individuals and his-torical totality. It acts on us; we are in it at a certain place and in a certain position; we respond to it. But we also live it, speak about it, and write about it. Our experience everywhere overflows our standpoint. We are in it, but it is completely in us. These two relationships are concretely united in every life. Yet they never merge. They could be brought back to unity only in a homo-geneous society where the situation would no more restrain life than life imprisons our gaze. All Marxism which does not make an epiphenomenon of consciousness inevitably limps, sometimes on one side, sometimes on the other.

Such, according to Lukács, is the philosophical read-ing of history. As we see, it does not have an overview of events, it does not seek in them the justification of a pre-established schema. Rather, it questions events, truly deciphers them, and gives them only as much meaning as they demand. By an apparent paradox, it is precisely this rigor, this sobriety, for which he was reproached by Marxists. Lukács rehabilitated consciousness in principle beyond ideologies but at the same time refused it the *a priori* possession of the whole. He never claimed to exhaust the analysis of the precapitalistic past, and for him the rationality of history was only a postulation of its capitalistic development. Most Marxists do exactly the opposite. They contest the existence of consciousness in principle and, without saying so, grant themselves the intelligible structure of the whole, and then discover all the more easily the meaning and the logic of each phase in that they have dogmatically presupposed the intelligible structure of the whole. The exceptional merit of Lukács—which makes his book, even today, a philosophical one —is precisely that his philosophy was not by implication to be understood as dogma but was to be practiced, that it did not serve to "prepare" history, and that it was the very chain of history grasped in human experience. His philosophical reading of history brought to light, behind the prose of everyday existence, a recovery of the self by itself which is the definition of subjectivity. But this philosophical meaning remained tied to the articulations of history, undetachable from them; and finally the operation of philosophical focusing had its ballast, its counterpart, in a historical fact, the existence of the proletariat. We are not changing direction. We are simply deepening the analysis by now showing that philosophy is history, as, before, we showed that history is philosophy.

The philosophical reading of history is not a simple application of concepts of consciousness, of truth and totality, badly disguised under historical rags, for this focusing, this placing in perspective, is accomplished in history itself by the proletariat. In creating an expropriated class—men who are commodities— capitalism forces them to judge commodities according to human relationships. Capitalism makes evident *a contrario* the "relations between persons" which are its reality but which it is very careful to hide, even from itself. It is not the philosopher who looks for the criteria of a judgment of capitalism in a conception of the "reign of freedom." It is capitalism which gives rise to a class of men who cannot stay alive without repudiating the status of commodity imposed upon them. The proletariat is commodity seeing itself as commodity, at the same time distinguishing itself from this, challenging the "eternal" laws of political economy, and discovering, under the supposed "things," the "process" which they hide—that is to say, the dynamic of production, the social whole as "production and reproduction of itself." [17] The proletariat is an "intention of totality" or the "totality in intention," [18] "the correct view of the over-all economic situation." [19] The realization of society that capitalism has sketched, left in suspense, and finally thwarted is taken up by the proletariat, because, being the very failure of the capitalistic intention, it is, by position, "at the focal point of the socialising process." [20] The "socialising" function of capitalism passes to the proletariat. At the same time, the proletariat *is* this philosophical meaning of history that one might have thought was the work of the philosopher, because it is the "self-consciousness of the object (*das Selbstbewusstsein des Gegenstandes*)." [21] It furnishes this identity of subject and object that philosophical knowledge perceives abstractly as the condition of truth and the Archimedes' point of a philosophy of history. "For this class the knowledge of self signifies at the same time a correct knowledge of the entire society. . . . Consequently . . . this class is at one and the same time the subject and the object of knowledge." [22]

> In the period of the "pre-history of human society" and of the struggles between classes the only possible function of truth is to establish the various possible attitudes to an essentially uncomprehended world in accordance with man's needs in the struggle to master his environment. Truth could only achieve an 'objectivity' relative to the standpoint of the individual classes and the objective realities corresponding to it. But as soon as mankind has clearly understood and hence *restructured* the foundations of its existence, truth acquires a wholly novel aspect.[23]

The "historical mission of the proletariat," which is the absolute negation of class, the institution of a classless society, is at the

17. GK, pp. 27–28; ET, p. 14. [In footnotes 17, 18, 22, and 37 I have followed Merleau-Ponty's translations of Lukács' German.—Trans.]
18. GK, p. 190; ET, p. 174.
19. GK, p. 88; ET, p. 75.
20. GK, p. 193; ET, p. 176.
21. GK, p. 195; ET, p. 178.
22. GK, p. 14; ET, p. 2.
23. GK, pp. 206–7; ET, p. 189.

same time a philosophical mission of the advent of truth. "For the proletariat the truth is a weapon that brings victory; and the more ruthless, the greater the victory." [24] It is not, first of all, as it is for Weber, in the existence of the man of culture or the historian but rather in the "object," in the proletarian, that rationalization and truth are elaborated. History provides its own interpretation by producing, along with the proletariat, its own consciousness.

But what do we mean when we say that the proletariat is the truth of the historical whole? We have already encountered the question and the following false dilemma. Either one truly places oneself in history, and then each reality is fully what it is, each part is an incomparable whole; none can be reduced to being a sketch of what is to follow, none can claim to be in truth what the past sketched. Or one wants a logic of history and wants it to be a manifestation of truth; but there is no logic except for a consciousness, and it is necessary to say either that the proletarians know the totality of history or that the proletariat is in itself (that is to say, in our eyes, not for itself) a force which leads to the realization of the true society. The first conception is absurd. Marx and Lukács cannot think of putting the total knowledge of history into the proletariat and into history, under the form of distinct thought and will, in the mode of psychic existence. In Lukács' terms, the proletariat is totality only in "intention." As for Marx, we have only to cite again the famous sentence: "The question is not what goal is *envisaged* for the time being by this or that member of the proletariat, or even by the proletariat as a whole. The question is *what is the proletariat* and what course of action will it be forced historically to take in conformity with its own *nature*." [25] But then, even if Marxism and its philosophy of history are nothing else than the "secret of the proletariat's existence," it is not a secret that the proletariat itself possesses but one that the theoretician deciphers. Is this not to admit that, by means of a third party, it is still the theoretician who gives his meaning to history in giving his meaning to the existence of the proletariat? Since the proletariat is not the subject of history, since the workers are not "gods," and since they receive a historical mission only in becoming the opposite, namely, "objects"

24. *GK*, p. 80; ET, p. 68.
25. Karl Marx, *The Holy Family*, cited by Lukács, *GK*, p. 57; ET, p. 46.

or "commodities," is it not necessary that, as with Hegel, the theoretician or the philosopher remains the only authentic subject of history, and is not subjectivity the last word of this philosophy? Just because the historical mission of the proletariat is enormous, and because it should, as "universal class" or "final class," end what was the unvarying regime of history before it, it is necessary that it be fashioned by an unlimited negation which it contains in itself as class. *"The proletariat only perfects itself by annihilating and transcending itself, by creating the classless society through the successful conclusion of its own class struggle."* [26] Does this not mean that its function prevents it from existing as a compact and solid class? In a society of classes it does not yet completely exist; afterwards, it no longer exists as a distinct class. To the extent that it is, it is a power of continuous suppression, and even its own suppression. Is this not to recognize that it is historically nearly unreal, that it chiefly exists negatively, which is to say, as idea in the thought of the philosopher? Does this not amount to admitting that one has missed the realization of philosophy in history that Lukács, after Marx, wanted to obtain?

On the contrary, for Lukács it is here that the essential and most innovative notion of Marxism appears. The difficulty exists only if the proletariat must become either subject or object for the theoretician. This is precisely the alternative that Marx puts aside by introducing a new mode of historical existence and of meaning: *praxis*. Everything that we have mentioned concerning the relationships between subject and object in Marxism was only an approximation of praxis. Class consciousness in the proletariat is not a state of mind, nor is it knowledge. It is not, however, a theoretician's conception because it is a praxis; that is to say, it is less than a subject and more than an object; it is a polarized existence, a possibility which appears in the proletarian's situation at the juncture of things and his life. In short— Lukács here uses Weber's term—it is an "objective possibility."

Precisely because this difficult notion was new, it was poorly understood. Yet this is what makes Marxism another philosophy and not simply a materialistic transposition of Hegel. Engels says in passing: "Practice, namely experiment and industry (*Die Praxis, nämlich das Experiment und die Industrie*)," [27]

26. *GK*, p. 93; ET, p. 80.
27. Cited by Lukács, *GK*, p. 145; ET, p. 131.

which defines it by contact with the sentient or the technique and carries the opposition between *theōria* and *praxis* back to the vulgar distinction between the abstract and the concrete. If praxis were nothing more, it would be impossible to see how Marx could make it rival contemplation as a fundamental mode of our relationship with the world. Experiment and industry put in the place of theoretical thought would result in a form of pragmatism or empiricism; in other words, the whole of *theōria* would be reduced to one of its parts, for experimentation is a modality of knowledge, and industry also rests on a theoretical knowledge of nature. Experiment and industry do not cover this "critico-practical revolutionary activity," which is the definition of praxis in the first of the *Theses on Feuerbach*. Engels does not see what Marx calls "the vulgar and Judaic phenomenal form of praxis." Lukács says that one should reach the "philosophical-dialectical" meaning of it,[28] which can be stated more or less as follows: it is the inner principle of activity, the global project which sustains and animates the productions and actions of a class, which delineates for it both a picture of the world and its tasks in that world, and which, keeping in mind exterior conditions, assigns it a history.[29] This project is not the project of some-

28. *GK*, p. 146; ET, p. 132.
29. In a review of Bukharin's *Theory of Historical Materialism* (*Archiv für die Geschichte des Sozialismus und der Arbeiterbewegung*, XI [1925], 216–24), Lukács shows that, far from exhausting the historical activity of society, the technical derives from it. From the classical through the mediaeval economies, it is not technical changes which explain changes in modes of labor; on the contrary, these changes are understandable only through social history. More precisely, it is necessary to distinguish the results of a technique (the results of classical techniques are sometimes superior to those of the Middle Ages) from its principle (that of mediaeval economy, regardless of its results, represents progress because the rationalization extends to modes of labor and the Middle Ages renounces servile labor). It is this new principle of free labor, the disappearance of the unlimited resources of servile labor, which demands the technical transformations of the Middle Ages, just as, in antiquity, it is the existence of servile manpower which blocks the development of corporations and professions and, finally, that of cities. In speaking of the change from the Middle Ages to capitalism, the decisive factor is not the coming of manufacturing, a completely quantitative change, but rather the division of labor, the relations of forces in the enterprise, the coming of mass consumption. Technical transformation happens when the "narrow technical base" of manufacturing comes into contradiction with the needs of production that it has engendered (*Das*

one—of some proletarians, of all proletarians, or of a theoretician who arrogates to himself the right of reconstructing their profound will. It is not, like the meaning of our thoughts, a closed, definitive unity. It is the cluster of relations of an ideology, a technique, and a movement of productive forces, each involving the others and receiving support from them, each, in its time, playing a directive role which is never exclusive, and all, together, producing a qualified phase of social development. As the milieu of these exchanges, praxis goes far beyond the thought and feeling of the proletarians, and yet, says Lukács, it is not a "mere fiction," [30] a disguise invented by the theoretician for his own ideas of history. It is the proletarians' common situation, the system of what they do on all levels of action, a supple and malleable system which allows for all sorts of individual mistakes and even collective errors but which always ends by making its weight felt. Thus, it is a vector, an attraction, a possible state, a principle of historical selection, and a diagram of existence.

It will be objected that the proletarians do not share a common situation, that their conduct has no logic, that the particulars of their lives do not converge, and finally that the proletariat has unity only in the eyes of an external spectator who dominates history, since by hypothesis the proletarians themselves can be mistaken. This brings back the alternative: either they are subjects of history, and then they are "gods"; or it is the theoretician who supposes a historical mission for them, and then they are only objects of history. Marx's answer would be that there is no *theoretical* way of going beyond the dilemma. In the face of contemplating consciousness, the theoretician must either command or obey, be subject or object, and, correlatively, the proletariat must obey or command, be object or subject. For theoretical consciousness there is no middle ground between democratic consultation of the proletarians, which reduces proletarian praxis to their thought and their feelings of the moment and relies on the "spontaneity of the masses," and bureaucratic cynicism, which substitutes, for the existing proletariat, the idea made of it

---

Kapital, I, 333; ET, p. 404, cited by Lukács in the same review, p. 221). Techniques realized apart from man would be a "fetishistic transcendental principle in the face of man" (*ibid.*, p. 219), but Marxism, on the contrary, wants "to reduce all economic and 'sociological' phenomena to a social relation of man with man" (*ibid.*, p. 218).
    30. *Ibid.*, p. 88; ET, p. 75.

by the theoretician. But in practice the dilemma is transcended because praxis is not subjugated to the postulate of theoretical consciousness, to the rivalry of consciousnesses. For a philosophy of praxis, knowledge itself is not the intellectual possession of a signification, of a mental object; and the proletarians are able to carry the meaning of history, even though this meaning is not in the form of an "I think." This philosophy does not take as its theme consciousnesses enclosed in their native immanence but rather men who explain themselves to one another. One man brings his life into contact with the apparatuses of oppression, another brings information from another source on this same life and a view of the total struggle, that is to say, a view of its political forms. By this confrontation, theory affirms itself as the rigorous expression of what is lived by the proletarians, and, simultaneously, the proletarians' life is transposed onto the level of political struggle. Marxism avoids the alternative because it takes into consideration, not idle, silent, and sovereign consciousnesses, but the exchange between workers, who are also speaking men—capable, therefore, of making their own the theoretical views proposed to them—and theoreticians, who are also living men—capable, therefore, of collecting in their theses what other men are in the process of living.

When one founds Marxist theory on proletarian praxis, one is not therefore led to the "spontaneous" or "primitive" myth of the "revolutionary instinct of the masses." The profound philosophical meaning of the notion of praxis is to place us in an order which is not that of knowledge but rather that of communication, exchange, and association. There is a proletarian praxis which makes the class exist before it is known. It is not closed in on itself, it is not self-sufficient. It admits and even calls for a critical elaboration and for rectification. These controls are procured by a praxis of a superior degree, which is, this time, the life of the proletariat in the Party. This higher praxis is not a reflection of the initial praxis; it is not contained in it in miniature; it carries the working class beyond its immediate reality; it expresses it, and here, as everywhere else, the expression is creative. But it is not arbitrary. The Party must establish itself as the expression of the working class by making itself accepted by the working class. The Party's operation must prove that beyond capitalistic history there is another history, wherein one does not have to choose between the role of subject and object. The proletariat's acknowledgment of the Party is not an oath of allegiance to persons. Its counterpart is the acknowledgment of the proletariat by the Party. This is certainly not to say that there is a submission of the Party to the proletarians' opinions just as they are; rather, there is the statutory aim of making them attain political life. This exchange, in which no one commands and no one obeys, is symbolized by the old custom which dictates that, in a meeting, speakers join in when the audience applauds. What they applaud is the fact that they do not intervene as persons, that in their relationship with those who listen to them a truth appears which does not come from them and which the speakers can and must applaud. In the communist sense, the Party is this communication; and such a conception of the Party is not a corollary of Marxism—it is its very center. Unless one makes another dogmatism of it (and how is one to do so, since one cannot start from the self-certainty of a universal subject), Marxism does not have a total view of universal history at its disposal; and its entire philosophy of history is nothing more than the development of partial views that a man situated in history, who tries to understand himself, has of his past and of his present. This conception remains hypothetical until it finds a unique guarantee in the existing proletariat and in its assent, which allows it to be valid as the law of being. The Party is then like a mystery of reason. It is the place in history where the *meaning which is* understands itself, where the concept becomes life; and, avoiding the test which authenticates Marxism, any deviation which would assimilate the relationships of Party and class to the relationships of chief and troops would make an "ideology" of it. Then history as science and history as reality would remain disjointed, and the Party would no longer be the laboratory of history and the beginning of a true society. The great Marxists realized so well that problems of organization command the value of truth in Marxism that they went so far as to admit that theses, however well-founded, must not be imposed on the proletarians against their will, because their rejection signifies that subjectively the proletariat is not ripe for them and, thus, that these theses are premature and, finally, false. Nothing remains to their defenders but to explain them anew, once the teachings of events will have made them convincing. Class consciousness is not an absolute knowledge of which the proletarians are miraculously the trustees. It has to be formed and straightened out, but the only valid politics is the one which makes itself accepted by the workers. It is not a question of entrusting to the proletariat the task of deciphering the situation and elaborating theses and the political line. It is not even a question of continually translating into clear language for the proletarians the full revolutionary implication of their actions. This would sometimes make them feel that the weight of the resistance to be overcome is too heavy —a resistance which they will overcome without being aware that they are doing so; and, in any case, this would amount to warning the enemy. The theoretician therefore is in front of the proletariat, but, as Lenin said, only a step in front of it. In other words, the masses are never the simple means of a great politics which is worked out behind their backs. Led, but not maneuvered, the masses bring the seal of truth to the politics of the Party.

In what sense are we employing the word truth? It is not the truth of realism, the correspondence between the idea and the external thing, since the classless society is to be made, not already made, since the revolutionary politics is to be invented, not being already there, implicit in the existing proletariat, and since, finally, the proletariat is to be convinced and not merely consulted. Revolutionary politics cannot bypass this moment when it dares to step into the unknown. It is even its specific character to go into the unknown, since it wishes to put the proletariat in power as negation of capitalism and as sublation of itself. Thus, the truth of Marxism is not the truth one attributes to the natural sciences, the similarity of an idea and its external *ideatum*;[31] it is rather *nonfalsity*, the maximum guarantee against error that men may demand and get. The theoretician and the proletarians have to make a history in which they are included. They are therefore, at the same time, subjects and objects of their undertaking, and this creates for them a simultaneous possibility of understanding history, of finding a truth in it, and of being mis-

31. In the already cited review of Bukharin's book, Lukács reproaches the author for having suggested that the date of events and the speed of the historical process are not predictable because we have "not as yet" the knowledge of their quantitative laws. For Lukács, the difference between history and nature is not this alone, which would be totally subjective: it is objective and qualitative. In social situations there are only "tendencies"; and this is so, not because we do not have sufficient knowledge of them, but because this mode of existence is essential to the social event. As he again writes in *History and Class Consciousness*, history is not "exact." The only exact sciences are those whose object is made up of constant elements. This is not the case with history if it is to be able to be transformed by a revolutionary praxis (*GK*, p. 18; ET, pp. 5–6).

taken as to its developing meaning. We can say, then, that there is truth when there is *no disagreement* between the theoreticians and the proletarians, when the political idea is not challenged by known facts, although one can never be sure that it will not be challenged at some future date. Truth itself is then conceived as a process of indefinite verification, and Marxism is, at one and the same time, a philosophy of violence and a philosophy without dogmatism. Violence is necessary only because there is no final truth in the contemplated world; violence cannot therefore pride itself on having an absolute truth. Certainly, in action, in revolutionary periods, violence has the aspect of dogma. But there remains a difference, which can be seen in the long run, between a new dogmatism and a politics which puts generalized self-criticism into power. The *Stimmung* of Lukács, and, we believe, of Marxism, is thus the conviction of being, not in the truth, but on the threshold of truth, which is, at the same time, very near, indicated by all the past and all the present, and at an infinite distance in a future which is to be made.

WE HAVE SEEN HISTORY trace a philosophical itinerary which is realized only through us and through our decision; we have seen the subject find its certitude in adhering to a historical force in which the subject recognizes itself because this force is the power of a principle of negativity and self-criticism. For Lukács the essential feature of Marxism as dialectical philosophy is this meeting of event and meaning. Josef Revai, one of his companions in this struggle, who hailed his book as an event [32] and who today has become one of his principal critics, went so far as to propose a sort of Marxist irrationalism. Lukács himself carries out Marx's program, which is to destroy speculative philosophy but to do so by realizing it. The problem of the thing-in-

32. Revai said that Lukács' book is "the first attempt to make conscious what is Hegelian in Marx, the dialectical 'it is'; by its depth, its richness of content, its art of testing apparently purely philosophical general propositions against concrete and particular problems, it is far superior to the works which until now have been dealing with the philosophical basis of Marxism as a special problem. Besides this, it is the first attempt to deal with the history of philosophy in terms of historical materialism, and, from a purely philosophical point of view, it is the first time we have indeed gone beyond a philosophy which hardens itself into a theory of knowledge" (Josef Revai, review of Lukács' *History and Class Consciousness, Archiv für die Geschichte des Sozialismus und der Arbeiterbewegung*, XI [1925], 227–36).

itself, say Revai, reappears in the philosophy of history under the form of a divergence between actual history and the image we ourselves make of it; to Lukács he objects that

> The identical subject-object of the capitalistic society is not identifiable with the unique subject of all history, which is postulated only as correlative and cannot be embodied concretely. . . . The modern proletariat which fights for communism is not at all the subject of ancient or feudal society. It understands these epochs as its own past and as stages which lead to itself. Thus it is not their subject.[33]

The proletariat "projects" a subject into the past which totalizes the experience of the past and undoubtedly projects into the empty future a subject which concentrates the meaning of the future. This is a well-founded "conceptual mythology," but a mythology, since the proletariat is not truly able to enter into a precapitalistic past or a postcapitalistic future. The proletariat does not realize the identification of subject and history. It is nothing but the "carrier" [34] of a myth which presents this identification as desirable. This extension offered by Revai reduces Lukács' philosophical effort to nothing because, if the proletariat is only the carrier of a myth, the philosopher, even if he judges this myth to be well founded, decides this in his profound wisdom or unlimited audacity, which becomes a court of last appeal. In such a situation the historical movement which puts the proletariat in power no longer has philosophical substance. It no longer has this privilege, which is also a duty, of being the realization of the true society and of the truth. Lukács' effort was precisely to show that the empirical proletariat, surpassed by the richness of a history which it cannot represent to itself either as it was or as it will be, retains, nevertheless, an implicit totality and is in itself the universal subject which, because it is self-critical and sublates itself, can become for itself only through the indefinite development of the classless society. The essential feature of Lukács' thought was no longer to put the total meaning of history in a mythical "world spirit" but on a level with the proletarians' condition in a provable and verifiable process without an occult background. Revai stated that Marx "introduced the future into the domain of the revolutionary dialectic, not as positing a goal or an end, or as the necessary advent of a natural law, but as an

33. *Ibid.*, p. 235.
34. *Ibid.*

active reality which dwells in the present and determines it." [35]
This hold on the future—and, moreover, on the past, which remains to be unveiled in its true light—was, for Lukács, guaranteed to the proletariat because the proletariat is the work of
negativity. If the proletariat is nothing but a carrier of myths, the
whole meaning of the revolutionary enterprise is in danger.

This meaning, according to Lukács, is not entirely defined by
any particular objective, not even those which revolutionary
politics proposes for itself day by day, not even by the ideology
diffused by this politics. The meaning of the revolution is to be
revolution, that is to say, universal criticism, and, in particular,
criticism of itself. The characteristic of historical materialism, he
said, is to apply itself to itself, that is to say, to hold each of its
formulations as provisional and relative to a phase of development and, by constantly refining itself, to proceed toward a truth
which is always to come. Take, for example, the ideology of historical materialism. When the foundations of capitalistic society
are destroyed and the proletariat takes power, said Lukács, the
doctrine "changes function." Its purpose before was to discredit
bourgeois ideologies (even if they contained some truth) by
unmasking the interests they defended. It was then one of the
weapons of the proletarian struggle. When the proletariat directs
its struggle from above, when the management of the economy
begins to obey its demands and to follow human norms, true
knowledge and a regression of ideologies, including those used at
first by the proletariat, inevitably accompany the development of
production. The solidarity of "matter" and spirit, which in the
capitalistic phase of history meant the decadence of a knowledge
which no longer expressed the social totality and served only to
mask it, now means a liberation of both knowledge and production. It is, then, the task of historical materialism to recognize
what was purely polemical in the representations of history with
which it had satisfied itself, and to develop into true knowledge
as society develops into classless society. And Lukács invited his
country's sociologists to rediscover the richness of the precapitalistic past beyond Engels' explanatory diagrams.[36]

The coming-to-be of truth, the core of history, gives to Marxism the validity of a strict philosophy and distinguishes it from

35. *Ibid.*, p. 233.
36. See "The Changing Function of Historical Materialism" in *GK*,
pp. 229–60; ET, pp. 223–55.

any kind of psychologism and historicism. In this regard, Lukács thinks that the vague slogan of humanism should be reconsidered. The very concept of man must be rendered dialectical; and if by "man" one understood a positive nature or attributes, Lukács would no more accept this idol than any other. We have seen that, if one goes deeply enough into relativism, one finds there a transcendence of relativism, and one would miss this transcendence if one were to absolutize the relative. Man is not the measure of all things if man is a species or even a psychic phenomenon equipped with a certain set of principles or an unconditional will. "The measure," says Lukács, "should itself be measured," [37] and it can be measured only by truth. Under the myth of Platonic recollection [38] there is this always valid view that truth is of another species than the positivity of being, that it is elsewhere, that it is to be made. "The criterion for correctness of thought is without doubt reality. But reality does not exist; it becomes; and it does not become without the collaboration of thought (*nicht ohne Zutun des Denkens*)." [39]

> . . . the criterion of truth is provided by relevance to reality. This reality is by no means identical with empirical existence. This reality is not, it becomes. . . . But when the truth of becoming is the future that is to be created but has not yet been born, when it is the new that resides in the tendencies that (with our conscious aid) will be realized, then the question whether thought is a reflection appears quite senseless.[40]

What worries Lukács in humanism is that it offers us a given being to admire. To put man in the place of God is to displace, defer, and "abstractly negate" [41] the absolute. Our task, rather, is to make the abstract fluid, diffuse it in history, "understand" it as process.

Nothing is further from Marxism than positivistic prose: dialectical thought is always in the process of extracting from each phenomenon a truth which goes beyond it, waking at each moment our astonishment at the world and at history. This "philoso-

37. *GK*, p. 204; ET, p. 187.
38. *GK*, p. 220; ET, pp. 201–2.
39. *GK*, p. 223; ET, p. 204 (modified).
40. *GK*, pp. 222–23; ET, pp. 203–4.
41. *GK*, p. 208; ET, p. 190. [Merleau-Ponty's reference is to the discussion on p. 208 rather than to a specific expression used there. —Trans.]

phy of history" does not so much give us the keys of history as it restores history to us as permanent interrogation. It is not so much a certain truth hidden behind empirical history that it gives us; rather it presents empirical history as the genealogy of truth. It is quite superficial to say that Marxism unveils the meaning of history to us: it binds us to our time and its partialities; it does not describe the future for us; it does not stop our questioning—on the contrary, it intensifies it. It shows us the present worked on by a self-criticism, a power of negation and of sublation, a power which has historically been delegated to the proletariat. Max Weber ended by seeing in our historical participation an initiation into the universe of culture and, through that, into all times. For Lukács, it is not only the thought of the historian or the theoretician but a class which thus transforms the particular into the universal. But for him, as for Weber, knowledge is rooted in existence, where it also finds its limits. The dialectic is the very life of this contradiction. It is the series of progressions which it accomplishes. It is a history which makes itself and which nevertheless is to be made, a meaning which is never invalid but is always to be rectified, to be taken up again, to be maintained in the face of danger, a knowledge limited by no positive irrationality but a knowledge which does not actually contain the totality of accomplished and still to be accomplished reality and whose ability to be exhaustive is yet to be factually proved. It is a history-reality [42] which is judge or criterion of all our thoughts but which itself is nothing else than the advent of consciousness, so that we do not have to obey it passively but must think it in accordance with our own strength. These reversible relationships prove that, when Marxism focuses everything through the perspective of the proletariat, it focuses on a principle of universal strife and intensifies human questioning instead of ending it.

IF WE HAVE UNDERTAKEN to recall Lukács' attempt (very freely, and emphasizing certain points that in his work were only indicated), it is not because something of it remains in today's Marxism or even because it is one of those truths which only by chance miss the historical record. We shall see, on the contrary, that there was something justified in the opposition it encountered. But it was necessary to recall this lively and vigorous attempt, in which the youth of revolution and Marxism lives

42. [In the French: "une histoire-réalité."—Trans.]

again, in order to measure today's communism, to realize what it has renounced and to what it has resigned itself. By thus remaining in the superstructures, by trying to find out how communism theoretically conceives the relationships between subject and history, one undoubtedly skims over political history, but a certain sense of its evolution appears with an incomparable distinctness. The intellectual history of communism is not indifferent—even, and especially, for a Marxist; it is one of the detectors of communist reality. Perhaps, in the end, the "detour" via philosophy is much less conjectural than a political, social, or economic analysis which, in the absence of sufficient information, is often only a construct in disguise. Let us try, then, to ask the communist question once again by confronting Lukács' attempt with the orthodox philosophy that was preferred to it.

3 / *Pravda*

LUKÁCS' ATTEMPT was very poorly received by the orthodoxy,[1] particularly the "Marxists-Leninists," who immediately pretended to consider the book—which only wanted to develop the Marxist dialectic—as a revision and a criticism of Marxism.[2] In *Pravda* of July 25, 1924, Lukács, Korsch, Fogarasi, and Revai were grouped together in the same reprobation and were confronted with what was called the ABC's of Marxist philosophy, namely, the definition of truth as "the harmony of representation with the objects which are outside it"—in other words, that vulgar Marxism in which Lukács saw rather a product of capitalistic reification. Lukács here came up against *Materialism and Empiriocriticism*, which was then becoming the charter of Russian Marxism. His adversaries were not wrong to criticize Lenin's philosophical ideas for being incompatible with what they themselves called, as Korsch says, "Western Marxism." Lenin had written his book in order to reaffirm that dialectical materialism is a materialism, that it supposes a materialistic diagram of knowledge (regardless of what the dialectic may be able to add

1. As Karl Korsch notes (*Marxismus und Philosophie* [Leipzig, 1930]), by the Social Democratic orthodoxy as well as by the Russian Communist Party. Kautsky's condemnation of Lukács' thesis (*Die Gesellschaft*, June, 1924) corresponds to Zinoviev's, who was then president of the Communist International (*Internationale Presskorrespondenz*, Year IV, 1924). The scientism, objectivism, and idolatry of the sciences of nature are equal on both sides. It would be interesting, says Korsch, to find out why.
2. Cf. Abram M. Deborin, "Lukács und seine Kritik des Marxismus," *Arbeiterliteratur* (Vienna, 1924).

to those premises). In saying again that thought is a product of the brain and, through the brain, of the external reality, in taking up again the old allegory of ideas-images, Lenin thought he was going to establish the dialectic solidly in things. He forgot that an effect does not resemble its cause and that knowledge, being an effect of things, is located in principle outside its object and attains only its internal counterpart. This was to annul all that has been said about knowledge since Epicurus, and Lenin's very problem—what he called the "gnostilogical question" of the relationship between being and thought—re-established the pre-Hegelian theory of knowledge. Hegel had indeed been able to show that, in a philosophy of history, the problem of knowledge is surmounted, because there no longer can be a question of timeless relations between being and thought, but only of relations between man and his history, or even between the present and the future, and the present and the past. For Lenin this was a dead letter; as Korsch notes, not once in the 370 pages of his book does Lenin put knowledge back among the other ideologies or try to find an internal criterion to distinguish them. He never asks himself by what miracle knowledge carries on a relationship with a suprahistorical object, a relationship which is itself removed from history.[3] This new dogmatism, which puts the knowing subject outside the fabric of history and gives it access to absolute being, releases it from the duty of self-criticism, exempts Marxism from applying its own principles to itself, and settles dialectical thought, which by its own movement rejected it, in a massive positivity.

To be sure, we have no way of knowing whether Lenin himself regarded this book as having any value beyond that of serving as a protective barrier. Marx and Engels, he says, especially wished to preserve materialism from simplifications [4] because

3. Similarly, H. Lefebvre categorically writes: "Physical discoveries are not superstructures of the bourgeois society; they are knowledge" ("La Pensée, Lénine philosophe," *La Pensée* [March 1, 1954]); and J. Desanti bursts out laughing when Laplace's nebula is put into the "cultural world"—but the readers are not told how historical determination respectfully stops on the threshold of science.

4. So that "the valuable fruits of the idealist systems [should not] be forgotten, the Hegelian dialectic, the veritable pearl that . . . Büchner, Dühring and company . . . did not know how to extract from the manure of absolute idealism" (V. I. Lenin, *Matérialisme et Empiriocriticisme* [Paris, 1949], p. 219; English translation, *Materialism and Empiriocriticism* (New York, 1927), p. 248.

they intervened at a moment when materialism was an idea commonly accepted among advanced intellectuals. If Lenin himself returns to the ABC's of "materialism" or to its "first truths," this, too, is perhaps nothing but an attitude dictated by circumstance. It would then be a shift in cultural politics rather than a rigorous philosophical formulation. That Lenin admitted tactics into philosophy, and that he distinguished them from research, is proven by a letter to Gorki [5] in which he claims the right as a party man to take a position against "dangerous" doctrines while proposing to Gorki a neutrality pact concerning "empiriocriticism," which, he says, does not justify a factional struggle. "A party must contain a whole gradation of nuances in its unity, and the extremes may even be absolute opposites." [6] The fact is that, after *Materialism and Empiriocriticism*, Lenin returned to Hegel. In 1922 he gave the cue for the systematic study of Hegel's dialectic,[7] and this meditation on Hegel would scarcely leave the succinct "gnosticism" of *Materialism and Empiriocriticism* intact. What he wanted to do in this earlier work was, therefore, to furnish a simple and efficacious ideology to a country which had not gone through all the historical phases of Western capitalism. The dialectic, the self-criticism of materialism, was for later on.[8] Here, as everywhere, communism after Lenin has stabilized, congealed,[9] transformed into institutions, and denatured what was, in Lenin's view, only a phase in a living development. This, however, does not settle the question. For even if there is a question of philosophical tactics in *Materialism and Empiriocriticism*, it would still be necessary, as with any tactics, for these to be compatible with the strategy they serve. Yet one does not see how a pre-Hegelian gnosticism or even a pre-Kantian one could introduce the Marxist dialectic. Tactics without principles —anywhere, but especially in philosophy—are a confession of irrationality, and this offhandedness with truth, this use of ex-

5. March 24, 1908.
6. V. I. Lenin, *Pages choisies* (Paris, 1937), II, 139. [Merleau-Ponty's reference is not to Lenin's March 24, 1908, letter to Gorki (Lenin, *Collected Works*, XXXIV, 388–90).—Trans.]
7. "We must organize a systematic study of Hegel's dialectic from a materialistic point of view."
8. Such is the interpretation proposed by Korsch (*Marxismus und Philosophie*, pp. 27 ff.; English translation by Fred Halliday, *Marxism and Philosophy* [London, 1970], pp. 109 ff.).
9. [In the French: "figé."—Trans.]

pedients in philosophy, must hide an internal difficulty of Marxist thought.

And indeed, one would find in Marx the same discordancy between naïve realism and dialectical inspiration, for Marx begins dialectical thought. It is complete in the famous principle that one cannot destroy philosophy without realizing it. To do so is to gather the whole heritage of philosophical radicalism, including Cartesian and Kantian radicalism, to incorporate it in Marxist praxis, and recover it, freed of formalism and abstraction. To realize it is, therefore, to want the subjective to pass into the objective, to want "the object" to snatch or incarnate the subjective and then form a single whole with it. Lukács' main theses (the relativization of subject and object, the movement of society toward self-knowledge, and truth seen as a presumptive totality to be reached through a permanent self-criticism) are already there as soon as one attempts to develop the Marxist idea of a concrete dialectic and a "realized" philosophy. But this Marxism which wishes to integrate philosophy is the pre-1850 one. After this comes "scientific" socialism, and what is given to science is taken from philosophy. *The German Ideology* already spoke of destroying philosophy rather than realizing it. One had to "put it aside" and become again an "ordinary man" in order to undertake the study of the "real world," which is to philosophy "what sexual love is to onanism." In the final paragraph of *Ludwig Feuerbach*, Engels writes that philosophy is "as superfluous as it is impossible." One still speaks of the dialectic, but it is no longer a paradoxical mode of thought, the discovery of an entangling relationship between the dialectician and his object, the surprise of a spirit which finds itself outdistanced by things and anticipated in them. It is the simple verification of certain descriptive features of history, even of nature.[10] *There are* "interactions," "qualitative leaps," and "contradictions." Like all the others, these particularities of the object are recorded by scientific thought. Each science therefore makes its dialectic, and Engels does not concede to philosophy even the right of putting the results of science into an original dialectic. Philosophy is itself a particular science which is concerned with the laws of thought. In the second preface to *Capital,* what Marx calls dialectic is "the affirmative recognition of the existing state of things." In

10. The two domains are not even distinguished. With respect to Darwin, Marx speaks of a "history of nature."

his later period, therefore, when he reaffirms his faithfulness to Hegel, this should not be misunderstood, because what he looks for in Hegel is no longer dialectical inspiration; rather it is rationalism, to be used for the benefit of "matter" and "ratios of production," which are considered as an order in themselves, an external and completely positive power. It is no longer a question of saving Hegel from abstraction, of recreating the dialectic by entrusting it to the very movement of its content, without any idealistic postulate; it is rather a question of annexing Hegel's logic to the economy. This is why Marx is at one and the same time very close to Hegel and opposed to him, why Engels can write that it is necessary to put Hegel "back on his feet," and why Marx says that his own dialectic is the direct opposite of Hegel's.[11] In this perspective, one sees today's Marxism at the end of this development. We are on the surface of an economic process far more extensive than what is embraced by consciousness. Except for knowledge of the economy, which does reach being, we are cut off from truth. What we are living is a result of long chains of economic causes and effects. We are not able to *understand* it, that is to say, to elucidate the implied human relationships in each historical phase and to situate them in relation to the "reign of freedom"; we are able to explain it only by the objective process of the economy. The action which will change the world is no longer undivided praxis-philosophy and technique, i.e., movement of infrastructures but also recourse to the whole criticism of the subject; rather, it is the type of action a technician would make, like that of an engineer who builds a bridge.[12]

11. In the second preface to *Capital*.
12. In the study we have already cited, J. Revai correctly notes that Plekhanov and Engels, by wanting to put the dialectic in nature, end up "naturalizing the dialectic," making a simple statement of certain characteristics of the object (development by contradiction, change of quantity to quality) a rhapsody of generalities. Revai says that Plekhanov "believed it possible to disregard the Hegelian theory of self-consciousness, which joins the isolated moments of the dialectic into an organic whole," and to replace Hegel's *Weltgeist* by the relationships of production (Josef Revai, review of Lukács' *History and Class Consciousness, Archiv für die Geschichte des Sozialismus und der Arbeiterbewegung*, XI [1925]). Going from Engels to Plekhanov, one easily arrives at the views of contemporary orthodoxy, which are that the dialectic is not a sort of knowledge; it is rather a group of verifications, and it is valid only in its "general context" (interaction, development, qualitative leaps, contradictions) (see L. Althusser, "Note sur le Matérialisme dialectique," *Revue de l'enseigne-*

The conflict between "Western Marxism" and Leninism is already found in Marx as a conflict between dialectical thought and naturalism, and the Leninist orthodoxy eliminated Lukács' attempt as Marx himself had eliminated his own first "philosophical" period. This circuit which always brings the dialectic back to naturalism cannot therefore be vaguely ascribed to the "errors" of the epigones. It must have its truth, and it must translate a philosophical experience. This circuit testifies to an obstacle that Marxist thought tries, for better or for worse, to get around. It attests to a change in the relations of Marxist thought to social being insofar as this thought theoretically and practically attempts to dominate social being. As Korsch notes, dialectical and philosophical Marxism is suited to soaring periods, when revolution appears close at hand, while scientism predominates in stagnant periods, when the divergence between actual history and its immanent logic gets worse, when the weight of infrastructures makes itself felt, as was the case at the end of the nineteenth century, when the capitalistic apparatus stabilized itself, or as is the case in the U.S.S.R. when the difficulties of a planned economy present themselves in practice. Then the "subject" and the "object" become disassociated, and revolutionary optimism gives way to a merciless voluntarism. The economic apparatus, whether to be overthrown or to be constructed, which according to Marx was a "relationship between persons mediated by things," practically ceases to appear as a relationship between persons and becomes almost completely a thing. The Marxism of the young Marx as well as the "Western" Marxism of 1923 lacked a means of expressing the inertia of the infrastructures, the resistance of economic and even natural conditions, and the swallowing-up of "personal relationships" in "things." History as they described it lacked density and allowed its meaning to appear too soon. They had to learn the slowness of mediations.

In order to understand the logic and the shifts of history, its meaning and what, within it, resists meaning, they still had to conceptualize the sphere proper to history, the institution, which develops neither according to causal laws, like a second nature, but always in dependence on its meaning, nor according to eter-

---

ment philosophique, October–November, 1953, p. 12). This mixture of positive spirit and dialectic transfers into nature man's way of being—it is nothing less than magic.

nal ideas, but rather by bringing more or less under its laws events which, as far as it is concerned, are fortuitous and by letting itself be changed by their suggestions. Torn by all the contingencies, repaired by involuntary actions of men who are caught in it and want to live, the web deserves the name of neither spirit nor matter but, more exactly, that of history. This order of "things" which teaches "relationships between persons," sensitive to all the heavy conditions which bind it to the order of nature, open to all that personal life can invent, is, in modern language, the sphere of symbolism, and Marx's thought was to find its outlet here.

The Marxist orthodoxy, however, does not frankly consider the problem. It is satisfied with placing things and the relationships between persons side by side, with adding to the dialectic a dose of naturalism, which, even though it is a moderate dose, immediately breaks it up, and with situating the dialectic in the place where it is least capable of residing, namely, in the object, in being. Marx had brought to the fore the problem of an open dialectic which would not eternally be founded on an absolute subjectivity. Lenin's gnosticism restores to the dialectic an absolute foundation in being or in pure object and thus returns not only to the side of the young Marx but also to the side of Hegel. This is the source of communist eclecticism, that thought without candor which one never completely knows, that unstable mixture of Hegelianism and scientism which allows the orthodoxy to reject, in the name of "philosophical" principles, all that the social sciences have tried to say since Engels and yet allows it to reply with "scientific socialism" when philosophical objections are raised. It maintains itself only by constant precautions, by paralyzing the spirit of research, and this is enough to explain why one rarely sees the Marxist side produce an interesting book. Lenin's gnosticism, by joining the dialectic with materialistic metaphysics, preserves the dialectic but embalms it, outside ourselves, in an external reality. This means replacing history as a relationship between persons embodied in "things" by a "second nature" which is opaque and determined like the first. On the theoretical plane, it means closing off any attempt at "comprehension," as, on the plane of action, it means replacing total praxis by a technician-made action, replacing the proletariat by the professional revolutionary. It means concentrating the movement of history, as well as that of knowledge, in an apparatus.

IF THIS EVALUATION IS CORRECT, and if philosophical Leninism is an expedient, the problems that elude philosophical Leninism must reappear, and the balance between dialectical and metaphysical materialism must remain precarious. Lukács' intellectual career since 1923 shows how difficult it is to maintain this balance. As early as the publication of *History and Class Consciousness*, Lukács admitted [13] that some of the essays [14] in it grant too much to the optimism of the revolutionary years and do not sufficiently take into consideration the long work which is necessary in order to bring history to express what is, nevertheless, its meaning. As L. Goldmann shows,[15] Lukács now thinks that the work is "apocalyptic," that it was wrong to postulate a spirit of the revolution all ready to appear as soon as the capitalistic foundations are shaken. It is therefore because his too supple and too notional dialectic did not translate the opacity, or at least the density, of real history that Lukács accepted the Communist International's judgment on his book and never allowed it to be reprinted. It is this feeling of the objective world's weight, which is acquired only in contact with things, which makes Lukács, as philosopher, appreciate Lenin and makes him write that "the Leninist period of Marxism" represents "philosophical progress." [16] Marx, writes Lukács, always considers the economic facts as relationships between persons, but these relationships are for Marx "hidden under a veil of things." The false evidences of ideologies, mental things which are part of the existing social system and under which true social relationships are hidden, impose themselves between the truth and us. Our knowledge of society is then "a reflection in the thought of this dialectic which unrolls itself objectively in men's lives, independently of their knowledge and their will, and whose objectivity makes a *second nature* of social reality." [17] Lukács thus indicates more energetically than before the distance between

13. Georg Lukács, Preface to *Geschichte und Klassenbewusstsein* (Berlin, 1923); English translation by Rodney Livingstone, *History and Class Consciousness* (Cambridge, Mass., 1971).

14. Particularly "The Changing Function of Historical Materialism."

15. Lucien Goldmann, *Sciences humaines et philosophie* (Paris, 1952); English translation by Hayden White and Robert Anchor, *The Human Sciences and Philosophy* (London, 1969).

16. Georg Lukács, *Der junge Hegel* (Zurich and Vienna, 1948), p. 7.

17. *Ibid.*, p. 25.

truth and consciousness, and he learned to do this from the school of Lenin. It remains to be seen whether consciousness as *reflection* and history as *second nature*—in short, the return to naïve realism—are a philosophical solution of the difficulty, whether one can accept this language except as an approximative way of posing a problem, and whether, taken literally, this gnosticism does not make all philosophical strictness, and all living thought, impossible and does not place truth completely beyond our grasp. From the moment when consciousness and being are put face to face as two external realities, when consciousness as simple reflection is struck by a radical doubt and history as a second nature is affected by an opacity which can never be completely eliminated, consciousness no longer has any criterion for distinguishing by itself what is knowledge and what is ideology; and naïve realism, as it has always done, ends in skepticism. If it escapes this consequence, it can do so only by a *coup de force*, by an unmotivated compliance with some external urgency—the social process in itself, the Party—and all productions of thought from now on will have to be measured by this standard, held for true or false according to whether or not they conform. No one can think this, and least of all Lukács, who is a philosopher and a scholar. He has come to an attitude which is not coherent but which is significant. Having, on the whole, accepted the lessons of philosophical Leninism, and speaking, like everyone else, the language of consciousness-reflection,[18] thus leaving the field open to the least understandable turns and opening up an unlimited credit to those who make history, he yet maintains in principle the autonomy of truth, the possibility of reflection, the life of subjectivity in the order of culture, where, under pain of death, they cannot be subordinated to tactics. It is quite as if, having cleared the ground—of action and historical work—he paid particular attention to defending the conditions of a sane culture for the future. But can one give what is due to both dialectic and realism? From the recent polemics surrounding Lukács, it is clear that his theory of literature brings back the dialectic in its entirety and puts him in conflict with the ortho-

18. In German this language allows for convenient ambiguities. The *Wiederspiegelung* is not only reflection as result but the act of reflection. This restores the act of conception. H. Lefebvre is less at ease in French and has to content himself with proposing to his readers the enigma of an "active-reflection" ["reflet-actif"] ("La Pensée, Lénine philosophe," article cited above, n. 3).

doxy at the same time as his concessions to philosophical realism lead him to a complete capitulation.

What remains of his dialectic philosophy is his theory of literature. When he writes that literature never expresses a class only, but the relationship of classes inside the social whole and thus in some measure the whole itself, one once again sees the idea that consciousness may well be false or falsified but that there is never a fundamental falsity of consciousness. On the contrary, in principle it contains its own rectification because the whole is always glimpsed in consciousness as an enigma; and thus, being always exposed to error, consciousness is faced with a permanent self-criticism, and, being always open to truth, it can and must proceed by immanent criticism and internal transcendence of errors rather than by peremptory condemnation. This conception of our relationships with the true and the false is the opposite of Lenin's "gnosticism," which, on the contrary, allows in principle for the coincidence of a subject and an object external to each other, even if one treats this coincidence as an inaccessible limit, since, in the end, it is clear that the subject cannot be witness to his relationship to a thing-in-itself. When Lukács allows that there is a truth to ideologies, provided they be put back into their social context, that even the theory of art for art's sake in an imperialistic regime is relatively legitimate because it shows the society's resistance to the rendings of history and because it maintains the principle of intensive totality which is that of art, what he is defending is still the idea that consciousness cannot be absolutely cut off from the true. Even an error such as art for art's sake has, in the situation where it appears, its truth. There is a participation of ideas among themselves that forbids them ever to be absolutely unusable and false. In a word, all this is the dialectical method. When he asks today's writers to take their models from the great preimperialistic bourgeois literature, when he defends the partyless sniper writers, when he writes that realism is not simple notation or observation, that it demands narration and transposition, this implies that the work of art is not a simple reflection of history and society. It expresses them not punctually but by its organic unity and its internal law. It is a microcosm, and there is a value of expression which is not a simple function of economic and social progress; there is a history of culture which is not always parallel to political history; and there is a Marxism which appreciates literary works according to intrinsic criteria and not according to the author's political conformity. This claim of a relative autonomy for art is one of the consequences of the famous law of unequal development, which holds that the different orders of phenomena existing at the same time—as elsewhere political and social facts which appear in different sequences—do not develop according to a uniform plan. This law in turn supposes a dialectical conception of the unity of history, that is to say, a unity rich in final convergence and not a unity by reduction to a single order of reality or a single genetic schema. The dialectical conception in the end supposes a logic of history based on the immanent development of each order of facts, of each historical sequence, and on the self-suppression of the false, and not on a positive principle which would govern things from outside. What Lukács wishes to defend by his theses on literature, and what one attacks in them, is therefore always the idea that subjectivity is incorporated in history, not produced by it, and that history—generalized subjectivity, relationships among persons asleep and congealed in "things"—is not an *in-itself*, governed, like the physical world, by causal laws, but is a totality to be understood. Putting it briefly, this is the relativization [19] of subject and object with which *History and Class Consciousness* began. If he now writes that the social is a second nature, it is by putting the word in quotation marks, by making it a metaphor, in order to express the fact that our consciousness is far from being coextensive with the historical dialectic, that it does not spring out of it as an effect out of its cause. If he speaks of it as a reflection, it is immediately to add that there is "extensive reflection" and "intensive reflection," [20] which is to say that we are not only in the whole of objective history but that, in another sense, it is wholly in us, and he reestablishes the double relation or ambiguity of the dialectic.

But can one, even in the limited domain of culture and under the cover of these equivocal elements, maintain the dialectical method if one has yielded on the principles of "gnosticism"? These principles have their logic, which is not long in making itself felt: if the subject is a reflection of the social and political process, there is no other urgency of truth than conformity to the demands of the revolutionary movement, represented by the Party; and any literary criticism which remains intrinsic, which

19. [In the French: "relativisation."—Trans.]
20. Georg Lukács, *Karl Marx und Friedrich Engels als Literaturhistoriker* (Berlin, 1947).

takes into account the modes of expression appropriate to literature and analyzes the internal organization of works, is to be
condemned as *diversion, idealization of bygone regimes,* and
separation of literature and history.[21] For a realist there is not a
plurality of viewpoints, a center and a periphery of the dialectic,
an intensive totality; there is only a historical process to be veri-
fied and to be followed. If Lukács, the dialectician, acknowledges
that the totality lived by each man always extends, in some sense,
beyond his class situation, realist thought, which has no means of
expressing what is intensive and in transition, will suppose that
Lukács believes in an art "above classes."[22] "What could the
watchword, 'Zola? No, Balzac!'—formulated by Lukács in 1945
—give to Hungarian literature, and what could the motto 'Neither
Pirandello nor Priestley, but Shakespeare and Molière'—advanced by Lukács in 1948—give to it? In both cases, nothing."[23]
Nothing, in effect, except culture. Is this so little for a literature?
Lukács acknowledges, of course, that philosophies are explained
by social circumstances as well as by the maturation of philosophical problems.[24] But if the social is a second nature, it cannot
be one of the work's components; and it is necessary that the
work spread itself out on this objective plane and there receive a
complete explanation. Realism will demand of Lukács that he
make the history of philosophy and general history move at the
same pace. For if one maintains, even as a partial view, the possibility of a *problemgeschichtlich* study of philosophers, in each
case one will have to measure knowledge and ideology, acknowledge that culture both precedes and trails the economy, and reinstate a counterpoint of truth and error. If one believes that
there is a dialectic in things and that it results in the Russian
Revolution, this effort to understand the history of culture in its
deviations, its regressions, and its leaps, instead of simply recording it as objective progress, this return to internal criteria, distinct
from immediate political criteria, becomes "lack of a combative

21. We are here reproducing Josef Revai's arguments from *La
Littérature et la démocratie populaire, à propos de G. Lukács* (Paris,
1950). The author was then assistant general secretary of the Hungarian Worker's Party and minister of culture. Comparing this indictment with the writings of 1923 that we have already cited [note 12,
above], the reader asks himself if there are not *two* Josef Revais?
22. *Ibid.*, p. 22.
23. *Ibid.*, p. 11.
24. Lukács, *Der junge Hegel,* Preface, pp. 6–8.

Marxist-Leninist spirit," that is to say, "aristocraticism." [25] It is inevitably the dialectic itself which is arraigned by realism. It is not attacked frontally; and the law of unequal development is too classic to be denounced, so it is put aside, and its application is postponed. The dialectic is admitted as a general thesis, but it is vaguely added that the dialectic does not apply in "the manner described by Lukács" in societies that have classes. This is to exclude in advance the idea that any production made by societies with classes could be worth more than what is produced in the Soviet society.[26] After this, the self-criticism of Soviet literature stands no chance of being rigorous: it has "as its point of departure the recognition of the superiority of Soviet literature and socialist realism." [27] Thus realism ends by substituting a simple schema of progress for the difficult reading of the anticipations and delays of history and for the rigorous examination of revolutionary society; and, because the germs of socialist production are enclosed in the infrastructures of the U.S.S.R., the finest literature of the world must needs bloom on its surface. Realistic and causal thought always ends up by eliminating any reference to an interior of history or of literature or philosophy. There must be only one urgency: the existing social process and its completion in the U.S.S.R. One does not see how Lukács, except through inconsistency, could refuse this conclusion; actually, for a long time, even in Russia, he resisted and contested the superiority of Soviet literature. In 1949 he ended up granting that, "as a whole, only Soviet literature shows the way." This was not enough. *As a whole*—this was still a *quatenus* and thus, for realism, a refusal to conform. This self-criticism, said his censor, had "neither enough depth nor method." [28] He was asked not only to give Soviet literature his approval but also to give up saying why he had done so. Orthodoxy does not allow for critical reflection, even if the purpose is to base it in reason and in dialectic. Orthodoxy does not want to be a higher truth or true for reasons which are not its own; it claims for itself the truth of the thing itself. Lukács' history is that of a philosopher who believed it possible to wrap realism in the dialectic, the thing itself in the thought of the

25. Revai, *La Littérature et la démocratie populaire*, p. 22.
26. "There is no society which would be economically superior to that which preceded it and whose culture would yet be inferior" (*ibid.*, pp. 15–16).
27. *Ibid.*, p. 14.
28. *Ibid.*, p. 8.

thing. The blade wears out the sheath, and in the end no one is satisfied, neither the philosopher nor the powers that be.

THE CONFLICT between dialectic and realism is therefore not overcome, for, as we have said, if communism gives lip service to the dialectic, it cannot bring itself to renounce it. In the end, communism's intellectual profile is a fast and loose philosophical system [29] which disarms the dialectic by denying to the subject the judgment of history and the intrinsic appreciation of literature and politics; but it is a system which leads one to believe that the dialectic continues to function in the infrastructures and in the mysterious future which the infrastructures are preparing; and it is a system which honors the dialectic from afar and, without practicing or disavowing it, annuls it as a critical instrument, keeping it only as point of honor, justification, and ideology. We have attempted to show elsewhere [30] that the 1937 trials had their principle in the revolutionary idea of historical responsibility but that, strangely, this was not admitted; rather, they were presented as criminal-law trials, and the defendants were presented as spies. The Moscow Trials were the revolution which no longer wanted to be revolution, or inversely (we left the question open) an established regime which mimics the revolution. It has often been shown that the Russian Revolution, defined by Lenin as the Soviets plus electrification, concerned itself primarily with electrification and set up a series of powers, apparatuses, and social priorities which partition the revolutionary society and little by little make it something else. In communist philosophy we find an analogous equivocation between, on the one hand, a dialectic that takes precautions against itself and installs itself in being, beyond debate but also beyond practice, and, on the other, a realism which covers itself by using the dialectic as a point of honor. In any case it is a thought in the shadow of which something else is being done. Thus Marxism could not resolve the problem that is presented and from which we started. It could not maintain itself at that *sublime point* which it hoped it could find in the life of the Party, that point

29. [The original is "un système de double jeu philosophique." In French "double jeu" gives the impression of being both questionable and a double cross, and of there being two things working at the same time.—Trans.]

30. *Humanisme et terreur* (Paris, 1947). English translation by John O'Neill, *Humanism and Terror* (Boston, 1970).

where matter and spirit would no longer be discernible as subject and object, individual and history, past and future, discipline and judgment; and therefore the opposites which it was to unite fall away from one another. Someone will say that it is difficult to enter into the positive and to do something while keeping the ambiguity of the dialectic. The objection confirms our reservation because it amounts to saying that there is no revolution which is critical of itself. Yet it is through this program of continual criticism that revolution earns its good name. In this sense the equivocalness of the revolution would be the equivocalness of communist philosophy writ large.

4 / The Dialectic in Action

IF THERE IS a theoretical equivocalness of materialism and of dialectic, it should appear also in action; and by finding it again there, we shall obtain an indispensable cross-check. Indeed, to have a conclusive example, it is necessary to consider a pure case in which the dialectic was truly put to the test. It seems to us that Trotsky offers this balance of both practical and dialectical sense, and it is therefore his fate that we shall consider. If he did not accomplish the revolutionary resolution of antinomies in practice, it is because he encountered an obstacle there, the same obstacle that Lenin's "philosophy" confusedly attempted to take into account.

Trotsky was not a philosopher; and when he speaks philosophically,[1] it is by taking up again as his own the most banal naturalism. At first glance his naturalistic convictions resemble those of many less important men, and one is surprised to find in

1. For example: "Consciousness grew out of the unconscious, psychology out of physiology, the organic world out of the inorganic, the solar system out of nebulae. On all the rungs of this ladder of development, the quantitative changes were transformed into qualitative. Our thought, including dialectical thought, is only one of the forms of the expression of changing matter. . . . Darwinism, which explained the evolution of species through quantitative transformations passing into qualitative, was the highest triumph of the dialectic in the whole field of organic matter. Another great triumph was the discovery of the table of atomic weights of chemical elements and, further, the transformation of one element into another" (Leon Trotsky In Defense of Marxism [New York, 1942], p. 51). [Merleau-Ponty here translates the English edition.—Trans.]

someone who had to the highest degree the sentiment of personal honor and rectitude a philosophy which gives so little place to conscience. But it is this astonishment which is naïve. Naturalism is a philosophy vague enough to support the most varied moral superstructures. Some look to it for permission to be virtually anything, since man is nothing but an effect of nature and since, driven by external causes, he cannot claim responsibility or impose it on himself. Others, on the contrary, and Trotsky is among them, find the surest basis for a humanism in the naturalist myth: if our thought, "including dialectical thought . . . is only one expression of matter in the process of change," it is the whole human order which receives in return the solidity of natural things, and the exigencies of the most eccentric personality lose their epiphenomenal character to become components of the world itself. The fact remains that when Trotsky is speaking of literature, ethics, and politics and not of pure philosophy, he never falls back into the mechanism which is the weakness in Bukharin's works; nor does he ever cease to perceive, in the most precise and supple manner, the most complex dialectical relations. It is only at the two limits of his thought, in pure philosophy and in action, that one finds him suddenly peremptory, schematical, and abstract. It is as if a man's ideas of the relations between subject and being expressed his fundamental choice—the attitude to which he returns in extreme situations—and sounded, beyond the middle and happy zones of thought and life, the same note as his decisions in dangerous proximity to action.

Let us take, for example, Trotsky's definition of revolutionary realism, which he defines with admirable sureness. The debate between the cynicism of "by all means" and the pharisaism of "pure means" was already under way thirty years ago. Trotsky says that a revolutionary politics does not have to choose between them. Since it is completely in the world, it is not attached to an "ideal," and it takes its share of the violence of things. What revolutionary politics does at each instant should be considered only as a moment of the whole, and it would be absurd to ask of each means "its own moral tag." [2] But because such a politics is still in the world, it does not have the excuse of good intentions and must prove its value on the spot. Due to the accumulation of

2. Leon Trotsky, *Leur morale et la nôtre*, trans. Victor Serge, 2d ed. (Paris, 1966), p. 31; English translation, *Their Morals and Ours* [New York, 1969], p. 14. [The 1966 French edition is the same as the 1939 one.—Trans.]

means, one is placed before a result which takes shape and appears as an end even if it was not intended as such. If our means do not announce even our remote ends, at least by some quality which distinguishes them, they change the direction of history. The ends then pass into the means, and the means pass into the ends. "In practical life as in the historical movement the end and means constantly change places." [3] Between them there is a "dialectical interdependence." In setting up the power of the proletariat as the rule of action, revolutionary politics is able to go beyond the dichotomy and to ground itself in both value and reality. This is so because the proletariat is not a natural energy to be tapped by some sort of manipulation; rather, it is a human situation which cannot become the principle of a new society if the politics which claims it makes it obscure to itself. For a Marxist, then, whatever helps to put the proletariat in power is moral, but

> precisely from this it follows that *not* all means are permissible. When we say that the end justifies the means, then for us the conclusion follows that the great revolutionary end spurns those base means and ways which set one part of the working class against other parts, or attempt to make the masses happy without their participation; or lower the faith of the masses in themselves and their organization, replacing it by worship for the "leaders." [4]

Revolutionary realism, unlike technical action, never aims at external results alone. It wants only a result which can be understood, for if its result were not understandable, there would be no revolution. Each revolutionary act is efficacious not only through what it does but through what it gives people to think about. Action is the pedagogy of the masses, and explaining one's actions to the masses is acting again. [5]

3. *Ibid.*, p. 32; ET, pp. 14–15.
4. *Ibid.*, pp. 96–97; ET, p. 37.
5. If the revolutionary politician does not succeed in holding back the proletariat, he will not refuse to follow it into adventure, even if it is doomed to failure, because it has a lesson to give; and it would be a worse problem to let the proletariat fight alone, for it might think itself betrayed. Revolutionary politics can therefore adopt a "do as you must" attitude, not because it is uninterested in what will happen, but because, in a politics that must give the governing of history to those who until now were subservient to history, failure itself is a lesson which will contribute to victory, and only equivocation is an absolute failure.

Universal history, with which Trotsky, like all Marxists, is concerned, is not in an unfathomable future. It is not the future revelation, once all has been accomplished, of a subterranean force which led us without our knowledge. We have the right to invoke it only insofar as it appears on the horizon of present action and to the extent that it is already sketched there. The revolutionary future can serve to justify present action only if the future, in its general lines and in its style, is recognizable in such action. "Seeds of wheat must be sown in order to yield an ear of wheat." [6] Totality and universality are seen in the increasing participation of the masses in revolutionary politics and in the increasing transparency of history. We have no other guarantee against non-sense than this step-by-step confirmation of the present by that which succeeds it, this snowballing accumulation of history that ever more forcefully indicates its sense. Historical reason is not a divinity which guides history from outside. Trotsky compares it to natural selection, to the immanent play of given conditions which render impossible and eliminate organisms incapable of adequate response. [7] The external conditions do not of themselves create the species which will be put to the test. Historical selection is therefore only that unconscious or spontaneous part of history where the comprehension of history has not yet intervened. It is a fact that there are convergences, phenomena which support and confirm one another because they obey the same law of structure; and this is the case of all those phenomena that can be grouped under the notion of capitalism. The internal contradictions which dissociate this structure, the affinity which, on the contrary, brings together and confirms the one by the other, the advances of the proletariat, such are the data of spontaneous history. It falls to man's consciousness to achieve this outline, to coordinate the scattered forces, to find for them the point of application where they will have maximum efficiency, and to justify in fact their candidacy for a role in the guiding of history. Thus there is an immanent logic in things which eliminates false solutions; there are men who invent and try the true solutions, but nowhere is there an already written future. The Party is voluntary history, the place where forces previously incapable of breaking the structures in which they

6. *Leur morale et la nôtre*, pp. 98–99; ET, p. 38.
7. Leon Trotsky, *Ma vie* (Paris, 1953), p. 500; English translation, *My Life* (New York, 1930), pp. 494–95.

were born are concentrated and attain consciousness. "History," says Trotsky, "has no other way to realize its reason." [8] The Party is not admitted to the supposed verdicts of historical reason: There is no ready-made historical reason; there is a meaning of history sketched in the convulsions of spontaneous history and a voluntary and methodological recovery of history which reflects this meaning back into history. The Party neither knows nor sees all; and yet its authority is absolute because, if spontaneous history has a chance to become manifest history, this can only be through the Party. History will become manifest on the condition that all that is lived by the workers is clarified by the politics which is proposed to them by the Party and which they then adopt as their own. In the absence of any metaphysic of history, the dialectic of the proletariat and the Party gathers together all others and bears them within itself. What most concerns Marxist philosophy is not what the workers think, or what the Party believes they should think, but rather the recognition by the proletariat of its own action in the politics which the Party presents to it. History would wander aimlessly, and all the dialectics would fall away, if the Party did not allow itself a certain distance from which to view objectively the situation of the proletariat in the confluence of forces and to impose the decisions of the majority on everyone, or, similarly, if it omitted having the proletariat legitimize the decisions proposed to it. The Party, then, is at once all and nothing. It is nothing more than the mirror where the proletarian forces scattered throughout the world are concentrated, and it is all, since, without it, truth "in itself" would never become manifest or fulfill itself as truth. It is all, because it is nothing less than the universal on the march:

It is true . . . that to a Bolshevik the Party is everything. The drawing-room socialist Thomas is surprised by, and rejects, a similar relationship between a revolutionist and revolution because he himself is only a bourgeois with a socialist ideal. In the eyes of Thomas and his kind, the party is only a secondary instrument for electoral combinations and other similar uses, no more. His personal life, interests, ties, moral criteria, exist outside the party. With hostile astonishment he looks down upon the Bolshevik to whom the party is a weapon for the revolutionary reconstruction of society, including also its morality. To a revolutionary Marxist

8. Quoted by Claude Lefort in "La Contradiction de Trotsky et le problème révolutionnaire," *Les Temps modernes*, IV, no. 39 (1948/49), 56, from Boris Souvarine, *Staline* (Leiden, 1935), p. 340.

there can be no contradiction between personal morality and the interests of the party, since the party embodies in his consciousness the very highest tasks and aims of mankind. It is naïve to imagine that Thomas has a higher understanding of morality than the Marxists. He merely has a base conception of the party.[9]

In practice, what does Trotsky do with these very precise theses, in which a concrete and mythless dialectic has been so well restored?

We will not even ask, for the moment, whether Trotsky respected these theses when he was in an uncontested position. But from 1923 to 1927, when he had to defend his politics against the rising power of Stalin, one might think that he would do everything possible to carry the discussion to the proletariat and to put into action, to his advantage, the dialectic of the Party and the masses. Yet it has been shown that he did nothing of the sort.[10] Convinced that he could carry the Party at the Twelfth Congress, "even if Lenin [took] no direct part in the struggle," [11] he limited himself to polemics in the Politburo. His articles published in 1923 and 1924 contain only allusions to political divergencies and no open appeals to the militants. Not only did he publish nothing against "Lenin's levy"—which introduced into the Party a mass of manageable and inexperienced militants and which, Trotsky was later to say, delivered "a death blow to Lenin's party"—but he declared at the Thirteenth Congress that it made the Party more similar to an elected one.[12] He did indeed formulate his ideas on "the new course," but in 1925 he refrained from opposing a comprehensive policy to that of the Central Committee and the Stalinist majority. Moreover, he was in agreement with the Central Committee's decision to hide from the militants the documents known as "Lenin's Testament." When they were published by Max Eastman, Trotsky called Eastman a liar and insinuated that he was an agent of international reactionary forces.[13] On three or four occasions between 1925 and 1927 he officially declared that it was scarcely possible to speak of "different points of view" in the Central Committee

9. *Leur morale et la nôtre*, pp. 86–87; ET, pp. 33–34.
10. Lefort, "La Contradiction de Trotsky et le problème révolutionnaire."
11. *Ma vie*, p. 203, quoted by Lefort, *ibid.*, p. 55.
12. Quoted by Lefort, *ibid.*, p. 57.
13. *Ibid.*

and that, in any case, there was "no programmatic difference" between the Left Opposition and the majority of the Party.[14]

Later, in *My Life*, Trotsky attempted to sum up his 1927 politics by saying that he was not then able to commit himself completely because the revolutionary ebb eliminated his line and that his only alternative was to prepare himself for the moment when a new flow of history would once again bring forth progressist ideas.[15] In reality, in 1927 he did not limit himself to obedience while biding his time and recalling his principles: we have just seen that he lent himself to the actions of the Central Committee. The account rationalizes after the event an involuntary equivocation. Furthermore, other passages of *My Life* give another version of the events: Trotsky avoided the struggle as long as possible because the action of Stalin's friends was at the beginning only an "unprincipled conspiracy" against his person [16] and because it was better to answer this aggression by "the greatest personal concessions" than to risk transforming an "imaginary peril" into a "real menace." [17] However strange this mention of a personal conflict—and, fundamentally, this lack of self-confidence—may appear in as strong a politician as Trotsky, it proves at least that he did not immediately see the political significance of Stalinism. If he did not commit himself to the struggle in 1927, it was not because he already saw the revolution ebbing; on the contrary, it was because he did not see this. As has been mentioned, Trotsky hesitated a long time before diagnosing a Thermidorian reaction. In 1923 he categorically rejected it; and in 1926, while a Thermidorian course did not appear impossible to him, he strongly criticized the leftists in "Democratic Centralism" who held it to be a *fait accompli*. In November, 1927, after a street demonstration in which the opposition was harassed, he wrote that a general rehearsal of Thermidor had just been seen. Also in 1927, he declared with the 121 that no one had ever accused the Party or its Central Committee of having brought about a new Thermidor. In 1928–29, however, there was a threat of Thermidor. In 1930 he suddenly wrote: "In Russia, Thermidor has dragged on." Finally, in 1935, in the pamphlet *Etat ouvrier: Thermidor et Bonapartisme*, he wrote, "The Thermidor of the great Russian Revolution is not in front of us, but already far

14. *Ibid.*, p. 59.
15. *Ibid.*, p. 50.
16. *Ibid.*, p. 53.
17. *Ma vie*, p. 209, quoted by Lefort, *ibid.*, p. 54.

behind. The Thermidorians can celebrate the tenth anniversary of their victory." [18] If Trotsky did not bring the Party's democracy into play against the Central Committee's maneuvers, it was not because of historical clairvoyance; it was because of blindness. What remains to be understood is this blindness in such an expert statesman and revolutionary.

His conception of the Party was not vague, and he never lacked courage or information. To have hesitated to apply such clear ideas to a situation known to him, he must have always known that an existing Party can move quite far from its theoretical schema without ceasing to be itself. The question was to know whether the degeneration of the Party touched its essence and whether this degeneration were irreversible. As is always the case when it is a question of a reality and not simply of an idea, it was a problem of proportion or degree. In 1927 he said, "That which separates us is incomparably less than that which unites us." [19] Now, as long as the Party, if not by what it does, at least by what it is—which is to say, by what it will be able to do— remains the Party of the proletariat and guardian of the heritage of October, 1917, it provides "the grounds for a common work," [20] and it is in the Party that one must act. But if the "revolutionary dictatorship" that it exercises is valid, then, in view of this task, deviations are secondary. Divergences fall to the level of personal differences and will be hidden if they endanger the dictatorship. "Democratic centralism" does not make the oppositionist drop or hide his ideas; while obeying, the oppositionist continues to defend them. And when Trotsky associates himself with the lies of the majority and helps it in maneuvers that disfigure the Party, he transgresses the recognized rule and capitulates. But the question precisely was to know whether the other attitude existed except on paper: is obeying while expressing one's judgment aloud still obeying? How does one rally half way? How does one give a dialectical, nuanced "yes" to the majority? How could public reservations coming from such an illustrious revolutionary not have been the equivalent of a "no"?

It will be answered that to observe the rule of discipline with respect to a party which no longer observed the rule of democracy, and which was going to eliminate Trotsky at any cost, was to

18. Quoted by Lefort, *ibid.*, p. 67.
19. Souvarine, *Staline*, p. 421, quoted by Lefort, *ibid.*, p. 60.
20. Quoted by Lefort, *ibid.*, p. 53.

play the loser and to surrender to the adversary. Under the pretext of fidelity to the Marxist idea of Party, it was to give in to those who were going to ruin the Party. There is no doubt about this. But what else was there to do? Say and write, from 1927 on, that the Party was no longer the Party of the proletariat? Proclaim Thermidor? What kept Trotsky from doing this was the fact that the materialistic dialectic did not envisage this eventuality, and the problem was thus to bring it up for consideration. The dialectic foresaw, of course, divergences in the Party, and it settled them by free discussion and the discipline of the majority. The minority kept its right to defend its ideas but not the right to act as a party within the Party. Such a rule can work only below a certain level of political tension, and thus only when the divergences do not touch what is essential. But what if these differences touch the very style which defines revolutionary action, this appeal to the workers' consciousness, this progress toward clarity, this universal in action, which makes the Party history's laboratory? If the Party rejects these criteria, then to confront it with true history, which it fails to recognize, is to confront it with history as thought by Trotsky. This is to say that the Party is no longer in the Party but is rather to be found totally in Trotsky and in those who think like him. But how would this be philosophically possible in the sphere of materialistic dialectic? The dialectic postulates that if truth is anywhere, it resides in the inner life of the Party, which the proletariat has created. And if the Party itself abandons the elaboration of truth through the confrontation of the *de facto* proletariat with the views of its most enlightened avant-garde, Trotsky can well say that he no longer understands, but he has no other procedure at his disposal to substitute for the methods of the Party. If he denounces the rule of discipline, he is playing the game of degeneration, and he pushes the Party still further away from democracy. If the Party is truly in the process of abolishing "democratic centralism," it is not up to Trotsky to provide the pretexts. Thus he must observe discipline even beyond what is required by "democratic centralism": he must allow himself to be eliminated rather than to lack discipline, and he must consider the creation of another organization, another revolutionary direction, only when the old one throws him out, because only then will the Party have proved that it is no longer the bearer of historical reason. Trotsky lacked neither the courage to speak a truth that he already knew nor the ability to defend it. He hesitated to situate truth outside the Party because Marxism had taught him that truth could not in principle reside anywhere but at the point where the proletariat and the organization which embodies it are joined. He sniffed Thermidor in the air, and he asked himself the question early on; but it is natural that he did not see or proclaim it until much later, for, while Thermidor is easily conceivable in a bourgeois revolution, which feels bypassed by its proletariat, in a proletarian revolution it raises a difficulty of principle: how can a separation exist between the proletariat and its Party? What remains in the country of the revolution which could support counterrevolution? There are indeed remnants of the former society, and its pressure is still felt at the borders of the U.S.S.R.; but these forces cannot make the Party turn definitively against its proletariat. It would be necessary for the bureaucracy to have become a caste, nearly the equivalent of a class. Now there is indeed in Marx a theory of bureaucracy, but as a reversible deviation. If it truly exploits the proletariat which put it in power, it is because, beyond capitalism and socialism, there is a third possibility, a third regime, and Marx did not speak of it. For if he had, this would have amounted to admitting that the revolution could betray itself and to renouncing the immanence of truth. It was only after the fact that Trotsky saw the premises of a system and of a regime in the "bureaucratic" traits of the year 1923, because, as a Marxist, he was not able to foresee a derailment of the dialectic in the country of the revolution and bowed to the fact only when constrained and forced to do so.

It is known that, even after he had been expelled from the U.S.S.R. and had founded a new International, he never came to consider the bureaucracy as a class [21] and consequently maintained his thesis of the unconditional defense of the U.S.S.R. as the country of collectivization and of planning. Claude Lefort writes: "He transferred to economic categories . . . the fetishism that he had previously professed toward political forms, the Party, and the Soviets." [22] Perhaps this was "fetishism." But what one must ask oneself is whether the materialistic dialectic allows one to distinguish between fetishes and true divinities. *It does not separate* collectivization and planning from the power of the pro-

21. "The dictatorship of the proletariat found its disfigured but incontestable expression in the dictatorship of the bureaucracy" (Trotsky, *Etat ouvrier: Thermidor et Bonapartisme,* quoted by Lefort, "La Contradiction," p. 52).

22. Lefort, *ibid.,* p. 67.

letariat, *it does not wish to choose* between them, *it does not allow* us to imagine them in conflict. But precisely because the dialectic does not separate them, because Marx never conceived of a collective and planned economy which was not for the benefit of the proletariat, because it postulates that the end of private property is the end of exploitation, that the relationships among men are the simple reflection of their relationships with nature, it leaves the Marxists without a criterion when they are faced with a regime which separates the two elements of socialism. Trotsky's circumspection in regard to the Russian Party and the U.S.S.R. teaches us that in materialism it is difficult to give the "objective" its due. Marx continually increased the weight of the objective factors of history, and the beautiful parallelism in the young Marx between the realization of philosophy and the realization of socialism was destroyed by "scientific socialism" to the benefit of the infrastructures. The sphere of revolution was less and less the relationships between persons and more and more the "things" and their immanent necessities. To crown it all, the revolution took place in a country where, as it happens, the proletariat had not been formed by a long period of industrialization, and Trotsky was among the first to make revolution relevant in these unforeseen conditions. The only revolution which succeeded was not, then, the appearance of a new society which had matured, in both body and spirit, inside the old society. If the historical dialectic functioned only in these paradoxical conditions, if the imperious thesis of permanent revolution came to replace that of progressive maturation, and if revolution, after the 1917 explosion, was the completely voluntary creation of a modern economy and not the advent of an already mature proletariat, how could Trotsky, who knew this better than anyone, have been astonished that the dialectic of the proletariat and the Party also had its paradoxes, that the dialectic of centralism and democracy had its crises, and that it ended in alternatives where one had hoped for a transcendence of antinomies? In order to look at the Soviet society in a positive manner, to refuse any occult quality, any virtual historical virtue, to planned and collective production, materialistic philosophy would have to be put into question, for it is this philosophy which transfers to economic categories virtues first attributed to certain political forms. When the revolution eliminates the latter and respects only the former, this is the fetish of fetishes. The "fetishism" of collectivization and planning is the aspect that dialectical materialism takes when history quarters the two pieces of which it is made. Passivity toward the Party is the stance that discipline and centralism take when the Party ceases to be democratic. In order to denounce the degeneration and to draw the consequences, one would have to give up putting the dialectic in things. Certainly, Trotsky contradicts himself when he endorses the Party's maneuvers, knowing that they falsify history. But, more than in Trotsky, the contradiction and the ambiguity are in the Russian Revolution and, ultimately, in Marx's realism.

In Marx, we repeat, and not only in Bolshevism. Claude Lefort admits that Trotsky's insight was clouded by Bolshevik practices. Centralization, the preponderance of committeemen and professional revolutionaries, the contempt for democracy—all those traits that Bolshevism owes to its illegal development in a backward country are accentuated when the Bolsheviks are in power. When Trotsky was in power, he maneuvered with his colleagues to dishonor all opposition and repressed the Kronstadt commune. Why, then, should he hesitate to slander Eastman? How could he get the militants to rise up against Stalinism, since he was the first to cut himself from the avant-garde? How could he have taken the offensive against Stalin, since he had "allowed himself to be locked in the contradiction of leading the proletariat, in the name of its higher interests, counter to its immediate interests?" [23] Lefort thinks that one must go back to the principles of Bolshevism to find the premises of the "degeneration." We wonder if it is not necessary to go even further back. It is Marxism, not Bolshevism, which bases the Party's interventions on forces which are already there and bases praxis on a historical truth. When, in the second half of the nineteenth century, Marx moved to a scientific socialism, the idea of a socialism inscribed in facts still more energetically guaranteed the Party's initiatives. For if revolution is in things, how can one hesitate to brush aside, by any means, oppositions which are only apparent? If the revolutionary function of the proletariat is engraved in the infrastructures of capital, the political action which expresses it is justified in the way the Inquisition was justified by Providence. In presenting itself as a reflection of what is, of the historical process itself, scientific socialism emphasizes again the knowledge that the *Theses on Feuerbach* subordinated. It grants itself the position of an absolute knowledge, and, at the same time, it authorizes itself to

23. *Ibid.*, p. 65.

take from history by violence a meaning which is there but profoundly hidden. The mixture of extreme objectivism and subjectivism (the one constantly supporting the other) which defines Bolshevism is already in Marx when he admits that revolution is present before it is recognized. When, therefore, the Bolsheviks (and Trotsky with them) say that at certain moments one must know how to force history's hand and bypass certain phases of development, that it is precisely the historical backwardness of a country which destines it to a revolution that will not stop at the bourgeois phase, when they compare history to a horse which one learns to train by riding it, when they deride the theoreticians of historical spontaneity and Kautsky waiting for the historical process to pass by his worktable, when they say with Lenin that the revolutionary is for a long time condemned to *hit heads* and that an interminable effort is needed to form a classless society and to bring history by iron and fire to express its meaning—this *Stimmung* of violence and truth, this voluntarism astride an absolute knowledge, simply develop the idea of a dialectical resolution inscribed in things, that is, the idea of a dialectical materialism. Trotsky's theses on permanent revolution are in turn only the consequent formulation of this. There was a vulgar Marxism which believed it could give a general genetic diagram and describe clearly distinct phases in an order of invariable succession. With the idea of permanent revolution, Trotsky holds that the proletarian revolution may be immanent in a society which itself did not plan this revolution, that the bourgeois-democratic revolution may open a cycle of transformations in society which will stop only with the socialist revolution, that perhaps in backward societies the proletariat has, even by itself, the force to realize the democratic revolution, that the proletarian revolution itself, once it has come, is the seat of a continual "crossgrowth" [24] of this sort, that, even if revolution is declared in only one corner of the world, it is a central issue in the entire world—in short, that there is an "internal mechanism" [25] of revolution which leads it beyond what the "average" objective conditions allowed one to foresee. Trotsky's formulation showed that, in addition to the objective conditions of history and the will of men, there is a third order, that of the internal mechanism of revolutionary action, and that,

24. [In the French: "transcroissance."—Trans.]
25. The expression is Daniel Guérin's (*La Lutte des classes sous la Ire République* [Paris, 1946]).

within this order, from the beginning to the end of space and time, the proletarian revolution is never completely absent. This idea of a transtemporal revolution—anticipated before its objective conditions come together, always to be remade even where these conditions are not joined, present everywhere in "embryonic" form and never completed anywhere, history's continual obsession and the permanent justification of the will, which provides the basis for renewed purgings by giving them the stamp of truth—this is nothing other than the Marxist idea of a world incomplete without praxis, of a praxis which is part of the definition of the world. One should not be astonished that Trotsky without hesitation took up Marxist naturalism and, with Marx, grounded value in being. It is this naturalism which, for better or worse, expresses the fundamental intuition which is common to them, that of a *being in revolution*, of a change which, beyond man's actions, never stops gnawing at history or at least silently shaking it, even when it appears to be at rest. Yes, Bolshevik practice and Trotskyism are of the same lineage and are legitimate consequences of Marx. If one questions Bolshevism, one must also question the objectivist-subjectivist philosophy of praxis. It was because this was Trotsky's philosophy that he was a Bolshevik and remained as long as he could in the Russian Party. This philosophy taught him that the dialectic is buried in historical matter, that it can fail to develop if not taken up by the will of the most enlightened, that this will cannot, at each moment and in the immediate, coincide with the will of all the proletariat's factions, and that it is only after the event, when the dialectic is victorious, that the whole proletariat rallies to it and the revolution appears as a maturation; thus, provided that it be only temporarily, the dialectic can lose contact with the proletariat. Trotsky further learned that an appreciable difference can exist between means and ends and that no exact criteria exist for defining acceptable differences. At certain moments the Party must listen to the revolution's profound voice and not to the noisy protests heard on the surface, and it must anticipate reversals that, considering appearances, seem improbable but which the hidden and continual dynamic of history will suddenly bring to light. Finally, Trotsky learned that even if the Party is mistaken and degenerates, even if it is caught in the revolutionary ebb, the internal mechanism of permanent revolution can suddenly bring it back to itself. A single hypothesis was excluded: that a Party born of the proletarian movement and brought to power by it might not only degenerate but might actually turn against the revolution. This hypothesis was excluded by materialism, by the idea that the classless society is inscribed in the structure of capitalist production, that it is already there, and that, as soon as the barrier of private appropriation is done away with, this future will weigh heavily on revolutionary politics and sooner or later will inevitably set it straight. Until he was thrown out of it, how could Trotsky, as a Marxist, not have continued to adhere to the Party which was supported by the freed productive forces? Even after his expulsion, he never drew the philosophical conclusion from his failure: he restricted himself to recreating Bolshevism outside of Bolshevism, Marxism outside of Stalinism. As for principles, he returned to the beautiful dialectical rectitude that he had somewhat jostled in action; he justified or rationalized his experience, rather than elucidated it.[26] In practice, as his theses on the defense of the U.S.S.R. testify, he remained as close as possible to orthodox objectivism. The problem is that, in order to truly understand his failure, Trotsky should have revised the permanent frame of his action and his thought, his philosophical conviction that the homogeneous and stateless society is virtually assured with the end of capitalism, that this dialectic is in things, and that no third system is possible, or in any case is not lasting. To admit, on the contrary, that the revolutionary suppression of capital does not necessarily signal the advent of the proletariat would have been to take away the dialectic's realist foundation as well as to deprive the revolutionary party of its authority. This, for Trotsky, would have been to disavow his Marxist action. He preferred to recreate this action in the realm of the imaginary—in a skeletal Fourth International—since he could go no further in the real world. But this was because he wanted to remain a Marxist, as do all those like him who try to create Marxism all over again, not only outside the paths of the U.S.S.R. but also outside those of Trotsky.

Let us say the same thing in another way: materialism affirms that the dialectic resides in the matter of the social whole, which is to say that the ferment of negation is supplied by an existing historical formation, the proletariat. From this comes the idea of the proletariat as *Selbstaufhebung,* or yet again the idea of

26. This is undoubtedly one of the reasons why the new organization never became important and why it attracted chiefly intellectuals fond of dialectic. It renewed the Marxism of 1850, which has never been that of the workers' organizations.

permanent revolution, of a continued negation immanent in the internal mechanism of history. Thus realized in the world, negativity can be tapped like a spring or a subtle matter. The Party which works to put the proletariat in power can take advantage of this negative force, and the society which the Party prepares is, by definition, permanently self-critical—a classless or true society. Unfortunately, a government, even a revolutionary one, a party, even a revolutionary party, is not a negation. In order to establish themselves on the terrain of history, they must exist positively. They do not do what they are doing *quatenus,* they do it absolutely; and at least in the immediate situation there is dictatorship only of the positive. Even should the Party and the revolutionary society remain as close as possible to the proletariat, the proletariat as "suppression of itself" is not to be found: one finds only proletarians who think and wish this or that, who are exuberant or discouraged, who see correctly or incorrectly, but who are in any case always in the world. The Party—animated in principle by the class which suppresses itself, justified in principle for the single reason that it *is* this class, organized—returns to the positive, as does the class itself, and then the historical representatives of negativity assert themselves ever more strongly in the name of positivity. The proletarians, and the Party even more so, have a tendency to think that revolution is a positive principle at work in things, not this handful of perplexed leaders and these hesitant masses. A political apparatus which functions on a day-to-day basis among men who are not all philosophers, who like to believe in their leaders or to lay the blame on them, and which, after all, acts in the positive and the immediate falls back into the positive with all its weight. All mediate identifications of the dialectic are transformed into real identities: the proletariat *is* the revolution, the Party *is* the proletariat, the leaders *are* the Party. This is not an identity in difference but, like being, is being; and thus double meanings and equivocalness are the laws of the system, since, from all evidence, there is no positive equivalent of negativity and since its representatives are positive to the extent that they can be. Now, this equivocalness was already present when Marx placed the dialectic in things themselves. Of course there are moments, justly called revolution, when the internal mechanism of history is such that the proletarians live in their Party, that the workers and peasants live in the destined community which the dialectic assigns them on paper, that the government is nothing other than the people's commissar. One is then at that sublime point which we have mentioned several times. Trotsky always draws his perspectives from these perfect moments. He emphasizes the fact that constraint is then barely necessary, because the will to change the world finds confederates everywhere and because, from the fields to the factory, each local demand is found to concur in the general action. He always remembered with happiness the days of the October insurrection, when the proletariat took power practically without bloodshed. Such is the miracle of the revolutionary flow, of negativity embodied in history. But can one conceive of a continued, of an established, flow, of a regime that would live at this level of tension, of a historical time which would be constantly agitated by this critical ferment, of a life without lasting attainments and without rest? Permanent revolution is this myth, the underground work of the negative which never ceases, especially not in the revolutionary society. All this may be the case for those who conceive universal history, for the leaders; in the thinking of Trotsky and Lenin, governmental lies, maneuvers, and repression were leading to world-wide revolution. But for those who are not professional politicians, there is work and leisure, war and peace, movement and rest, and for them permanent revolution is a pretext for violence. In principle, therefore, it is only in privileged moments that negativity actually descends into history and becomes a way of life. The rest of the time, it is represented by bureaucrats. This is a difficulty not only of Bolshevism but of any Marxist organization, and perhaps of any revolutionary organization. Revolution as continued self-criticism needs violence to establish itself and ceases to be self-critical to the extent that it practices violence. Revolution is a realized or indefinitely reiterated negation, and there is no pure or continued negation in things themselves. Marx was able to have and to transmit the illusion of a negation realized in history and in its "matter" only by making of the noncapitalistic future an absolute Other. But we who have witnessed a Marxist revolution well know that revolutionary society has its weight, its positivity, and that it is therefore not the absolute Other. Must we retain, by simply extending it to infinity, the limiting-idea [27] of the homogeneous society, of the last society? This would be to create the illusion all over again and to provide, to a society that has its relative merits, an absolute distinction to which it has no right. This is what

27. [In the French: "l'idée-limite."—Trans.]

Trotsky did, and it is correct to say that there is not much sense in trying Bolshevism all over again at the moment when its revolutionary failure becomes apparent. But neither is there much sense in trying Marx all over again if his philosophy is involved in this failure, or in acting as if this philosophy came out of this affair intact and rightfully ended humanity's questioning and self-criticism.

We therefore cannot agree with Claude Lefort when he supposes that Trotsky's fate poses no philosophical problem and that his contradictions are only those of Bolshevism, those of a historical form linked to the particularities of a backward country. How can one be sure that the proletarian revolution—the revolution of the "last" class, the revolution which must create the *true* society —only accidentally took place in a backward country? If, on the contrary, the proletarian revolution was by its nature destined to occur in backward countries, one should expect to see the problems of Bolshevism reappear in any proletarian revolution. Now this is indeed a hypothesis to consider: Marxism first presented revolution as a fact of maturation or maturity. Subsequently, when revolution appeared in countries where it was "premature," Marxism rationalized the event by linking it to a law of unequal development: the historical backwardness of a country which did not experience bourgeois development, the pressures exercised on it by advanced countries, the implantation of a semi-colonial regime, and the sudden appearance of a new proletariat amassed in it the conditions of a revolution which would pass beyond the democratic stage and leap over the bourgeois phase. For the Marxists, however, this analysis, which returned to the dialectic its flexibility and to history its unforeseen character, remains in the framework of a general plan of development: even if history goes from precapitalism to socialism, it remains understood that the socialism in which it ends is the very socialism to which the maturity and the decadence of capitalism should lead. The development leaps over certain phases, is abridged, and avoids certain transitions, but the end to which it leads is always conceived as it was by Marx; the schema of historical maturation is not changed. One simply introduces a supplementary condition: the "internal mechanism" of revolution in backward countries, which explains certain historical anticipations. Since the revolution did not appear in advanced countries, the question is precisely to know whether it is not Marx's basic schema which should be called into question. Isn't the proletarian revolution, contrary to that schema, essentially linked to the structure of backward countries, and isn't it, instead of an *anticipation* of the canonical phases to which the development of capitalism would "ineluctably" lead, a formation which comes in its time and place, in the sense that the revolution is possible only where there is a historical delay and that it in no way represents the future promised to capitalist societies? Proletarian revolution in a backward country could be called, if one wished, "premature," but in the sense that psychoanalysts say that an infant's birth is premature: not that, had it come later, it would have been "fully natural" but, on the contrary, that, however late and well prepared it may be, birth is always a wrenching-forth and a re-creation. Revolution and revolutionary society would be premature— they would possess an *essential* prematureness—and their analysis should therefore be redone from that point of view. In principle a revolutionary society would be one which was born, not of a seed long since deposited in the previous society, ripened and "hatched," as Marx said, in its objective functioning, but, on the contrary, through "crossgrowth," through the "internal mechanism" of a conflict which has grown by itself to the point of destroying the social structures in which it had appeared. In a sense, we have said that the theses of unequal development and of permanent revolution extend and develop certain of Marx's thoughts; but they also "revolutionize" them, because they introduce a new idea of revolution and its relation to history. Revolution is no longer history's fulfillment; it also takes shape in societies which did not "hatch" it; it is always there and also never there, since even in mature societies it can be indefinitely late, and even in the revolutionary society it must always be repeated. Revolution becomes continued rupture with history; it is seen everywhere but can never be approached or overtaken. The dialectic had established a double relationship of continuity and discontinuity between the present and the past. Capitalism creates its own gravediggers, itself prepares the regime by which it will be overthrown; the future thus emerges from the present, the end from the means of which it is only the sum and the meaning. But can a revolution be born in this manner? Is it history itself that changes history? Must not revolution, as rupture, first of all renounce what preceded it? Does it not create among men, and even among proletarians, such a tension that democracy of the Party, freedom of discussion, revolutionary fraternity, salvage of the past, and the unity of history can come only much later, if they come at all, and then only as ends and as justifications in the leaders' minds rather than inside the revolutionary movement itself? Marxism does not want to choose between the two aspects of the dialectic. Sometimes it speaks of revolution as a wave which picks up the Party and the proletariat where they are and carries them beyond the obstacle; sometimes, on the contrary, it puts the revolution beyond everything that exists, in a future which is the negation of the present, at the end of an infinite refinement. In Marxism these two views are not reconciled; rather they are juxtaposed. Marx counted on the growth of the proletariat in its Party to make the synthesis. The idea of permanent revolution declares that revolution is not so much a result of the past or a transcendence of its problems in the present as it is an immanence in each of its moments of the furthest-removed future; in other words, it proclaims a sort of original delay of history. It is therefore not surprising that the idea of permanent revolution applies well to revolutions in underdeveloped countries. But it would be astonishing if these "premature" revolutions, like those that the old societies were said to be "hatching," were capable of creating *the true* society. The dialectical schema must be retained: things must be realized and things must be destroyed, revolution saves everything and changes everything. In practice, depending on the moment, one or the other predominates; a zigzag movement replaces dialectical development. Purgings and the easing of tensions are made to alternate. The result is that each of these attitudes becomes the simple mask of the other. One creates from nothing in the name of truth, one uses violence with little scruple, since it is said to be inscribed in things. This is the Bolshevik mind, the thought of Trotsky; it is the crisis of Marx's thought and and its continuation. Trotsky's fate is outlined in this philosophy which was to unite truth and action, but where one is simply an alibi for the other.

The "accidents" of Bolshevism and of "socialism in one country" provoked such consequences in the U.S.S.R. and in world-wide communism and so completely shifted the perspectives of proletarian revolution that there is no longer much more reason to preserve these perspectives and to force the facts into them than there is to place them in the context of Plato's *Republic*. Even if Bolshevism is only the expression of an epoch, it so imperiously fashioned the epoch which followed that the problem is to know whether, in order to consider the latter, we should still keep the coordinates of proletarian society. Expelled from the Party, Trotsky kept his philosophy of history, his theory of the Party and the revolution, and even the "fetishism" of the collective and planned economy. This is why he criticizes the U.S.S.R. as a "disfigured" revolution, as one not without hope. For Lefort the deviation began with Bolshevism. Along with the thesis of the "bases of socialism," he renounces the Bolshevik practices of the Party and evaluates Bolshevism as a disfigured Marxism. But he leaves the proletarian philosophy of history uncontested: Bolshevism caricatured it, being a "historical anticipation" and ahead of its time. Lefort, also, thus proceeds *minimo sumptu*. He is Trotsky's Trotsky. But where does he get this certitude of a maturation point of history, the point when the proletariat, having taken power, will not let it fall from its hands? As for the Bolsheviks, they believed in only a relative maturity and, so to speak, in a minimum of maturity. Once certain objective conditions had come together, they did not hesitate to force history's hand. A proletarian philosophy which allows itself these infringements will return to the contradictions of Bolshevism, and a proletarian philosophy which completely refrains from them will become wholly contemplative. When Lefort writes that Bolshevism was a "historical anticipation," the formula is ambiguous. If it means that history in 1917 was not ripe for proletarian power in Russia, this is hardly questionable, for all the reasons he gives. But this does not prove—and yet this is what "anticipation" suggests—that tomorrow, somewhere else, a proletarian power will be "mature," nor does it prove that a revolutionary power will ever be other than "premature."

5 / Sartre and Ultrabolshevism

THUS, SINCE MARXIST PHILOSOPHY believes it possible
to express the weight of social reality only by situating the
dialectic wholly in the object, the dialectic in action responds to
adversity either by means of terror exercised in the name of a
hidden truth or by opportunism; in either case, the dialectic
wanders from its own line. But it is one thing to experience this
and yet another to recognize and formulate it. It was only im-
plicitly that Trotsky resigned himself to this when, in his last
years, he said that the course of things would perhaps call into
question the Marxist thesis of the proletariat as ruling class and
of socialism as heir to capitalism. The communists are very far
from this admission. For them, to the very degree that the
dialectic is a failure, it must remain in force: it is the "point of
honor," the "justification" of an immense technical labor in which
it never appears in person. In both meanings of the word, one
does not "touch" the dialectic, because one does not change anything and because one does not use it. If, as Lukács says, the
social is a "second nature," the only thing to do is to govern it as
one governs nature: through a technique which allows discussion
only among engineers, that is to say, according to criteria of
efficiency, not according to criteria of meaning. The meaning will
come later, only God knows how. This will be the business of the
future communist society. For the moment it is only a question of
"laying the foundations," using means which no more resemble
their ends than the trowel does the masonry which it serves to
construct. Once the machinery of production, which Marx took
for granted—and which was indeed not present in Russia and is

even less evident in China—has been built, State production will of itself put forth its socialist and communist consequences, and one will see humanism and the dialectic bloom and flower, while the State fades away.[1] This would be fine if Soviet society, in order to create the machinery of production, did not establish machinery of constraint and did not organize privileges which, little by little, make up the true shape of its history. But this the communists do not see, because their eyes are fixed on the dialectic. They take its failure into consideration (and in this sense they know it is a failure), since at every opportunity they avoid the dialectic with great care. But *with the same movement* they place it in the future. It is the same thing to no longer believe in the dialectic and to put it in the future; but it is seen to be the same thing by an external witness, who contents himself with the present, not by someone who commits the fraud and who lives already in his intended ends. The dialectic thus plays precisely the role of an ideology, helping communism to be something other than what it thinks it is.

Given this state of affairs, it was good that an independent philosopher attempted to analyze communist practice directly, without the mediation of ideology. The language of the dialectic and of the philosophy of history has been so fully incorporated into communism that it is a completely new undertaking to describe communism without using it. Such is the extreme interest of the essays recently published by Sartre.[2] Here the dialectical

1. In his later years Stalin once again took up the thesis of the withering-away of the State.
2. "Les Communistes et la paix" (Parts I, II, and III) and "Réponse à Claude Lefort," which appeared as articles in *Les Temps modernes*. ["Les Communistes et la paix," Part I, appeared in Vol. VIII, no. 81 (July, 1952), pp. 1–50; Part II appeared in Vol. VIII, nos. 84–85 (October–November, 1952), pp. 695–763; and Part III appeared in Vol. IX, no. 101 (April, 1954), pp. 1731–1819. "Réponse à Claude Lefort" appeared in Vol. VIII, no. 89 (April, 1953), pp. 1571–1629. They were later published in book form—"Les Communistes et la paix" in *Situations VI: Problèmes du marxisme, 1* (Paris: Gallimard, 1964), pp. 80–384, and "Réponse à Claude Lefort" in *Situations VII: Problèmes du marxisme, 2* (Paris: Gallimard, 1965), pp. 7–93. Quotations from these essays in the present volume are taken from the English translation, *The Communists and Peace*, trans. Martha Fletcher, John Kleinschmidt, and Philip Berk (New York: Braziller, 1968). (The book includes both essays.) In all footnotes "The Communists and the Peace" will be abbreviated as *CP;* "A Reply to Claude Lefort" will be abbreviated as *RL*. The page numbers cited

cover is drawn back, communist action is considered as it is at present, as it would be by someone who had forgotten its history; in short, it is "understood" in itself. Here, for the first time, we are told what a communist should say to defend communism clearly and without recourse to the presuppositions of tradition.[3]

Sartre "understands" communist politics, justifies it from the proletarian point of view, and thus (to a degree to be specified) makes it his own for reasons quite different from those of the communists and, as he says, "by reasoning from *my* principles and not from *theirs*." [4] His principles are, in truth, not only different from those of the communists, they are practically opposed to them; and what Sartre contributes is a brief on the failure of the dialectic. While the communist philosophers, Lukács among them, formally preserve the principle of a historical dialectic and simply drive it back into the in-itself of the "second nature"—which, it is true, infinitely extends the field of mediations, separates the communist enterprise from its final meaning, and defers their confrontation indefinitely—Sartre founds communist action precisely by refusing any productivity to history and by making history, insofar as it is intelligible, the immediate result of our

---

will refer first to *Les Temps modernes* and then to the English translation ("ET").—Trans.]

3. In Part II of *CP*, Sartre writes, ". . . the purpose of this article is to declare my agreement with the Communists on precise and limited subjects" (*CP*, p. 706; ET, p. 68). The title of the work indicates that in the beginning he was looking for agreement with them based on the single question of peace. Yet, in order to justify unity of action, Sartre attempts to say as much as one can say in favor of communist politics when one is on the left but is not a communist. This leads him to present it as the only politics possible for a communist party, to concentrate his criticism on the Marxist adversaries of the Communist Party, and finally to challenge their Marxism. On the terrain of Marxist discussion, this is to take a position. It is true that this is not Sartre's terrain and that he envelops Stalinists and Trotskyites in another philosophy—his own; but even when he stops arbitrating Marxist discussions to speak in his own name, the advantage given to the C.P. is not withdrawn. The C.P. remains grounded in Sartrean philosophy (although as we will see, this is for reasons which are not its own). Sartre's accord with the Party thus goes beyond the "precise and limited subjects" with which it started: "[I] do not hide my sympathies for many aspects of the Communist enterprise" (*RL*, p. 1615; ET, p. 282); and it is necessary to seek in *The Communists and Peace*, beyond the formulas of unity of action, for an attitude of sympathy.

4. *CP*, p. 706; ET, p. 68.

volitions. As for the rest, it is an impenetrable opacity. To be sure, this extreme subjectivism and this extreme objectivism have something in common: if the social is a second nature, it can be modified, like the other, only by a technician, in this case a sort of political engineer. And if the social is only the inert and confused residue of past actions, one can intervene and put it in order only by pure creation. Whether it be in the name of a theoretical knowledge which the Party alone possesses or in the name of an absolute nonknowledge (since, if history is chaos, then anything is better than what exists at present), the Party's action is not subject to the criteria of meaning. The philosophy of pure object and the philosophy of pure subject are equally terroristic, but they agree only about consequences. As for their motives, these remain in a position of rivalry. The ruin of the dialectic is accomplished openly with Sartre and clandestinely with the communists, and the same decisions that the communists base on the historical process and on the historical mission of the proletariat Sartre bases on the nonbeing of the proletariat and on the decision which, out of nothing, creates the proletariat as the subject of history.

Sartre then relatively justifies the communists, in their action rather than in what they think and in the philosophy they teach; moreover, if this philosophy is itself "understood" as an auxiliary myth, the kind of truth that one attributes to it is symbolic and not the kind that it lays claim to. One feels that for Sartre the dialectic has always been an illusion, whether it was in the hands of Marx, of Trotsky, or of others; differences arise only in the manner of speaking, of justifying action, of staging the illusion; in its essential features, Marxist action has always been pure creation. The "truth" of history has always been fraudulent and the discussion of the Party always a ceremony or an exercise. Marxism has always been the choice of the proletariat, which, historically, does not exist, in opposition to the Other, which does; and the pretense of transcending internal oppositions has always been Platonic: one can only leap over them. Sartre, then, does not see any reason to distinguish in the history of Marxism between important and decadent periods, between founders and epigones. He never confronts communism with the dialectic which it claims. Better equipped than anyone to understand and explain communism as it is, in relation to the traditional ideologies with which it covers itself, Sartre does not do this, precisely because, for him, the profound meaning of communism lies—well beyond dialectical illusions—in the categorical will to bring into being that which never was. He never asks himself why no communist would dream of writing what he is writing, even though communists *do* it every day, or why no communist would base his action on repudiation of the dialectic, even though this is the only thing to do if those who are nothing historically are to become men. It is enough for him that communism should finally be like this within the context of his thought. That communists conceive and justify it otherwise, this, he is sure, changes nothing in the meaning of communism. Communism is here "understood" and relatively justified to a second degree, not as it sees itself, but as it is—in other words, as Hegel teaches it, as the philosopher sees it. If Sartre would openly give his reasons, if he would say that communism is a more profound pragmatism, he would expose to broad daylight the divergence between theory and practice, the crisis of communist philosophy, and, beyond philosophy, the change in meaning of the whole system. If he "understands" communism correctly, then communist ideology is deceitful, and we can ask the nature of the regime which hides itself in the philosophy it teaches instead of expressing itself there. If Sartre is right in grounding communism as he does, communism is wrong in thinking of itself as it does; it is not, then, entirely what Sartre says it is. Ultimately, if Sartre is right, Sartre is wrong. Such is the situation of the loner who incorporates communism into his universe and thinks of it with no regard for what it thinks of itself. In reading *The Communists and Peace,* one often wonders—without finding an answer, since the quotations from Marx are so equitably distributed—what distinction Sartre makes between Marx, the ideologies of Soviet communism, and his own thought. As a good philosopher, Sartre packs this whole company into his thought. In it and in it alone—once his negation of history and historical truth and his philosophy of the subject and of the other as intrusion are supposed—Marx, Lenin, Stalin, and Duclos are, in the main, indistinguishable from one another and indistinguishable from Sartre. But even that is left unsaid: in saying it he would emphasize the change in communism from Marx to the present day, and this change is for him only apparent. His interpretation remains implicit. From this there results a certain reticence in him, and, in us who read him, a certain uneasiness. We would very much like it to be said that if Duclos and Trotsky are equally legitimate heirs of Marxism and if non-Stalinist Marxists are traitors, it is only so for someone who does not believe in the dialectic. Because of a lack of precision on this point, Sartre's analysis, which was to enlighten the reader, simply adds to the confusion.

In the above, we were anticipating, and indeed we had to in order to place Sartre's theses within our own study. In *The Communists and Peace*, then, we will look for the indication of this new phase, which we will call ultrabolshevism, in which communism no longer justifies itself by truth, the philosophy of history, and the dialectic but by their negation. Next we shall have to ask ourselves whether one must draw from Sartre's premises the conclusions he does, whether they can ground any form of communism, whether this completely voluntary communism is tenable, and whether it is not based on an idea of revolution which such a form of communism in itself renders impossible.

Someone may object that it is premature to appraise Sartre's first analyses; we cannot know precisely what implications he himself attributes to them, since they are to be completed later. He has stated that, after he has shown how the Communist Party expresses the proletariat, he will show in what way it does not, and it is only then that one will be able to see how communism and noncommunism are reconciled in his mind and in his action. The problem is comparable to Christian philosophies confronted with historical Christianity. One always wonders whether for them religion is the true philosophy or whether, on the contrary, philosophy is the truth of religion, which includes the former; or rather one wonders how a peaceful coexistence is established between them, for if truth is on only one side, the cold war continues. Sartre will thus leave behind the terrain of historical terror. He will say why he does not become a communist, in what way his "understanding" is different from adherence, in what way his reasons for approving the communists remain distinct from their own, and finally he will construct a mixed universe where the action of communists and that of a noncommunist left can unite.

But still, the published analyses must leave room for these developments, and this is the point toward which our study is directed. It seems to us that if we accept Sartre's analyses, the debate is closed by a desperate justification of communism which does not admit of restriction, nuance, or motive, properly speaking, because it belongs to the sphere of morality: communism is not to be judged, to be put in place, or to be reconciled with anything other than itself. Its action is not to be measured by any criterion other than itself because it is the only consequential attempt to create, out of nothing, a society where those who are nothing become men and because this "anti-physis," as Sartre readily says, this heroic enterprise, tolerates no sort of condition or restriction. If indeed for him these views represent only the thoughts of a communist sympathizer, and if they must be joined to others to arrive at his true conclusion, our discussion will do no more than anticipate his own. If, on the contrary, he accepts them as they are, we are justified in saying even now why they do not convince us. Briefly, this is so because (1) the conception of communism that Sartre proposes is a denunciation of the dialectic and the philosophy of history and substitutes for them a philosophy of absolute creation amidst the unknown; (2) if this philosophy is accepted, communism is an undetermined enterprise of which one knows only that it is absolutely *other,* that, like duty, it is not subject to discussion, nor is it subject to rational proof or rational control; (3) finally, this action without criteria, precisely because it is without criteria, can obtain from those who are undecided only a reserved sympathy, an absent presence. This action will scarcely be strengthened by them and still less will it be changed. Finally, the noncommunist left will be "noncommunist" in its reasons, not in its actions. This is exactly why, instead of serving it, it can be harmful to the coexistence of communism and noncommunism.

I

SARTRE'S STUDY is first of all an appeal to the facts. It is true that today the most active part of the working class adheres to the C.P. and C.G.T.[5] It is thus true that any failure of the C.P. lessens the weight of the working class in the political struggle and that those who celebrate as a victory of the working class the failure of a strike called by the C.P. are abandoning the existing working class, which is in the majority communist. The anticommunist leftist extricates himself by calling the working class's weariness "lucidity" and by calling its disgust "revolutionary

5. [C.G.T. is the abbreviation for the Confédération générale du Travail, which is the French communist trade union and one of France's largest unions.—Trans.]

spirit." He advances with an imaginary proletariat toward a revolution finally freed from communist tutelage, and he dignifies with the name "proletarian politics" a politics which triumphs or suffers at the same time as the government of Mr. Pinay.[6] Sartre asks him: *What are you doing?* If the world were to stop at this instant and you were judged by your perverse glee, you would be one who applauded the collapse of the working class. You say that a distinction must be made, that you celebrate the event as a defeat of the C.P. and as the awakening of a liberated working class, but you know very well that most of the time politics is the art of organizing equivocations and attacking the adversary's flank. When the government arrests J. Duclos and organizes a test of strength, it is not openly after unionism or the working class: it is only a question of a party leader. But when the strike called to defend him fails, general strikes are thereby assailed in advance, apathy is established in the working class, and it is the working class which is weakened. In the moment, and facing the event, this failure of the C.P. is a failure of the working class. If you treat the Communist Party as enemy number one and conceive your politics accordingly, your enemy number two, capitalism, is relatively your ally; for if you are *first of all* concerned with weakening the Communist Party, you will have neither the time nor the taste to weaken its adversaries. If today the Communist Party is against you, the existing proletariat is against you, and you speak only in the name of an ideal proletariat; at this minute you express only thoughts—not, as your Marxism would demand, the worker's movement itself.

All of this is true and had to be said. Sartre poses the question in urgent terms and in the present moment: he who is not with the C.P. is against it and against the proletariat which surrounds it. One can reply, however, that any opposition accepts the risk of destroying the movement that it wants to reform and that, if it did not accept this, no organization would ever reform its politics. If one did not at times compare today's proletariat to that of tomorrow's, if one did not thus dare to prefer the ideal proletariat to the existing one, there would be no proletarian politics. There would then be in each case only a blind fidelity to what the proletariat's Party does, and one would not even know if the Party still merited its name. No politician, and, indeed, especially

6. [Antoine Pinay was prime minister during the Fourth Republic.—Trans.]

not those of the Communist Party, will accept being judged on an isolated moment of his action. No politics responds to an event simply by "yes" or "no," none renounces the right of posing the problem in a different way than it is posed in the moment; for there is the past, where this trap has been prepared, and there is the future, where one can work to remove its bait and render it harmless. A politics which would lack any recourse against the factual situation and its dilemmas would not be a living politics; it would be that of a dying man reprieved, yet threatened at each moment with appearing before his judge. "I was abroad, my relations with the communists were good but certainly not excellent . . . all the more reason to hear of the failure of the strikes with indifference . . . yet the news produced just the contrary effect on me." [7] All right. Everyone thinks in terms of the event, but it is from afar, while traveling, that the crisis is a clap of thunder in the midst of silence. The politician saw it coming, and when it bursts he is already thinking of tomorrow. In short, he thinks it and he lives it, he is not in the position of saying "yes" or "no."

Sartre reserves in principle the right to refuse the ultimatum of facts: "To be a traitor, you don't have to be accused of treason by the Communists." [8] The Communist Party can cause the working class to be against us, but not us to be against it. The entreaty of consciousness remains and, with it, the right for us to step back, consider the event, and ourselves give a meaning to what we are doing. But the situation, the "smiles from the Right," put us in imminent peril of treason, for—and this is the decisive point—the consciousness which withdraws from the dilemma and wishes to confront the C.P.'s politics with a certain idea of revolution *will find nothing in the facts which permits it to decide whether or not the C.P.'s politics is revolutionary* or to sketch another revolutionary line. The solidarity between the working class and the C.P. is not an accident, a jumble supported by the C.P. and exploited by the government. It is legitimate and will never cease, for there is no way to distinguish Communist politics from the proletarian movement. They say that the strike of June 2 bears the mark of the C.P.: the preference given to illegal means, the confusion of the political and the economic, the devotion to Soviet diplomacy—this is Communist, not proletarian. For

7. *CP*, p. 705; *ET*, p. 67.
8. *CP*, p. 5; *ET*, p. 8.

Sartre there is no assignable difference between the C.P.'s politics and proletarian violence. It is not only mentally and through a regrettable error that the workers' movement forms a coalition with the C.P. and the U.S.S.R., it is in reality. And it is not only by a correctable oversight that the anticommunist of the left allows his hatred of communism to overflow to include proletarian violence; it is because, even though he is a "Marxist," he has, as a result of being outside the working class, such as it is, stopped thinking as it does, and, through communism, it is the working class that he is rejecting. Certainly one cannot demonstrate that the revolutionary end requires a June 2, *this* illegality, *this* mixture of the economic and the political, *this* support of the security of the U.S.S.R.; but neither can one demonstrate the contrary. Equivocalness is in things. It is history that is equivocal. "As always, the facts say neither 'yes' nor 'no.'" [9] The use of illegal means? But they are the proletariat's means, since bourgeois law is made against the proletariat. The jumble of the economic and the political? But it is the very law of the proletarian, because he never has access to pure political life (particularly when an electoral law annuls a good part of the Communist suffrage), because political action is simply that which aims at the whole of the social apparatus, and because, in abstaining in this domain, the proletariat would be like a body without consciousness. The devotion to the U.S.S.R.? But the U.S.S.R. is the country of the revolution; and even if the revolution is everywhere, and everywhere inescapable, how can it measure the support it owes to its first bastion? If Communist politics can always by some expedient attach itself to revolutionary violence, though it cannot be derived from it, a consciousness which attempts to evaluate it freely cannot make any effective use of its freedom. It is "yes" or it is "no," and that is all. The "yes," just like the "no," is willful and is uttered equivocally. The C.P. is always justifiable by the permanent reason that its violence is *perhaps* nothing other than proletarian violence. The "yes" is barely distinguishable from the "no," just as, with Kierkegaard, faith was barely distinguishable from incredulity. The C.P. has, in any case, a negative mission: it is perhaps not the revolution, but surely it is not capitalism. It is perhaps not pure proletarian violence, but that certainly is not absent from what it does. Consciousness as pure negation, when confronted with facts which,

9. *CP*, p. 8; ET, p. 11.

on the contrary, say "neither 'yes' nor 'no,' " can engage itself outside only if it finds a negation there which resembles it and in which it recognizes itself: as negation of bourgeois society and emblem of proletarian violence, the Party is a double of consciousness. Consciousness can discuss what the Party does; it will, in fact, never finish discussing it. It remains free. But it will employ this right of scrutiny only with respect, for such a right must never compromise the essential esteem that consciousness holds for the Party as the vehicle of its negations. This decision is *a priori* and of another order.

Thus from an observation, the solidarity of the working class and the C.P., one has passed to a principle, because the facts have, as one might say, several meanings or none at all, and they receive a single meaning only through freedom. Sartre's entire theory of the Party and of class is derived from his philosophy of fact, of consciousness, and, beyond fact and consciousness, from his philosophy of time. He often says that he is not making a theory or speaking of either the ideal proletariat or the Party in general; rather, he looks at what is taking place in France today. But it is this reference to the present as such which is theory. There is theory precisely in this manner of treating the event as ineffaceable, as a decisive test of our intentions and an instantaneous choice of the whole future and of all that we are. This is to imply that political questions can and should be posed and resolved in the moment, without looking back to the past or repeating it. It is to accept the confrontation with the singular. This twisting, which in the event forever unites what appeared separable, places in opposition what was only other. Not to speak of the proletarian, of the class in itself, or of the eternal Party is here to make a theory of the proletariat and of the Party as continued creations, that is to say, as the dead reprieved from death.

The militant, the party, and the class are going to be born out of similar urgencies. They will be the replies that a will which has no basis in things gives to the trap of events. Let us not even speak of birth, for they come from nowhere, they are only what they have to be, what they make themselves. The militant is not a worker who militates; he is not a certain past of suffering which makes itself political action. The sufferings belong to the producer, to "the concrete man," [10] and it is beyond the concrete man that the active proletarian appears. His sufferings would re-

10. *CP*, p. 731; *ET*, p. 96.

duce him to yielding if a pure refusal did not make him a militant. Sartre has always thought that nothing could be the cause of an act of consciousness. In the past Sartre spoke at least of "mild forces" and "motives." Today he still speaks of "the reciprocal conditioning of both progressive impoverishment and permanent revolution," [11] but for him this is statistical and secondary thought. In all strictness, the proletarian is not the condition of the militant, and the fact that the revolutionary will does not arise completely armed out of misery is enough for Sartre to act as if it did not arise from it at all, and to see it appear *ex nihilo* as an "invention," a refusal of the worker's condition,[12] a "conversion" by which the worker "dies and is reborn." Lagneau said that to live will always be to take the trouble to live.[13] He who takes this trouble is not the worker overwhelmed with misery and fatigue. It is that in him, beyond despair and also beyond hope, that says "no" to this life and transforms it into another. One must not even speak of decision here, that is to say, of the deliberation between possibilities and of the motives which prefigure it. "Freedom has descended on me like an eagle" is more or less what Orestes said in *The Flies*. In the same way, the revolutionary will of the militant is more himself than his life. It does not come out of what he was but out of the future, out of nonbeing, where from now on he places himself. ". . . if action takes hold of him, he will believe: action is in and of itself a kind of confidence. And why does it take hold of him? Because it is possible: he *does not decide* to act, he acts, he *is* action, subject of history." [14] The militant believes in the revolution and the Party as Kant's moral subject believes in God and immortality: not that the will attaches itself to an external being, but, on the contrary, because it is gratuitous, prior to any motive, and pure affirmation of value, the will additionally postulates in being what is necessary for its

---

11. *RL*, p. 1611; ET, p. 278.

12. In his *A Reply to Claude Lefort,* Sartre explains that the worker refuses the wage system, not manual labor. Yet he had written in his first article: "Is there a worker's interest? It seems to me that the interest of the worker is to be no longer a worker" (*CP*, p. 27; ET, p. 31) Sartre understands the revolution of existing conditions, of which Marx spoke, almost as a change in professions.

13. [Jules Lagneau (1851–94) was a highly influential spiritualist and idealist philosopher known for his method of reflective analysis, which, starting with the "I," moved to universal spirit.— Trans.]

14. *CP*, p. 717; ET, pp. 80–81 (modified).

fulfillment. The will believes only in itself, it is its own source. The revolution cannot come from the worker, and especially not from the skilled worker. He has a recognized value, he is encumbered with his talent, he is not ready for the rape of freedom. He supposes that man exists and that all that is necessary is to arrange society. Liquidate merit, says Sartre. The only valid humanism in that of absolute destitution, just as Lagneau's God was the more acceptable since he had no basis in being. "Man is yet to be made: he is *what man lacks,* what is *in question* for each one of us, at every instant, what, without ever having been, continually risks being lost." [15] In other words, man is a duty-to-be [*devoir-être*] and even a pure duty, since it is difficult to see how man could *be* man without losing his value. It is the bite of duty or of nothingness into being, into freedom—the bite that Sartre once called "mortal," "deadly"—which constitutes the militant.

It will be asked why the militant is active in the Communist Party and not, like Lagneau, in the Union pour l'Action morale. [16] It is because, for Sartre, the will as absolute is only the interior truth and because there is a different view of the subject (different and the same, since it is his own freedom which is affected and compromised by the gaze of one in misery): the view the other has of him and, in particular, the most miserable of the others. Freedom recognizes itself in this misery, which is, as it were, its derision or caricature, a destitution which is not its own but which, on the contrary, invites it to capitulate. Because for Sartre the other is not a vague double of myself, because, born in the field of my life, the other overturns it, decenters my freedom, and destroys me in order to make me reappear over there, in a gaze which is fastened on me, it is not, as with Kant, beyond this life, or even, as with Lagneau, prior to life, within oneself, on the level of the pure relations of friendship and the society of minds, that *making* imposes its postulates; it is in this life, in the space that separates me from and links me to the other, and which gradually envelops the whole world.

Yet, at this very moment and in this passing to the outside, something attests to the fact that we remain within the philosophy of the subject. It is precisely that the Party, like the militant, is pure action. If everything comes from freedom, if the workers are

15. *CP*, p. 1792; *ET*, p. 200.
16. [Also see his posthumous works, *Fragments* and *L'Existence de Dieu.*—Trans.]

nothing, not even proletarians, before they create the Party, the Party rests on nothing that has been established, not even on their common history. Either the party of the proletarians never will exist or, if it exists, it will be their continued creation and the emblem of their nonbeing, itself a pure act or relationship, like the categorical imperative from which it was born. There will thus be a single party,[17] and no factions within it. "The linking organism must be pure action; if it carries with it the least seed of division, if it still conserves in it any passivity—sluggishness, self-interest, divergent opinions—who then will unify the unifying apparatus?"[18] If there is only one organization, its decisions being "the only possible ones,"[19] then that organization is the proletariat itself, and in it the proletariat is all that it can and should be.[20] If there are several organizations, their decisions, even majority decisions, are no more than accidents. Since other decisions are possible, the leaders are no longer the proletariat itself; and to say that the leaders are good is already to say that they could be bad.[21] The masses, "instead of asserting themselves in a unanimous reaction, are made to choose one of several likely politics."[22] Since it destroys the proletariat, pluralism is not even to be discussed. One must therefore say that the Party is by definition the bearer of the proletarian spirit. It is an order in the sense of monastic and professional orders. It has received the sacred trust of a certain inspiration or of a certain honor and administers it with full powers. In it the three meanings of the word "order" are united. "[It is] an Order which makes order reign and which gives orders."[23] It should not be said that it expresses the proletariat *because* the militants elect the leadership or even *because* they tacitly approve it. It has an eternal and total mandate from the single fact that without it there would be no proletariat. The Hegelian State is society in substance because it is the emergence of an idea pre-existing in society. The Party, on the contrary, is the proletariat in substance because before it there was no proletariat. What one calls the confidence of the proletarians is thus not a state of mind or a feeling which could de-

17. *CP*, p. 760; *ET*, pp. 128–29.
18. *CP*, p. 766; *ET*, p. 129.
19. *CP*, p. 716; *ET*, p. 78.
20. *Ibid.*
21. *CP*, p. 716; *ET*, p. 79.
22. *Ibid.*
23. *CP*, p. 759; *ET*, p. 128.

crease or increase; it is like a condition of being: [24] if there is a proletarian, he has confidence in the Party. It is a feeling which does not need to be felt. It is inscribed or implicated in the necessity for the proletariat, which is nothing, to have a Party if it is to exist historically; and finally it is inscribed in the thought of Sartre, who conceives these possibilities and their relationships. Proletarian history is thus or it is nothing: it is made not of opinions which are expressed and communicated but of missions entrusted as a bottle is thrown into the sea, of investitures received as a consecration, formed in the absolute by a will without means and without condition, because the creation of a proletariat and of a proletarian society is itself an unprecedented enterprise, contrary to everything that until now has been called nature and history. Any idea of controlling the leaders is therefore out of the question. What does the opinion of a majority, and, even less, that of a minority, mean with regard to the Party's infinite task, which is to make something out of nothing? They are only opinions, while the Party has at each instant no other choice than to be or not to be. They are thus "almost nothing: soreheads, outsiders: the majority disregards them and declares unanimity." [25] The liquidation of minorities [26] is already germinating at the birth of the proletarian Party. Because the unanimity of decisions in the Party is only a way of saying that the decisions were taken at the risk of the death of the Party, that they carry all the chances of the proletariat's survival, and because this condition of risk is permanent, any decision is, by nominal definition, "unanimous." This regime without secret ballot, without a minority, without an opposition, calls itself

24. [In the French: "un sentiment d'état."—Trans.]
25. *CP*, p. 715; *ET*, p. 78.
26. In Part III of his study, Sartre describes this as a trait of mass trade unionism (*CP*, p. 1812; *ET*, p. 223). But not a word indicates that no one knows where trade unionism is going on this path or that there is a problem that needs to be posed once again. On the contrary, sarcasm rains on the skilled workers. Does Sartre mean that we must just go along until chaos reigns and then begin everything anew with a system about which we know only that it will be something different? This is, perhaps, his perspective. Or does he mean, as one might believe from reading his third article [Part III], that a renovated capitalism would come out of the impasse, giving at least to the French proletarians the benefits of a type of production of which until now they knew only the slavery? Sartre "understands" mass trade unionism so well that one does not see to what extent he is actually following it.

"real" democracy—not because it extends the formal guarantees of a bourgeois regime to the realities of government and production, but because it creates out of nothing the power of the powerless, an enormous undertaking which cannot afford contestation. The militant's function is, therefore, to "obey orders." [27] It is true that Sartre does not identify the proletariat with the Party apparatus.[28] With good reason he protests that the apparatus would be nothing if it were not supported by the proletarians, but they in turn would be nothing if they did not support it. They do not obey it as an external urgency: it is rather that the militant is, in the philosophical sense, in ecstasy in the Party and is completely transformed in it, so that obedience to orders is his highest activity, making him in turn pure action: "the Party is his freedom." One may ask whether to obey without criticizing, without examining, without taking a certain distance, is still to be active. But in the urgent situation—which is always the case for the proletariat—to act is not to choose or to decide:

> To criticize is to stand back, to put oneself outside the group or the system, to consider them as *objects*.[29]

> Doubt and uncertainty: these seem to be intellectual virtues. But [the worker] must struggle to change his condition, and these virtues of the mind can only paralyze action . . . and he, precisely, needs to believe that there is a truth. Since he cannot work it out alone, he must be able to trust his class leaders profoundly enough to believe he is getting the truth from them.[30]

Action does not come from the worker, who existed before the Party; it is localized in the life of the Party. Only starting with his

27. "They [the workers] give birth to the class when they all obey the orders of the leaders" (*CP*, p. 760; ET, p. 128).
28. "Where have I written," he asks, "that the Party is identical to the working class?" (*RL*, p. 1572; ET, p. 236). When he writes, however, that the Party is only the *means* by which the class is formed, or the string on the bunch of asparagus (*RL*, p. 1572; ET, p. 236), he is speaking of the apparatus. On the other hand, the entire Party— the apparatus, the militants, and the sympathizers—is identical to the proletariat: "In a word, the Party *is* the very movement which unites the workers by carrying them along toward the taking of power. How then can you expect the working class to repudiate the C.P.? It is true that the C.P. is nothing outside of the class; but let it disappear, and the working class falls back into dust particles" (*CP*, p. 761; ET, p. 130).
29. *CP*, p. 755; ET, 123.
30. *CP*, p. 758; ET, p. 127.

initial conversion will he discuss, within the framework of the Party, "the problems which the Party submits to him and . . . within the context of the principles which the Party gives to him." [31] In other words, the question can only be one of "enriching," of "going beyond" Party politics in its own direction, of accelerating this politics and preceding it toward its goal. Resistance to Party action never comes from a proletarian, for the worker disqualifies himself as a proletarian as soon as he resists. Resistance, therefore, never has the value of a judgment but exists in the Party only as the remains of inertia, as a relic of its prehistory. The militants and even the masses are justified in respect to the Party if they go further in their attack than it does.[32] For once, they have felt more clearly than the Party the alternative between action or death which is the perpetual law of the Party and have felt the original *delay* [33] of all proletarian action, which occurs because its action is not founded in an existing class and because it is the invention of a future. But the outdistancing of the Party by the masses presupposes them already formed and organized by it; the current which overflows the Party comes from the Party. Even then it is not subject to proceedings other than its own or judged according to other criteria than its own: it is their haste and feverishness, which are justified in respect to it, it is the state of urgency, of which, nine times out of ten, it is the most sensitive detector, it is the law of all or nothing, its fundamental law, which bring it back to itself. This exception cannot by definition be extended to the case where the masses leave the Party, nor can it found a control of the Party by the masses.[34]

31. *CP*, p. 761; ET, p. 130.
32. The masses "judge their leaders when their leaders follow them, but not when they don't follow their leaders" (*CP*, p. 752; ET, p. 120).
33. *RL*, p. 1606; ET, p. 272 (modified).
34. In truth, this concession puts everything back in question because, if the masses are permitted to invoke the teaching of the Party against its decisions, its essence against its existence as it is, one passes from the brute urgency which takes one by the throat to an appraisal of the urgency; and from then on, the discussion, previously limited to a contest of activism, will extend to everything. The apparatus will be able to maintain that the offensive is provocation and treason. The premium on activism is no longer in order as soon as one distinguishes strategy from tactics and as soon as the notion of offensive and defensive are relativized. The Party, as Sartre conceives it, excludes even this rudiment of dialectic.

A fabric of imperious wills which do not allow gradations, itself pure action or nothing, the Party does not leave much of anything to the class. There is a way of living, of dressing, of eating, of envisaging life and death, love and work, finally a way of thinking which comes from the worker's condition as producer. These are the traits that one can describe like the habits of a species, they are the wrinkles of the proletariat, the marks of its enslavement. It is the class as discouraged, inactive and historically dispersed. It is the class which "objective" sociology willingly describes in order to keep the proletariat inactive. For indeed, Sartre says, when sociology returns to primitive societies, it willingly takes the class as a living and significant whole. One could reply that the class in primitive societies is in fact largely constituted by participation in mythical relationships and that, on the contrary, in advanced capitalism the relationships of production predominate, and that in the former case one must "understand" and in the latter case describe objectively. It is labor lost. One is suspect for being too interested in what the proletarians eat and think. This is to push them down into what they are, to distract them from what they have to be and from the Party. And the only way to escape the reproach completely would be to renounce, as communism does, saying anything about the proletarians. Let us rather speak of the Party, where they die and are reborn. But what will there be even to *say* about the Party? Thus duty closes the mouth of knowledge. Let us not even say that the class shows or hides itself, that it strengthens or weakens itself. Let us say that it "makes, unmakes and remakes itself endlessly." [35] History is voluntary or nothing. "Classes don't just happen to exist, they are made." [36] The proletariat "exists only by acting. It is action. If it ceases to act, it decomposes." [37] "The class is a system in motion: if it stopped, the individuals would revert to their inertia and to their isolation." [38] "A class *organizes itself*," [39] says Sartre, probably meaning to say, not that it organizes itself, not that others organize it, but that in a single movement which is without subject, being the exchange of the workers and the Party, the workers invent themselves as militants and pure action comes into being. Between the worker and the militant,

35. *RL*, p. 1573; ET, p. 237 (modified).
36. *CP*, p. 732; ET, p. 96.
37. *CP*, p. 732; ET, p. 97.
38. *CP*, p. 733; ET, p. 98.
39. *Ibid.*

the unbeliever and the converted, the militants and the Party which "tolerates" their discussion, the relationships are inflexible because they are inflexible to the highest degree between the proletariat and the bourgeoisie. It is the entire social fabric which becomes as fragile as glass. It is all history which becomes a duel without intermission, without oversights, without chance, under the accusing gaze of the moral imperative. The passivity of the workers is the activity of the bourgeoisie working on the worker's world and setting out there, like so many traps, near occasions of treason. To invoke the class against the Party, to judge the Party by the measure of the class, is the bourgeoisie's cleverest victory, since it scatters the proletariat from behind and spares the bourgeoisie a frontal attack. In order to reply to this bourgeois aggression which comes from everywhere, Sartre does not seem to count very much on a counteroffensive: but the bourgeoisie also has its "slippery customers," and a conquering politics would sweep them along and rebuild the unity of the Party in action. Perhaps he will speak of it later on. But this dialectic dissolves the contours; one no longer knows where the enemy is, where the ally is. For the moment, Sartre stresses them; to pass a judgment on the C.P. that was a political *act* would require nothing less than the C.P. Thus, by virtue of the principle of identity there is no judgment of the C.P., especially not in the name of the class. At the very moment when the proletariat evades a Party-directed strike, Sartre solemnly writes that it *"recognizes itself* in the test of strength which the C.P. institutes in its name." [40] This is because "recognition," like "unanimity," no longer designates verifiable relationships. These words are no more than a manner of expressing a solidarity which *would* be realized in death, or an oath exchanged outside of life. Those that did not strike put the proletariat in danger, since the Party went the distance for the proletariat; and as the Party can always completely commit itself and play double or nothing, it is threatened with death and infallible any time it wishes to be. But as this common peril of Party and class unites them, not in what they are and do but only in defeat, the general and formal approbation that Sartre gives to the Party does not tie him to a particular policy that the Party may decide to follow at a particular moment. If, instead of the lighting of death, in which the shadows of the proletariat and the Party merge, the sun of discussion were to reappear in broad

40. *CP*, p. 49; ET, p. 55.

daylight, as it does in Sartre's third article, the reader would perhaps find Sartre preparing a wise politics of a united left against
economic Malthusianism.

II

HE CLEARLY DIFFERS FROM MARX by his conception of
the equivocalness of facts. We have seen that in the area of facts
Sartre dismisses both sides, communism and anticommunism,
that for him there is no rigorous confrontation of idea and fact
and no means of establishing whether or not the idea is realized
in fact. With a few dialectical modifications, the idea covers any
fact; and indeed it must, for it is the expression of the existing
proletariat, and, in a given moment, the Party action is the entire
existence of the proletariat. "Facts" are always circumvented by
decisions. They give us no means of appeal against decisions
which, in any case, do not *result* from discussion and which, regardless of what they may be, continually engage the fate of the
proletariat and are thus its decisions. From time to time there is,
of course, an external verdict—the Party fails, the masses ebb,
pure action stops and reconsiders itself. But even then one never
knows exactly to what the facts said "no." The failure allows of
opposing interpretations, and it is still in obscurity that one makes
one's choice. The fact, insofar as it exists, does not carry its meaning, which is of another order: meaning is dependent on consciousness and, just for this reason, can in all strictness be
neither justified nor excluded by the facts. We encounter, therefore, only facts invaded by consciousness. Nothing can enlighten
the Party or its militants. They never have to deal with truth but
with views which already are biases. There is no mediation between "pure fact," which has whatever meaning one wants to give
it, and decision, which gives the fact only one meaning. The
mediation would be the probable, the meaning that the facts
seem to recommend. But this shaky meaning cannot ground the
politics of the proletariat, which itself is improbable and which
begins to exist only by lightning-quick decisions against all facts.
One does not even see here on what basis a discussion could be
carried on, for discussions suppose a situation to which one attempts to fit a meaning. One applies a meaning and then another
and takes whichever works the best, but it is not a question of
doing it for the best. Under pain of leaving the universe to the

bourgeoisie, it is a question of doing what will work, and why would this be what is most probable? Sartre does not even think that the Party unravels the situation; it gropingly tries its keys.[41] What would one discuss, since it is not a question of interpreting the world but of changing it, since pure data (if there were any) and a decision are without common measure, and since, finally, the data themselves are not pure and give us only the reflection of other decisions?

Marxism well knows that any situation is ambiguous. How could it be otherwise, since the consciousness that one has of a situation is still a factor of that situation, since there is here no separation of the observer and the observed or any objective criterion for knowing whether one should wait or forge ahead toward the future? Nothing is more Marxist than the mixing of fact and meaning, with the exception that Marxism does not mix them in an equivocation but in a genesis of truth, does not crush two adversaries into each other, but makes of them two stakes along the same road. For Sartre conscious awareness is an absolute. It gives meaning; and in the case of an event, the meaning it gives is irrevocable. For Marx, conscious awareness, that of the leader like that of the militants, is itself a fact. It has its place in history, it either answers to what the period expects or it does not, it is complete or partial. At its birth it is already *in* a truth which judges it. And if, at the moment, we do not indeed have any external model with which we can compare it, the trial that it undergoes in Party discussion, the reception it receives there, the power that it either does or does not have to carry the proletariat along, to increase consciousness and power in it— these are the criteria of truth. Not in the sense of conformity of theses to a ready-made reality—that, indeed, would not be Marxist. Truth is to be made, but to be made according to what the proletariat and its adversaries are and do in the same moment. What is this dubious relationship, Sartre would say? Is or is not the meaning of the present given in it? It is neither given in it nor created out of nothing. It is elicited from the present, and such is the function of a congress. Here it is a matter of confronting theses and an existing proletariat, not as one compares two things, but by explaining the theses, by speaking to the pro- letariat, by giving it an understanding of itself and of its worldly situation that it does not have. If in the end it recognizes itself in

41. *RL,* p. 1587; ET, p. 253.

these views, they become true, not by nominal definition and because the proletariat stakes its life on them, but because in a philosophy of praxis, where the world does not exist completely without man, this view that the proletariat has of itself—once it has taken stock of its strengths and everything has been accounted for—is the present form of the truth. Ideas are neither received from the proletariat by the Party nor given by the Party to the proletariat; they are *elaborated* in the Party, and it is on this condition that they represent the maximum clarity that the proletarian present has of itself. Sartre does not envisage this adjustment of action to the situation because he always considers only decisions that are already made. Considered at its birth, however, action is first of all a *view;* it proposes immediate and distant objectives, it follows a line, it has a content, it supposes an examination, it is not "pure action." Reading Sartre, one would believe that the Party's action is a series of *coups de force* by which it defends itself against death. But such action would be mere convulsions. If there is *action,* it is necessary to elicit information, facts, a discussion (even when it would be only the discussion of the leader with himself), arguments, a preference given to this rather than that—in short, the probable, which Sartre does not want because he looks at it as a pure rationalist and sees it as a lesser certitude. And yet he has elsewhere said, profoundly, that the whole of the perceived world is probable. Let us add that that is its way of existing: the probable is another name for the real, it is the modality of what exists. In this sense the Party's line is probable: not as an uncertain opinion, but as the position which has been disengaged through the confrontation of the proletariat and its "consciousness" and to which this confrontation gives an absolute authority, since, right or wrong as regards the future, the "line" is at the moment the maximum of truth that history can claim. This is all very fine, Sartre would say, but where, then, are these criteria, where is this truth to which one subordinates the Party? Where is this revolutionary line when, without the Party, there would be only fluctuating masses? Where is this proletarian history on which the Party is dependent when, without it, there would be no proletariat at all? A truth always means that someone is judging. It must be either the militants or the leaders—and if one leaves it to the militants, the proletariat is lost. Who will judge the *true* line, the *true* situation, the *true* history? The Marxist reply is: no one, *which is to say,* the Party as laboratory of history, as contact with the proletariat and its consciousness, as elucidation of the present, of itself the becoming of truth. There is no external criterion by which one can measure the Party's action, but there is an internal logic by which one recognizes it. Sartre is at the highest point of realism, since he reasons under the category of pure fact and since political time is atomized for him into a series of decisions taken in the presence of death; he is also at the highest point of formalism, since what is put indiscriminately into question each time is the unqualified and naked existence of the Party and the proletariat. Marxism wanted to be a philosophy of contents. If Sartre is right, history has separated what Marxism had united: that is to say, the proletariat or the Party and a certain sense of their becoming, the existing proletariat and the leaders' idea of it. The Party's Marxist fidelity is not a fidelity to a wager but to general outlooks which the majority and the opposition have in common and which are not *continually* questioned. For a Marxist the meaning of events is to be found only in the Party, not by virtue of a permanent equivocalness—because the Party manufactures meaning and the proletariat is always compromised by what is done in its name—but rather by virtue of an immanent truth which magnetizes the Party's decisions.

All of Sartre's divergences with regard to Marx are given in this one, for his rigid conception of the Party is only the counterpart of the equivocalness of facts: it is the answer of consciousness, all the more peremptory [42] because the course of things is so indecisive. The Party as pure action is nothing but an ideal, says Sartre. But it is difficult to see how pure action could have gradations in reality: it is either completely pure or it is nothing. On these grounds, it is aggression and tends toward physical struggle. In fact, it will have to transform itself into a "line," situate itself according to a certain perspective, and direct this perspective. On the day after the June 2 strike, Sartre said buoyantly that the Central Committee had already solved its family quarrel with the working class. Subsequent events have shown that things are not so simple. Whether it is in the Central Committee or in the Party—and it is ordinarily in the Central Committee at the same time as in the Party—a perspective must be developed. In order to struggle, it is not enough to know that capitalism is the enemy.

42. "Marx saw the necessity of a constant effort of emancipation *which needed to be all the more sustained as the working class saw its condition worsen further*" (*RL*, p. 1611 [our emphasis]; *ET*, p. 277).

This enemy must be found here and now; one must know under what disguise it hides itself, whether a given strike is a provocation or whether, on the contrary, it foretells a movement of the masses. This examination knocks the wind out of pure action, because several estimations are possible and because the best one is subject to discussion. Besides, if the proletariat, which is nothing, can count only on itself, it is defeated in advance. It must assail the adversary, not in a frontal attack, but on its flanks or its rear; it must understand the bourgeoisie's internal functioning. Here again there are many probabilities to be evaluated. There is no action worthy of the name which is "pure action." Pure action, the "unanimous" Party, are the action and the Party seen from outside; and if Sartre entered within, he, like everyone else, could no more abstain from discussing than from breathing. Ultimately, pure action is either suicide or murder. Generally, it is an imaginary (and not, as Sartre believes, an ideal) action. When it tries to impose itself on things, it suddenly returns to the unreal from which it was born. It becomes . . . theater. From this come both the extraordinary description of the May 28 demonstration as "street theater," in which the Parisian population plays the part "Parisian population," [43] and Sartre's sympathy for the demonstrations in which the proletariat "shows itself." [44] The ardent negation which was to inspire a pure action becomes an exhibition, the duel becomes a show or an exchange of gazes. And Sartre says correctly that this is only a last resource, to which one resigns oneself when there is nothing else to be done. But starting from his principles, any action tends to end in such a way. It remains to be seen whether the working-class leaders can in any case give the excuse that there was "nothing else to be done," if they are ever allowed to organize shows, since the police weapons are not made of pasteboard. The May 28 demonstration was indeed something of that sort. The analysis of the neo-proletariat and of mass syndicalism given by Sartre in his third article makes it clear that we have come to this point. Unskilled workers, who very often are not militant and do not elect or control their leaders, do not have any political action. They do not know, says

43. *CP*, p. 696; ET, p. 57.
44. *CP*, p. 710; ET, p. 73. In Italy, after the assassination attempt against Togliatti [former Italian Communist Party leader], "the working class manifested its existence by an *act* before the nation, before Europe; . . . the barriers explode and the proletariat *shows itself*" [modified].

Sartre, how to maneuver in the face of capitalism, how to exercise pressure on it, how to use tactics, much less strategy. Suddenly they move to explosive strikes from which it is extremely difficult to predict whether or not a mass movement is heralded, strikes which the apparatus therefore hardly controls and with regard to which it is always either ahead or behind. All this is somewhat likely and reflects fairly well the ways of the working movement and of today's communist action. It remains to be seen whether this indeed is action as Marxism has conceived and practiced it. Sartre writes [45] that the neoproletariat has lost its grip on history, that the distance between everyday problems and the revolution has increased tremendously. During the great periods of the working-class movement, the demands and problems of the working class formed a whole, they were leading to an overthrow of capitalism which was to resolve them and, with them, the problem of modern society. It was not then a question of pure action. For the Party, the question was to organize the proletariat's hold on the social whole and to transform this into victory, to extend, concentrate, and push to its maximum effectiveness a struggle already inscribed in the relationships of production and in their partial demands. "Already inscribed?" Sartre will say. "But this is the retrospective illusion. You are projecting into a former reality what has been accomplished by the Party's action." Not at all. We are saying that the working class, guided by the Party, endowed by it with differentiated means of perception and action, was nonetheless functioning in the Party in a completely different way than as a driving force for which the Party invented the means of operation and determined the use. In an organism there is no action without a nervous system, but the nervous system endows an organism with a life which it is not adequate to explain. There is also the part played by humoral regulation, by experience, and most of all by a mobilization of all these resources in the face of a perceived situation to which one must respond. In the Party, without which, indeed, it would be inert and virtually like a body without brains, the working class accomplishes real work. Its choice is not only between a conversion that would identify it with the apparatus and a discouragement that would reduce it to a state of mass; it more or less takes part in the action, and the Party takes account of this action and considers it not mere caprice, but like the indications of a thermometer.

45. *CP*, pp. 722–23; ET, p. 83.

Sartre writes that the Party gives "orders" to the workers. The Marxists used to say "watchwords," and the whole difference is there. The Party gives the militant something to will beyond himself: a line, a perspective of action, both established after an examination, not only of the relations of force, but also of the way the proletariat lives and interprets the situation. There is an ebb and flow of the proletariat living politically in the Party. Sartre once said that the Party itself has a history. Yes, and to speak like Max Weber, it is made up not only of its *zweckrational* actions, of their consequences, and of the new decisions taken by the Party in their presence. It is the history of the Party's efforts to utilize the ebb and flow that are the respiration of the class and of the entire society. The class's history does not explain the Party's, nor does the Party's history explain the class's. They are coupled to each other; together they are only one history, but one in which class reactions count as much as Party actions. It is therefore essential for the Party to include this plurality or this inertia which Sartre refuses it and which is its flesh, *the principle of its strength and, in other moments, of its weakness,* and the control wheel which for the moment holds it back but which tomorrow may take it beyond the ends which it proposed. For the historical ebb and flow, of which the Party is the interpreter and consequently a very special component but never the cause, Sartre substitutes the conversion of the masses to the Party and their atomization when they withdraw. It is thus natural for him to conceive the Party's action [46] as a "technique for the masses," which "churns" them like an emulsion, makes them "curdle" like butter, or maintains them in a state of "affective erethism." [47] It is just the opposite of an action in which the Party and the working class jointly live the same situation and thus make the same history—not because all the proletarians see their action as clearly as the leaders, not because the Party alone conceives it, but because the action works on them and disposes them to understand the Party's watchwords and carries the apparatus itself to its highest degree of tension. Sartre intends to prove that the workers' abstention during the June 2 strike does not amount to a judgment of the C.P.'s politics by showing that they all had personal motives: one says that he was tired of politics, another

46. In the neoproletariat phase. But not a word to say that this is a crisis of Marxist politics and a dead-end situation.
47. *CP*, Part III.

that the Workers' Federation [48] did not budge, a third that one does not strike during a month of paid holidays, and finally another that he has three children and his wife was recently ill. But it is precisely this recourse to personal motives which *is* a political judgment. If the Party had a hold on the masses (and the masses a hold on history), personal motives would be outflanked. Sartre reasons as if the political life of the masses were on the level of judgment; and before admitting that they disapprove of the Party, he waits until they say that the Party is wrong. But neither adherence nor divergence, neither working-class history nor revolutionary history are of this order: the Party's watchwords do or do not count, do or do not exist for the worker, depending on their relation to the situation that he is living and on this situation itself. The judgments he makes of the Party and the importance he gives to his private life convey this tacit engagement, which is the essential factor. Marxism believes that in ordinary moments history is an accumulation of symbols that day by day inscribe themselves more or less clearly on the record of the past, fade or intensify, leaving a practically unreadable residue; but at other moments history is caught in a movement which attracts and submits to its rhythm an increasing number of facts. Political decisions prepare these moments and respond to them, but they do not create them. In the so-called revolutionary situations, everything works as a system, the problems appear to be linked, and all the solutions seem included in the proletariat's power. In the chaos of history these moments of truth furnish Marxist action its landmarks, and it guides itself by them. Marxist action never sets up the revolution as a goal that one can imagine but rather makes it spring out of the concatenation of the demands, of their convergence, of their collaboration, a process which calls the entire State apparatus into question and finally makes a new power emerge in opposition to the old. Not that the Party does away with politics by means of a fortuitous confluence of favorable circumstances, but because at these privileged moments all its initiatives succeed, the social whole responds marvelously, and the logic of the struggle makes the proletariat emerge into a revolution that they would have perhaps not dared make if it had been proposed to them as an end. It is this life of the Party and of the proletariat in the historical situation, this event which confirms itself as it goes along, like a

48. [Force Ouvrière.—Trans.]

fire or a snowball, that one cannot express by the idea of pure action. Sartre sometimes admits of degrees of historical equivocalness,[49] as he sometimes speaks of proletarian currents that the Party decodes [50] and even of a dialectic between the Party and the masses.[51] This is odd if the masses are nothing politically and if the Party is their political existence. One asks what is left of the dilemma: stick to the Party or disappear, and of the formal condemnation: whoever distinguishes the proletariat from the Party betrays the proletariat. But never does he consider, in order to reduce these tensions, anything but "concessions, accommodations, compromises," [52] or perhaps, when they are not possible, pure action, which is to say, force. Yet he never evokes the basic Marxist hope of resolution in *true* action, that is to say, action fitted to internal relations of the historical situation, which await nothing but action to "take," to constitute a form in movement. In other words, Sartre never speaks of revolution, for the truth to be made is in Marxist language precisely the revolution. He undoubtedly feels that such is not the order of the day, and this appears unquestionable to us. But what is the C.P.'s action without the revolution? What is left of the immanent guarantee that the revolution brought to the Party? The stratagem of men substituted for that of things, pure action substituted for the conflagration of a society, this is perhaps the expedient of communism confronting a history in crisis. But the expedient, produced by the crisis it attempts to hide, will not bring history back to a Marxist course; it prepares *something else*, and what it is remains to be seen.

49. He who refused to distinguish between the U.S.S.R. and the revolution, the C.P.'s and the proletariat's violence, ends up speaking of a permanent tension between the U.S.S.R. and the fraternal parties, between the Party and the proletariat (*RL*, p. 1616; ET, pp. 282–83)—and a tension is not a mediation, but it does mark differences, and it poses a problem. He who refused as bourgeois the distinction between politics and economics now says that they are dissociated in contemporary history and that strikes with dual objectives are the artificial means invented to compensate for this quartering of history (*CP*, pp. 1778, 1815; ET, pp. 189, 227). Thus equivocalness in the strict sense—the indistinguishability of contraries—appears as a limiting case, and the problem of dialectical unity is posed.
50. *RL*, p. 1607; ET, p. 273.
51. *RL*, p. 1572; ET, p. 236.
52. This is said with regard to the relations between the U.S.S.R. and the fraternal parties (*RL*, p. 1615; ET, p. 282).

What opposes Sartre's theses on class are not only "optimistic nonsense," the monadic class, spontaneity which "needs only to be directed," [53] the "proletariat which grows all alone like a very gifted student," the "fruit-proletariat," the "flower-proletariat," which "has to do only with itself, with its own activity"; [54] rather it is the Marxist conviction that the class is not placed before the militant like an object that his will molds or manipulates but that it is also behind him, ready to understand his politics, if this politics is explained to it. The question is not to know who, from the class or the Party, makes the proletariat's political history. These problems of causality, which have very little meaning in nature, have even less when dealing with society. No one holds that in advance of the Party the class contains a complete proletarian politics folded up inside it and that all that is necessary is to unfold it. But neither does the Party's general staff have such a plan; it invents proletarian politics in contact with the masses and as their expression. "This is quibbling," says Sartre, "for if expression could determine this immense tidal wave, then expression is also action." [55] Who says the contrary? But it is an action of the proletariat, not by nominal definition and because it is the Party's action, not by the inspiration of the "revolutionary instinct," but because the proletariat adopts it, finds itself in it, and makes it its own. Sartre writes that even in 1936 the movement expanded only when *L'Humanité* (May 20 and 24) had analyzed the first three strikes and underlined "the novelty and the similarity of the methods of combat." Thus the Party's press plays an essential role in "a supposedly spontaneous movement." [56] But who said that the proletariat cannot see without eyes or that

53. It is true that Claude Lefort concluded in a previous article that revolutionary leadership poses a problem, and he indicated that a leadership was needed that would not isolate itself from the class, as the Party does. But he never said that the class could act without organization or leadership.

54. Lefort wrote: "The proletariat has nothing to do with anything but itself, its own activity, and *the problems posed by its own situation in capitalistic society*" ("Le Marxisme et Sartre," *Les Temps modernes*, VIII, no. 89 [April, 1953], 1555) [italics added]. He thus did not forget the struggle. He said that it begins at the level of production, that this struggle, which is the proletariat's condition, is the ground or ballast of its political action, and that therefore the Other cannot, as Sartre says, "at any minute" pulverize the proletariat.

55. *RL*, p. 1609; ET, p. 275.

56. *CP*, p. 1807, note; ET, 218, note.

political facts do not count in the movement of the masses? It has been said, and it is quite another thing, that through the Party's apparatus, using its means of information and communication, the proletariat is born to a political life which is not to be confused with the general staff's orders. What stops Sartre from admitting this substantial action—in which there is neither pure authority nor pure obedience and which, in its culmination, is called revolution—is a philosophy in which meaning, seen as wholly spiritual, as impalpable as lightning, is absolutely opposed to being, which is absolute weight and blindness; and certainly this philosophy is the opposite of Marx's. "No one believes any longer in the proletariat fetish, a metaphysical entity from which the workers might alienate themselves. There are men, animals, and objects." [57] Marx, on the other hand, thought there were relationships between persons "mediated by things," and for him revolution, like capitalism, like all the realities of history, belonged to this mixed order. For Marx there was, and for Sartre there is not, a coming-to-be of meaning in institutions. History is no longer for Sartre, as it was for Marx, a mixed milieu, neither things nor persons, where intentions are absorbed and transformed and where they decay but are sometimes also reborn and exacerbated, tied to one another and multiplied through one another; history is made of criminal intentions or virtuous intentions and, for the rest, of acceptances which have the value of acts. Sartre today is as far away from Marx as when he wrote *Materialism and Revolution,* and there is nothing inconsistent in his work. What he disapproved of in the communists was materialism, the idea, well or poorly formulated, of a dialectic which is material. What he today appreciates in them is the disavowal of historical "matter," of class as the measure of action, and of revolution as truth. [58]

Truth, revolution, and history, then, are the things at stake in

57. *CP*, p. 725; *ET*, p. 89.
58. In a completely prospective philosophy such as Sartre's, the very formulas which rooted action in the class end up rooting the class in action. When Marx said to the proletariat that "its goal and its historical action are irrevocably and visibly traced out for it in the very circumstances of its life," one might have believed that the proletariat's historical role was already prepared in its existence. Sartre uses this text, but to describe the proletariat organized in a single labor union; the "circumstances of its life" which assign the proletariat a goal are thus those that it has first created in organizing itself (*CP*, pp. 715–16; *ET*, pp. 78–79).

the confused, or too clear, discussion that Sartre bases upon the notion of *spontaneity*. There is indeed one meaning of this word that Marxism does not have to consider. This involves what Lenin called "primitivism," the myth of a revolution based completely on economic premises and of workers' action limited exclusively to this domain. But there is another sense of the word which is essential, not only for Marxism but even for Bolshevism, since it merges with the sense of proletarian revolution: the masses' entry into politics, the common life of the masses and the Party. If Lenin never renounced the word or the thing called spontaneity,[59] it was for a reason which he makes implicit in a farsighted passage: all things considered, "spontaneity" and "consciousness" are not alternatives, and if one eliminated spontaneity from the Party's theory, one would deprive it of any means of being the proletariat's consciousness. Lenin wrote that

> the very talk of "estimating the *relative* significance" . . . of spontaneity and consciousness itself reveals a complete lack of "consciousness." If certain "spontaneous elements of development" can be grasped at all by human understanding, then an incorrect estimation of them will be tantamount to "belittling the conscious

---

59. Precisely in *What Is To Be Done?*, where he strongly criticized "primitivism," one can read: "Whoever doubts this lags in his consciousness behind the spontaneous awakening of the masses" (V. I. Lenin, *Collected Works*, V [Moscow, 1961], p. 430); "the wave of spontaneous indignation, as it were, is sweeping over us, leaders and organizers of the movement" (p. 441); "we were right in our opinion that the principal cause of the present crisis in the Russian Social Democracy is *the lag of the leaders* ('ideologists,' revolutionaries, Social Democrats) behind *the spontaneous upsurge of the masses*" (p. 446); "the revolutionary movement is rapidly and spontaneously growing" (p. 476); "[for] a circle of leaders . . . is capable of coping with political tasks in the genuine and most practical sense of the term, for the reason and to the extent that their impassioned propaganda meets with response among the spontaneously awakening masses, and their sparkling energy is answered and supported by the energy of the revolutionary class. Plekhanov was profoundly right, not only in pointing to this revolutionary class and proving that its spontaneous awakening was inevitable, but in setting even 'the workers' circles' a great and lofty political task" (p. 447). The organization is thus at one and the same time made to amplify a spontaneity which is already political and to render political thought and action "natural" for the proletariat. Sartre, on the contrary, takes for granted that "the very essence of the masses forbids them from thinking and acting politically" (CP, p. 1815; ET, p. 226).

126 / ADVENTURES OF THE DIALECTIC

element." But if they cannot be grasped, then we do not know them, and therefore cannot speak of them.[60]

These lines, directed against those who advocated spontaneity,[61] also work against the worshipers of consciousness, since they show that, in spite of some momentary lags, spontaneity and consciousness vary in the same sense. The general staff does not have supersensible faculties, and it is difficult to see on what the Party itself could be based in order to decide upon a politics if not on the proletariat's situation in different countries and on their "spontaneous" reactions. And even if it is necessary to coordinate and rectify them, it is still to the proletariat that one must speak, it is to the proletariat that the Party line must be explained and made familiar and natural. Lenin never imagined the relationship of Party to proletariat as that of a general staff to its troops.[62] The class has an apprenticeship in political life which enables it to understand what the Party does and to express itself in the Party, as we express ourselves in what we say, not without work and effort but not without profit to ourselves as well. It is not enough for the proletariat to follow; the Party must direct it, to quote a well-known text, "in a way so as to elevate and not to lower the general level of consciousness, of revolutionary spirit, of

60. Lenin, Collected Works, V, 394.
61. [In the French: "les 'spontanéistes.' "—Trans.]
62. Sartre says that democratic centralism means permanent mobilization. But one joins one's military unit under pain of death, and, at least in this regard, no mobilization is democratic. For Lenin "democritism" was impossible under an autocratic regime and in a clandestine party. But the elective principle "goes without saying in countries where there is political freedom." A completely straight-faced picture of the democratic control of the German Social Democratic Party follows. One will see that it is not a question of a formality: "Everyone knows that a certain political figure began in such and such a way, passed through such and such an evolution, behaved in a trying moment in such and such a manner, and possesses such and such qualities; consequently, all party members, knowing all the facts, can elect or refuse to elect this person to a particular party office. The general control (in the literal sense of the term) exercised over every act of a party man in the political field brings into existence an automatically operating mechanism which produces what in biology is called the 'survival of the fittest'" (Lenin, Collected Works, V, 478). Here is biology again, Sartre will say, and the fruit-proletariat. Not biology, but history, and the historical mission of the proletariat.

the capacity to struggle and of proletarian victory." [63] The Party is not the Calvinist Church: means which are too human precisely because they are in the service of a being beyond being. It is the initiation of the proletariat into political life, and in this regard it is neither end nor means for the proletariat. It is not an end, as Sartre implies when he writes that the Party gives orders, nor is it "means," as he ends up writing in completing his first analysis.[64] Are my profession and my children ends or means, or both? They are nothing of the sort, certainly not means for my life, which loses itself in them instead of using them; and they are much more than ends, since an end is *what* one wants, and since I want my profession and my children without measuring in advance where this will lead me, which will be far beyond what I can know of them. Not that I dedicate myself to something I do not know—I see them with the kind of precision that belongs to existing things, I recognize them among all others without completely knowing of what they are made. Our concrete decisions do not aim at closed meanings. The Party has value for the militant only through the action to which it calls him, and this action is not completely definable in advance. It is, like everything which exists, like everything we live, something in the process of becoming an expression, a movement which calls for a continuation, a past in the process of giving itself a future—in short, a being we can know in a certain *way*. We have said elsewhere that a proletarian power leads toward internationalism, to appropriation by the workers of production and the State, and to modern production, even though the necessary detours are to be explained to the workers. Anti-Semitism or police masquerades are excluded because either one of them clouds proletarian consciousness. Sartre somewhere makes fun of those purists who still speak of the day when Stalin proclaimed socialism in one country. He says that on that day the angels cried. It is, however, true that Marxism is touchy about certain points because it believes that history is a whole, that each detail counts, and that together they make a healthy or unhealthy historical landscape. For a Marxist, to speak on behalf of the proletariat does not mean one has unlimited powers; and precisely because a democratic consultation in the bourgeois manner is impossible, it is even more

63. Lenin, *Collected Works* (1966), XXXI, 74.
64. *RL*, p. 1572; ET, p. 236.

necessary to ballast the Party's action with the counterweight which guarantees against historical delirium: the proletariat's agreement. The workers are not gods, but neither are the leaders. The joining of the proletariat and the leaders is the only certain sign in a history full of irony; as Lukács said—using Weber's expression—it is here that the proletariat's *objective possibility* appears, not the proletarians' thought, not the thought the general staff believes they have or attributes to them, but what is left, completely hammered down, after the confrontation between the Party and the proletariat. Lenin never sacrificed spontaneity to consciousness; he postulated their agreement in the common work of the Party because he was a Marxist, that is to say, because he believed in a politics that attests to its truth by becoming the truth of the proletarians. He went very far in the art of compromise, maneuver, and trickery. He was not one of those supercilious ideologues who endlessly confront the Party's line with a concept of revolution, that is to say, with a revolution in ideas. But precisely because he was not an ideologue, he did not put consciousness or conception on one side and obedience or execution on the other. Contrary to Sartre, he did not give a free hand to the leaders "at their own risk." For him the leaders were ahead of the working class, but "only a step ahead." There was no criterion or geometrical definition which, in the abstract and outside a given situation, permitted one to say what is or is not proletarian. But there was a practical criterion: whatever can be explained to and be accepted by the proletariat, not through pure obedience but in conscience, is proletarian. The Party's action is not to be judged on a detail any more than a man is to be judged on a tic or a mole; rather it is judged on a direction taken, on a way of doing things, and, in the last analysis, on the militants' relationships with it.

One might answer that the Bolshevist pretension of making a *true* politics was never more than an illusion, that it served only to ground the authority of power more solidly. For if it is true that the classless society is already present in the infrastructures of capitalism, if the internal mechanism of capitalist production is like a particular and aberrant case of socialist production, in terms of which it must be understood and which is in some sense already there, then the initiatives of proletarian power find their guarantee once and for all in things and are justified in advance. How could one limit them? They are only there to liberate a revolution toward which the productive forces are moving. The "delivery" can be difficult. There is a logic in things which tends to make the remnants of capitalism regenerate themselves, even if only in people's minds. Revolution, then, is not made all at once; it comes at the end of an endless purification, it demands a party of iron. But the underground reality of socialism guarantees these violences and grounds them in truth. Since socialism is true, endowed with a truth which is accessible only to the readers of *Capital*, the Party of the proletariat, and more exactly its leaders (who have read *Capital*), see better than anyone else the true path toward socialism; the orientation they give to the Party also *must* be true, the consciousness they have of the proletarian situation *must* coincide with the spontaneous reactions of the properly enlightened proletariat. Ultimately, how could they want something which was not true? The assurance of being the carrier of truth is vertiginous. It is in itself violence. How can I know what God wants unless I try it out, asked Coûfontaine? [65] If I succeed, it is because God was with me. In the same way, the Bolshevik in power, assailed as he is by contingencies, is even more tempted to dare because, being in the darkness of everyday politics and incapable of getting from universal history a solution for today's problems, he is assured of acting according to truth only if he succeeds: it was then permitted by things and by the ineluctable truth of socialism. Here the relationship is reversed: at the start, the action of the Party and its leaders succeeded because it was true, but the truth of the moment is accessible only through action; one must try things out, and what *will* succeed *was* true. When one identifies spontaneity and consciousness, Bolshevist vertigo is not far away; and this is what Sartre pushes to its limit. One is not far from thinking that the Party's decisions are *eminently* "spontaneous" and that, *by definition*, they translate the movement of history. This is what Sartre says, but this is not what Lenin intended. Lenin gave consciousness the obligation of informing itself about everything the proletariat spontaneously does or says and of explaining to the proletariat its own direction. But in the end his formula, which we recaller earlier—consciousness *cannot* be unaware of spontaneity, the leaders *cannot* lose sight of the proletariat's spontaneous reactions—suddenly authorizes a state of frenzy belonging to the leader alone, if indeed he is the one who estimates the importance and the

65. [A character in Paul Claudel's play *L'Otage* (*The Hostage*). —Trans.]

meaning of these spontaneous reactions. And how could it not be he, since he has the best knowledge of long-run and short-run perspectives? The workers do not understand? They will understand tomorrow, and they will be grateful to the leader for having preceded them toward truth. It is not only truth in the sense of "scientific socialism" which grounds violence. Even when the truth is dialectical, it is dogmatic. It is understood that revolutionary action conserves in sublating, destroys only for the sake of realizing, that it saves everything, that it reconciles the individual and the Party, the past and the future, value and reality. But this return to the positive takes place only after negation: first of all, it is necessary to destroy, to sublate; and in order to put into motion the dialectical functioning that so delights classical minds, the revolutionary power must be solidly established. The classless society reconciles everyone, but to get there it is first of all necessary that the proletariat affirm itself as a class and make its own the State apparatus which served to oppress it. Those who will be shot *would understand* tomorrow that they did not die in vain; the only problem is that they will no longer be there to understand it. Revolutionary violence insults them most grievously by not taking their revolt seriously: they do not know what they are doing. Such are the poisoned fruits of *willed truth*: it authorizes one to go ahead against all appearances; in itself it is madness. "A spectre is haunting Europe—the spectre of communism." [66] Communism is not only in things; it is even in the thoughts of the adversary. There is a historical imagination which forces communism into his dreams. And the proletarian power would hesitate?

> The theoretical conclusions of the Communists are in no way based on ideas or principles that have been invented, or discovered, by this or that would-be universal reformer. They merely express, in general terms, actual relations springing from an existing class struggle, from a historical movement going on under our very eyes.[67]

Knowing this, how could one hesitate to step over an obstacle?

This is indeed how the Bolshevik in power reasons, this is why he has to collide with Stalin someday, and this development, as

66. *Manifesto of the Communist Party* (Moscow, 1952), p. 38.
67. *Ibid.*, p. 61.

we have already said, was prepared by the idea of a materialistic dialectic. But between Stalinist communism and Lenin, and even more so between Stalin and Marx, there remains the difference that Lenin, who was not a philosopher but who understood the Party's life in the most precise Marxist sense, broke up the *tête-à-tête* between truth and the theoretician and slipped a third party in between the dialectic of things and its reflection in the leader's mind. This third party was the proletariat, and the golden rule was to do nothing which could diminish its consciousness or its power. This was not a rigorous conceptual criterion, and one could ask for yet another criterion to guide its application; but the rule was very clear when applied to a long enough development, and it was explicit, at least as far as the Party's style was concerned, that is to say, pedagogic, not military. The *Theses on Feuerbach* philosophically defined Marxist action as "objective activity." The materialism of former times had understood matter only as inertia and left the monopoly of activity to idealism. It was necessary to arrive at the idea of activity on the part of the object, and particularly on the part of the historical object. This heavy activity was the counterweight to the dialectical exploits of the theoretician confronting truth alone. These fragile barriers defended the essence of Marxism, the idea of a truth that, in order to be completely true, must be *evolved*, not only in the solitary thoughts of the philosopher who ripened it and who has understood everything, but also in the relationship between the leader who thinks and explains it and the proletariat which lives and adopts it.[68] The barriers have been swept away, but one cannot speak of communism without mentioning the incident. Sartre describes a communism of pure action which no longer believes in truth, revolution, or history. The October generation, like the young Marx, believed in an action which *verifies itself*, in a truth which comes to be in the life of the Party and the proletariat. It was, perhaps, a chimera. At least it was—to speak as Sartre does, but without smiling—the Marxist "something or other."

---

68. The Marxists had a word (which is no longer used except ritually) for designating the line which takes into account the objective situation as well as the spontaneous reactions. It was the *accurate* line, not the arbitrary one, not exactly *true*, as if the question were to copy an already-made history, but accurate—that is to say, at one and the same time efficacious and proletarian.

III

ONE COULD SHOW that Sartre strips this halo from each of the Marxist notions that he uses by placing each in the light of his philosophy and, moreover, that he accounts in this way for today's communism point by point. The same term "praxis" that the *Theses on Feuerbach* used for designating an activity immanent in the object of history Sartre uses for designating the "pure" activity which makes the proletariat exist in history. The Sartrean "something or other"—radical freedom—takes possession of praxis. Sartre used to say that there is no difference between imaginary love and true love because the subject, being a thinking subject, is by definition what he thinks he is. He could say that a historically "true" politics is always an invented one, that only by a retrospective illusion is this politics seen to be prepared within the history where it intervenes, and that, in a society, revolution is self-imagination. According to Sartre, praxis is thus the vertiginous freedom, the magic power that is ours to act and to make ourselves whatever we want, so that the formula "everything which is real is praxis, everything which is praxis is real" [69]—in itself an excellent way of specifying the relations between Marx and Hegel—ends up meaning that we are what we contrive to be and, as for everything else, we are as responsible for it as if we had done it. The possibilities are all equally distant —in a sense at zero distance, since all there is to do is to will, in another sense infinitely distant, since we will never be *them,* and *they* will never be what we have to be. Transferred to history, this means that the worker who adheres to the Party at the same time rejoins a possibility which is nothing other than himself, the external reflection of his freedom, and that yet he will never be this militant that he swore to be because he is the one who swears. In both cases—because the Party and the revolution are both very close and infinitely far apart—there is no path which leads from that which was to that which will be, and this is why Party politics cannot be, properly speaking, "just" or "false." There are, of course, foolish decisions and wise decisions, the Party either is or is not informed; but the question is never, as it is in battles, one of knowing the adversary's strength and weakness; there are no internal collusions to break it up, just as there is no internal

69. *CP*, p. 741; *ET*, p. 107.

norm of action in the proletariat. Action is *the only possibility,* not because it rigorously translates the themes of proletarian politics into today's terms, but because no one else is proposing another possibility. If, in an opaque history, rationality is created by Party action and you are in conflict with the Party—the only historical agent (all the more so if it eliminates you)—you are historically wrong. If it gets the better of you, it knows better than you do.[70]

70. To this effect Sartre quotes a sentence of ours which places definitive judgment of each decision at the end of history. What appears to us to be outside the accurate line might, within the whole, appear indispensable. For our part, we immediately added: "But the resort to a judgment based on the future is indistinguishable from the theological appeal to the Last Judgment, unless it is simply a reversal of *pro* and *contra,* unless the future is in some sense outlined in the present, and unless hope is not simply faith and we know where we are going" (Merleau-Ponty, *Humanisme et Terreur* [Paris, 1948], pp. 153–54; *Humanism and Terror,* trans. John O'Neill [Boston, 1969], pp. 142–43), and this brought back the necessity of a comprehensible line. The recourse to a universal history that one imagines accomplished is pragmatism and nominalism in disguise. If we imagine ourselves to be spectators of a completed history, which, therefore, is the picture of all that humanity *will have been,* one can indeed say that we have before our eyes *all that was possible.* Hypothetically, the picture is complete; it is the picture of humanity; any other "possibility" we might like to imagine is out of the question, just as the particularities of a different species show nothing about those of a living species. But human possibility intermingles in this way with man's effective history only for a judge who, by hypothesis, is placed outside humanity and who is making its balance sheet—that is to say, for an absolute mind contemplating a dead humanity. No one who writes or makes history is in this position: they all have a past and a future, that is to say, they *continue.* For them, therefore, nothing that has been is completely in the past; they relive as their own the history they recount or to which they give a sequel, and they evoke at decisive moments in the past other decisions which would have had a different sequel. There is history only for a historical subject. A universal, completed, and externally contemplated history makes no sense, nor does the reference to this definitive balance sheet or the hypothesis of a rigorous necessity in which, by hindsight, our decisions would solemnly be cloaked. "The only possible decision" means and will always mean only one thing: the decision that, in a field of action opening onto the future, and with the uncertainties which that implies, orients things within the realm of the probable in a direction desired by us and permitted by them. Universal history never is and never will be the total of what humanity has been. It will always be in process; it will be what humanity has been *plus* what it

WHEN HE IS NOT GIVING an absolutely new and Sartrean meaning to Marxist notions, Sartre takes them as they present themselves in today's communism (and the two operations are not by any means mutually exclusive). So is it with the idea of revolution. He observes, as we have said, that in the great periods of working-class history revolution was the culminating point or the horizon of everyday demands. The everyday struggle opened onto the social totality, and there was a dialectic of demands and of revolution. Today, he adds, revolution has withdrawn; it is out

---

wanted and still wants through the one who speaks of it. There is, therefore, a play on words in saying that in universal history reality is all possibilities. It would be more precise to say that there is no universal history, if by that one means a completely real and accomplished history, because the historical reality of which we can speak has meaning only for a man who is situated in it and wants to go beyond it and therefore has meaning only within a framework of possibilities. We evoked the dream of an absolute justification of what is because it is, and the attitude "You are historically wrong since I liquidate you," only as traits of historical terror. We then showed that, precisely if the future is to be made, not to be contemplated, Marxism has no transcendent view at its disposal to justify its action and that, therefore, terror must open onto a "humanistic perspective" and revolutionary action must announce this future by certain unchallengeable signs in order that one may speak of a Marxist and revolutionary politics. It is just this confrontation of terror with a humanistic perspective that until now has been lacking in Sartre's studies. An immediate desire to change the world, resting on no historical buildup and including neither strategy nor tactics, is, in history, sentimentalism and vertigo of "doing" [la loi du coeur et le vertige du "faire"]. Sartre notes that Marxism has always admitted the dialectical necessity of the whole and the contingency of everyday history. From this he deduces that the militant, but not the theoretician, has the right to evoke diverse possibilities. "The theoretician can claim to provide us with an indubitable truth, on the condition that he confine himself to what is and does not concern himself with what *might have* been" (CP, p. 741; ET, p. 107). Is it granting Marx too much to suppose that he never admitted this dualism of theory and practice, that he believed in a practical value of theory and a theoretical value of practice? And that, therefore, instead of opposing the dialectical necessity of the whole and the contingency of the details, it would be better to see whether there is truly a *necessity* in Marxism, whether the dialectic does not in its very definition include contingency? This is not the way Sartre reads Marx: he maintains the dichotomy of radical contingency and mythical rationality from which one easily arrives at Sartre's own conceptions. All that is necessary is to consciously recognize the myth as a myth.

of sight. Nowhere does he ask if, when revolution withdraws to infinity, it truly remains the same.[71] Like the communists, he continues to speak of "reformists" and of "revolutionaries."[72] He retains the language of 1917 and thus keeps the moral benefit of the proletarian revolution for the communists. Now, if the revolution is the horizon of labor struggles, it is already present when the proletariat emerges, and the movement toward emancipation does not stop with it; revolution is a process, a growth. If, on the contrary, everyday action does not have a hold on history, revolution is a convulsion, it is at once explosive and without a future, and the revolution of which one still speaks becomes a future *state,* of which one knows only that it will reverse the present relationships. It is no longer the truth of the existing society and of every society; it is a dream which passes itself off as truth but which, as far as everyday life is concerned, is only a comforting beyond. In a word, it is a myth. Sartre does not say so, but this is where his thought leads.[73] Skilled workers, the neoproletariat, who do not know how to struggle,[74] are, he says, still revolutionaries. What could they expect from the existing order? But the question is precisely to know whether revolutionaries and a revolution still exist in the Marxist sense when there is no longer a class which, because of its situation, possesses, in addition to the will to change the world, the means of doing it and of giving life to a new society. When one bases a politics on the neoproletariat's historical nonexistence, it cannot be the same politics as one which was based on the proletariat's political existence. What one will have is not the already present and never completed revolution, the permanent revolution, but rather continu-

71. Concerning the neoproletarian he writes: "True, he still believes in the Revolution, but he only believes in it; it is no longer his daily task" (*CP*, p. 1718; ET, p. 185).

72. *CP*, p. 1819; ET, p. 231. He remarks, however, that certain professional workers revolt against "mass democracy" and yet agree with the C.G.T. on objectives and tactics. Must we say that they are "reformists" or "revolutionaries"? And is it not proof that these two common notions no longer enable us to understand today's history?

73. We have already quoted the text: "He, precisely, needs to believe that there is a truth. Since he cannot work it out alone, he must be able to trust his class leaders profoundly enough to believe he is getting the truth from them. In short, at the first opportunity, he will chuck these freedoms which strangle him" (*CP*, p. 758; ET, p. 127).

74. "Need is only a lack: it can be the foundation of a humanism, but not of a strategy" (*CP*, p. 1815; ET, p. 225).

ous acts of rupture in the name of a utopia. "The revolutionary *élan* . . . postulates the ends all at once in order to call for their immediate realization." [75] Of course, this radicalism is an illusion, and the explosion of revolt has a future only if it puts itself in the Party's service. The power which is lacking in the proletariat must pass to the Party which fights in its name. Then serious action begins, and Sartre lets it be understood that the proletariat is not to control it; [76] and just as the Party, in organizing strikes with dual objectives, artificially connects the daily struggle to the revolutionary ends, so, too, will the revolution itself be the Party's concern. It is for the same reasons that the masses want everything right away and that they will have to wait indefinitely on the Party's wisdom for that which their madness demands immediately. The revolution is in an incalculable future precisely because it is wanted immediately and unconditionally. It is thus really Utopia, with the single exception that a Party of iron receives the mission of realizing it. The revolution of which Sartre speaks is absent in the sense in which Marxism said it was present, that is to say, as the "internal mechanism" of the class struggle; and it is present in the sense in which Marxism believed it distant, that is to say, as the "positing of ends." The notion of permanent revolution, which Sartre gladly takes up, changes meaning in his hands. It was the sometimes premature action of the revolutionary class against the power of the possessing class, an action prolonged beyond the insurrection and directed against the inertia of its own apparatus; for Sartre it becomes the permanent anxiety of a Party which torments and tears itself apart, because, being the proletariat's Party, it rests on nothing and because it itself lives in terror. Self-criticism, which was the definition of the proletariat as *Selbstaufhebung* and which was to confront the apparatus with its sustaining historical forces, with the revolution already present, is falsified when one leaves to the apparatus the task of organizing it. [77] Revolution, not as truth and

75. *CP*, p. 1815; ET, p. 226.
76. The strike which includes occupying factories "in a socialist society no longer has a *raison d'être*" (*CP*, p. 44; ET, p. 50).
77. We have attempted to indicate this decline of self-criticism (Merleau-Ponty, "Lukács et l'autocritique," *Les Temps modernes*, no. 50 [December, 1949], pp. 1119–21 [see also Merleau-Ponty, *Signes* (Paris, 1960), pp. 328–30; *Signs*, trans. R. McCleary (Evanston, 1964), pp. 261–64—Trans.]) and to show how a dialectical process becomes its own opposite when a "pure" authority is put in charge of

as history's horizon, but as the Party's staging of a future without antecedents, is not *the same revolution* carried to another moment in time; it is another enterprise, which has in common with the first only the negation of bourgeois society. In the only passage in which he defines it, Sartre calls revolution "outstripping the Other toward the unlimited task." Marx thought: outstripping the Other *and itself*. Without these two words, revolution is defined only by its antagonism toward the class that it eliminates. This is no longer the Revolution, the founding anew of all things under the aegis of the last class, a creative imbalance which, once in motion, will not stop—history supporting itself on itself to rise above itself.

SARTRE, HOWEVER, is not unaware of the historical field in which the revolution, and consequently all Marxist politics, is established. The apparent paradox of his work is that he became famous by describing a middle ground, as heavy as things and fascinating for consciousness, between consciousness and things —the root in *Nausea*, viscosity or situation in *Being and Nothingness*, here the social world—and that nonetheless his thought is in revolt against this middle ground and finds there only an incentive to transcend it and to begin again *ex nihilo* this entire

---

administering it. Lukács thought that the proletariat is self-critical because it is its own suppression as a class. The proletariat's power is, or will be, a power which is self-critical. He profoundly justifies self-criticism as the true faithfulness to self which is that of a life which makes attempts, corrects itself, and progresses as it goes. But what happens when, instead of wandering through the social body, negation and criticism are concentrated in power? When there are functionaries of negativity? What happens is that the criticism is only nominally self-criticism; the functionaries give to the person in question the task of pronouncing the very sentence which they were passing on him and, in the name of negation, organize for themselves the most positive power on earth. It cannot be stressed strongly enough that in Marxism's classical period the oppositionist was bound by the majority's decision but was justified in keeping his theses if he believed them to be right while waiting for the lesson of events to force their acceptance, with the single condition that he not use them as the emblem of a party within the Party. It was a first sign of decadence to have erected it as a principle that the oppositionist should be broken, that is to say, forced to disavow his theses and charged with carrying out the decisions of which he disapproved. A second sign was the affirmation that true self-criticism is self-accusation and that the militant should dishonor the man he once was.

disgusting world.[78] Once again in the present work he sketches one of the horrified descriptions which make him an incomparable showman of enigmas, even if one does not agree with his way of going beyond them in a *coup de force* of action. There is, then, a social field onto which all consciousnesses open; but it is in front of them, not prior to them, that its unity is made. My own field of thought and action is made up of "imperfect meanings, badly defined and interrupted." [79] They are completed over there, in the others who hold the key to them because they see sides of things that I do not see, as well as, one might say, my social back, my social body. Likewise, I am the only one capable of tallying the balance sheet of their lives, for their meanings are also incomplete and are opening onto something that I alone am able to see. I do not have to search very far for others: I find

78. The paradox is only apparent, since it is necessary to have another background—the transparency of consciousness—in order to see the root, the viscous, or history in their obscene evidence. Husserl, who gave the first descriptions of embodiment and its paradoxes, offers another example of it, all the while continuing to place the philosophizing subject beyond their grasp as the one who constitutes them or, at least, reconstitutes them. He acknowledged only that there was an enigma there: in what conceivable sense can one say, he wrote, that a philosopher's thoughts move with him when he travels? It was only at the end of his career that he propounded as primordial fact that the constituting subject is inserted within the temporal flow (what he called *sich einströmen*); that it is even his permanent condition; that consequently, when he withdraws from things in order to reconstitute them, he does not find a universe of ready-made meanings, rather he constructs; and that, finally, there is a *genesis of sense*. This time the paradox and the dualism of description and reflection were transcended. And it is toward the same result that Sartre turns. For him also, consciousness, which is constitution, does not find a system of already-present meanings in what it constitutes; it constructs or creates. The difference—and it is immense—is that Husserl sees even in this praxis an ultimate problem: even though consciousness constructs, it is conscious of making explicit something true anterior to itself, it continues a movement begun in experience, "It is voiceless experience, which must be brought to the pure expression of its own meaning." Thence the "teleology" (in quotation marks) of consciousness, which led Husserl to the threshold of dialectical philosophy, and of which Sartre does not want to hear: there are men and things, and there is nothing between them except cinders of consciousness. There is no other truth than the truth of consciousness, and *doing* is absolute rootless initiative.

79. *RL*, p. 1581; ET, p. 245.

them in my experience, lodged in the hollows that show what they see and what I fail to see. Our experiences thus have lateral relationships of truth: all together, each possessing clearly what is secret in the others, in our combined functioning we form a totality which moves toward enlightenment and completion. We are sufficiently open to others to be able to place ourselves mentally in their perspective, to imagine ourselves in them. We are in no way locked inside ourselves. However, the totality toward which we are going together, while it is being completed on one side, is being destroyed on the other. Despite the fact that we accept others as witnesses, that we make our views accord with theirs, we are still the ones who set the terms of the agreement: the transpersonal field remains dependent on our own. The open, incompleted meanings that we see in the social world and that, in acting, we allow to be seen are nearly empty diagrams, far in any case from equaling the fullness of what others and ourselves are living. These meanings lead an anonymous life among things, they are indecisive actions which run off the track along the way or even change into their opposites as soon as they are put into circulation. There is practically nothing left in them of our precise aims, which go directly to their meaning and of which they are the external mark. "Intentions without consciousness, actions without subjects, human relationships without men, participating at once in material necessity and finality: such are generally our undertakings when they develop freely in the dimension of objectivity." [80] This is what Marx had in mind when he spoke of relations among persons mediated by things.

> Marx sees . . . that the very work of man, becoming a thing, manifests in turn the inertia of a thing, its coefficient of adversity; he sees that the human relationships which man creates fall back again into inertia, introducing the inhuman as a destructive force among men. We dominate the environment by work, but the environment dominates us in turn by the rigidified swarm of thoughts we have inscribed there.[81]

Yet, far though Sartre appears to be from his dichotomy between things and men, he has not gotten any closer to Marx, because for Marx this suspect environment can ignite. Just as it vegetates and proliferates in false thoughts and pseudo-things, it can also

80. *RL*, p. 1624; ET, p. 292.
81. *RL*, p. 1605; ET, p. 271.

escape from equivocalness when what happens here answers to what happens over there, when each event projects the process further in the very direction it was already moving, when an "internal mechanism" leads the system beyond any immobile balance; this is what one calls revolution. For Marx, good and evil come from the same source, which is history. For Sartre, the social whole never starts moving by itself, never yields more movement than it has received from "inassimilable" and "irreducible" consciousnesses; and if it escapes from equivocalness, it can only be through an absolute initiative on the part of subjects who go beyond its weight and who decree, without any previous motive and against all reason, that precisely what was not and did not seem possible to be, be done. This is why Sartre, who so well described "intentions without consciousness, actions without subjects, human relationships without men, participating at once in material necessity and finality"—but as residual phenomena, as furrows or traces of consciousness in what is constituted—uses all his severity to call to order those who look for something between being and doing, object and subject, body and consciousness.[82] It is because in reality, for him, as soon as one reflects, there is nothing there. Intentions without consciousness are phantasms. Intention without consciousness: this monster, this myth, is a way of expressing that, reflecting on events, I find a meaning which could have been put there either by myself or by another subject, or again, considering a complex of signs, I find myself obliged to give to each one a meaning which depends on the meaning of all the others, which itself is not yet fixed, and thus that the totality of meaning precedes itself in its parts. But of course it is I who make my passivity out of nothing. There is no real intention in the social whole, no meaning immanent in signs. Sartre has not changed since *The Psychology of the Imagination*,[83] where he rigidly distinguished between the "certain," the meanings of pure consciousness, and the "probable," that which emerges from the phenomenological experience; or, if he has changed, it is in the sense that he expects even less of the probable. He is the same philosopher who, analyzing the act of reading, saw nothing between scribbling, a book in its

82. *CP*, p. 739; ET, p. 103. He has against them this argument, which is not absolutely decisive: "We know the stock answers" (*RL*, p. 1599; ET, p. 265).
83. J.-P. Sartre, *L'Imaginaire* (Paris, 1940); English translation by Bernard Frechtman (New York, 1948).

physical existence, and the meaning attributed to it by the reader's consciousness. The in-between, that is to say, the book taken according to the meaning ordinarily given to it, the changes of this reading which take place with time, and the way in which these layers of meaning accumulate, displace each other, or even complete each other—in short, the "metamorphosis" of the book and the history of its meaning, and my reading placed within this history, understood by it, included by it as a provisional truth of this book—none of this, for Sartre, prevents the canonical form of meaning from being the one I personally bring into existence by reading or prevents my reading, expressly considered, from being the measure of any other. We cannot avoid putting the thoughts we have formed in reading it into the pages of the book resting on the table, and this is what one calls a cultural object. At a higher level we imagine Julien Sorel as a wandering ghost haunting generations, always different in each one, and we write a literary history which attempts to link these apparitions and form a truth of Julien Sorel, a genesis of his total meaning. But, for Sartre, this universe of literature or of culture is an illusion: there is only the Julien Sorel of Stendhal, *and* that of Taine, *and* that of Léon Blum, *and* that of Paul Bourget; and they are so many incompossible absolutes. The idea of a truth of the whole is vague. It is an idealization of *our* view, which indeed takes in all things but only from one point of view. The total Julien Sorel has no more reality than the haze of consciousness we see appearing beneath the steel forehead of the electronic automaton when he responds too well to what *we* see as promises or threats around him. At most one can accept a sort of consolidation by which the intentions without consciousness (that is to say, the thoughts that *I* would formulate if I let myself be guided by a certain common meaning of the signs) manage to compose themselves or, rather, mass together and weigh on our perception of the social world and on our action. A residue of residues, a distant effect of drowsy thoughts, this mechanism of significations could not in any case create a new meaning or bring history toward its true meaning. If there is truth—one should rather say that, for Sartre, *there will be truth* [84] when praxis has completely destroyed and rebuilt this jumbled world—it will come with the spark of consciousness which will bring us into being, myself and the

84. "Is it . . . irrationalism? Not at all. Everything *will be* clear, rational" (*RL*, p. 1588; ET, p. 253).

others, in the only comprehensible way, that of being-for-itself. Contrary to appearances, being-for-itself is all Sartre has ever accepted, with its inevitable correlate: pure being-in-itself. The mixed forms of the For Others [du Pour Autrui] urge us at every moment to think about "how nothingness comes into the world." But the truth is that it does not come into the world or that it remains there only for a moment. Ultimately there is pure being, natural and immobile in itself, a limpid mystery which limits and adds an outside to the transparency of the subject or suddenly congeals and destroys this transparency when I am looked at from outside. But even then there is no hinge, no joint or mediation, between myself and the other; I feel myself to be looked at immediately, I take this passivity as my own but at the same time reintegrate it into my universe. All the so-called beings which flutter in the in-between—intentions without subjects, open and dulled meanings—are only statistical entities, "permanent possibilities" of present thought; they do not have their own energy, they are only something constituted. If one wants to engender revolutionary politics dialectically from the proletarian condition, the revolution from the rigidified swarm of thoughts without subject, Sartre answers with a dilemma: either the conscious renewal alone gives its meaning to the process, or one returns to organicism.[85] What he rejects under the name of organicism at the level of history is in reality much more than the notion of life: it is symbolism understood as a functioning of signs having its own efficacy beyond the meanings that analysis can assign to these signs. It is, more generally, expression. For him expression either goes beyond what is expressed and is then a pure creation, or it copies it and is then a simple unveiling. But an action which is an unveiling, an unveiling which is an action—in short, a dialectic—this Sartre does not want to consider.[86] The relationship between persons can indeed become

85. RL, p. 1608; ET, p. 272. And also: "If one wanted to expose the shameful finalism which is hidden under all dialectic" (RL, p. 1575; ET, p. 239). Sartre does not even seem to admit that at the level of the organism there is a problem of organicism or that, no matter how they may finally be grounded, meanings are operating before they are known. He speaks of Goldstein with an irritation which applies also to the Critique of Judgment, the idea of an agreement between understanding and its object, strangely prepared in the object itself.

86. Indeed, of literature he says spitefully that it is an "unveiling action, a strange action."

caught in social "things," can be degraded in them, and can extend its bleak consequences endlessly; this relationship is not visible in things, it is *made* and not observed. In Sartre's thought, as in *The Critique of Pure Reason*, the consciousness of a connection comes from the consciousness of a pure connecting principle. From there comes the Kantian question which he always asks: Who will decide? Who will judge? From where does the synthesis come? And if one wants to measure the Party against a historical norm: "Who will unify the unifying principle?" The absolute authority of the Party is the purity of the transcendental subject forcefully incorporated into the world. This Kantian or Cartesian thought sees only organicism in the idea of an unconstructed unity. Yet Marx was not an organicist. For him it is indeed man who makes the unity of the world, but man is everywhere, inscribed on all the walls and in all the social apparatuses made by him. Men can see nothing about them that is not in their image. They therefore do not at every moment have to reassemble and recreate themselves out of an absurd multiplicity; everything speaks to them of themselves, and this is why there is no sense in asking whether the movement comes from them or from things, whether it is the militant who makes the class or the class which makes the militant. Their very landscape is animated; it is there, as well as in them, that tensions accumulate. That is also why the lightning flash which will give its decisive meaning to all this is not for Marx a private happening in each consciousness. It goes from one to the other, the current passes, and what is called becoming conscious [87] or revolution is this advent of an interworld. If, on the contrary, one thinks that the social world is "obscure and all too full of meaning" [88]—obscure because it does not of itself indicate its meaning; too meaningful because it indicates several of them, none of which is truer than the other (which amounts to the same thing), and the truest, if such exists, is not the revolutionary meaning—that would tend to justify a liberal rather than a revolutionary politics, for one cannot sanely attempt to recreate history by pure action alone, with no external complicity. Pure action, if it wants to remain pure, can only arrange the world and obliquely intervene by opposing, not force to force, but the trickery of freedom to the force of being. To want to change the world, we need a truth

87. [In the French: "prise de conscience."—Trans.]
88. *RL*, p. 1588; ET, p. 253.

which gives us a hold on adversity; we need, not a world that is, as Sartre says, opaque and rigidified, but rather a world which is dense and which moves.

Because he always moves from open and uncompleted meanings to the pure model of a closed meaning, such as it offers itself to lucid consciousness, Sartre is obliged to ascribe all historical facts to actions dated and signed by persons, and he is led to a sort of *systematic mythology*. For example, he says that, in order to show that the politics of the U.S.S.R. and that of the C.P. are not revolutionary, it would be necessary to "show that the Soviet leaders no longer believe in the Russian revolution or that they think the experiment has failed." [89] The reader asks himself how, even if confided to us, disillusioned confessions could ever settle the question. Could one not take exception to them by showing that, whatever the leaders' beliefs, they have inherited a system which is neither that of the Russian nation nor within reach of a universal solution? And if, on the contrary, their intentions are still revolutionary, how could this knowledge allow one to judge the system, which either does or does not exploit the workers, which either does or does not express the historical mission of the proletariat? But the fact is that for Sartre there is no deciphering or truth of a society, because no deciphering ever expresses anything but a personal, more or less ample, *perspective* and because degrees of truth are worth nothing when it comes to deciding, that is to say, to presuming everything. The idea of a party being revolutionary in spite of itself seems to him the height of absurdity,[90] like the idea of Stalinism without Stalin.[91] The reader says to himself that, nevertheless, in the countries it occupied at the end of the war, the U.S.S.R. was by its position in conflict with the interests of the bourgeoisie without, for that reason, calling upon the proletariat to manage the economy; or that the same revolutionary ebb which made Stalin possible prepared in all countries the mold for the same type of politics, the alternation of opportunism and terror. But this kind of analysis looks for the content of the historical fact: revolution is the negation of the bourgeoisie and the power of the proletariat, Stalinism is the alternation of rotten compromise and pure violence. Yet as soon as one examines the content, the historical

89. *CP*, p. 10; *ET*, p. 13.
90. *CP*, p. 742; *ET*, p. 108.
91. *RL*, p. 1614; *ET*, p. 281.

reality unfolds: each fact is this, but also that; one can decide only through balanced considerations, according to the *dominant* characteristic; in short, one penetrates, according to Sartre, into the order of the probable and the equivocal, one no longer measures revolution by its own standard. If one wants to understand it, one must not begin the infinite analysis of a society, one must not ask oneself what communism *is*, for that is questionable and thus immaterial. One must return to its sources in the will of one or several men and thereby restore a pure negation, because freedom is only secondarily will of this or of that: these are its momentary aspects, and revolution distinguishes itself from power only as a power of not doing. Thus historical judgment returns from revolution to the negation which is its principle, from Stalinism to Stalin, and here hesitation is not in order: one will readily agree that the power of the U.S.S.R. is not that of the bourgeoisie, that Stalin's fundamental choice was not the return to capitalism. The revolutionary ebb, the equivocal character of a regime which is new but which is not the revolution, these flowing notions have no place in a negative analysis or in an analysis of *pure intentions*. They would have a place only in analyses of dulled actions, of "intentions without subject." Revolutionary ebb and flow—bastard notions in which actual conditions, negligences, abstentions, and decisions are mixed—have no place in a universe where there are only men, animals, and things. Either *things*—"*historical* circumstances," the "*vital* necessity to intensify production" [92]—explain the decisions of the man Stalin, and then one is not "allowed" [93] to speak of exploitation and one must continue to speak of revolution, since the choice was between Stalinism and nothing; or else Stalin could have done something different, he chose badly, he is guilty, but then one must not try to "understand" him. In any case, there is no Stalinism without Stalin, nor any revolutionary in spite of himself. That Stalin's action was a reply to certain external "quasi-necessities," but a reply which exacerbated them and prepared for tomorrow new dilemmas in which, little by little, the revolution's meaning was changed and, with it, that of all the Marxist institutions and notions; that this very dialectic of wills and fortune is to be found throughout the world, because everywhere the signs of things have changed and, besides, what is done here serves as

92. *RL*, p. 1618; ET, pp. 284–85.
93. *RL*, p. 1621; ET, p. 288.

a model over there—Sartre does not have to consider these hypotheses because they are placed at the juncture of men and things, where, according to him, there is nothing to know, indeed nothing at all but a vague adversity which one must face up to in every possible way.

Now his reduction of history to personal actions authorizes unlimited generalizations, since Stalin or Malenkov, brought back to their fundamental choices are probably [94] the Revolution itself in new circumstances, and since Stalin the individual and Malenkov the individual thus with a single stroke rejoin Lenin and Marx beyond all the verifiable differences in their politics.[95] For Sartre it is illusory to attempt to judge history according to its "objective meaning": in the last analysis there is no objective meaning; all meanings are subjective or, as one might also say, they are all objective. What one calls "objective meaning" is the aspect taken by one of these fundamental choices in the light of another, when the latter succeeds in imposing itself. For example, for the proletariat, the bourgeoisie consists of those signed and dated acts which instituted exploitation, and all those who do not call these acts into question are considered as accomplices and coresponsible, because objectively—that is to say, in the eyes of the exploited—they assume these acts as their own. For the bourgeoisie, the proletariat is the worker who wants the impossible, who acts against the inevitable conditions of the social world. Between these two fundamental choices, no reading of history can arbitrate, no truth can decide. Very simply, one of them is the demand of life for all, the other for a few. The bour-

94. For once, Sartre here speaks in terms of the probable and the improbable. The Soviet leaders no longer believe in the Russian revolution? "It goes without saying that, even if this were true, which I strongly *doubt,* to prove it *would not be possible* today" (*CP,* p. 10; ET, p. 13). But this is because here the probable is only a polite form of the *a priori* an *a priori* which becomes shy around facts.

95. One will remark that Sartre says much about the working class, very little about communism or revolution, and nothing about Soviet society. He even gives as an argument in favor of communism our ignorance of the internal life of the U.S.S.R., whose side he readily takes. For him, the question does not lie there. One can forever discuss the nature of Soviet society, the right and left opposition, Bolshevism and revolution as a social fact. None of this is decisive. What is decisive is the fundamental choice which lies behind these appearances. As for the rest, he says tranquilly, "the discussion is open." For him, communism is not something one makes or lives; rather, it is a human posture with which one "sympathizes."

geois choice is ultimately murder or, worse still, degradation of other freedoms. The revolutionary choice is ultimately freedom for all. The decisive reading of history depends, then, on a moral option: one wants to exist against others, or one wishes to exist with everyone; and the true perspective in history is not the one that accounts for all the facts, because they are equivocal, but that which takes into account all lives. "To look at man and society *in their truth,* that is to say," Sartre writes, "with the eyes of the least-favored." [96] Thence comes the necessity of a mythological reading of history which reassembles into a single bundle wills scattered throughout the world; some are courageous and cynical, others are insipid and timid, but little matter: this is the share of things, of circumstances; the intention does not vary, it is virtue or crime, emancipation or exploitation. Since men and things are face to face (let us forget animals, for which Sartre, as a good Cartesian, should not care very much), wills do not continue living a decadent or fertile life in the things they mark. They are the brief signals a consciousness makes to another consciousness, separated from it by the wall of being. If those who receive them are thereby inspired, they have the entire merit or blame of what they are doing; they are not continuing anything, they are beginning anew. The 1954 Malthusian bourgeois really committed the Versailles 1871 crime. On May 28, 1952, the Communist Party was really the same people who acted in 1848 and who formed the Commune. Neither the politics of the bourgeoisie nor that of the C.P. is to be examined historically as the exact or inexact renewal of a tradition, the meaning of which perhaps changes, like a near-sighted action, starting from a well or badly understood present which would have to be confronted with its truth. In replacing men in a historical scenario, one could find them less noble or less base. For Sartre, on the contrary, Duclos [97] is Marxism, and Mr. Pinay is Mr. Thiers, since Pinay and Duclos live off what Thiers and Marx did, take it upon themselves, and are responsible for it, and since infinitely distant men pierce the wall of things and live in the same world, suddenly reappearing very close, identified, lost, and saved together. By this inevitable reversal, extreme personalism makes history into a melodrama, smeared with crude colors, where the individuals are types. There

96. *CP,* p. 1793; *ET,* p. 201.
97. [Jacques Duclos: French politician born in 1896, Communist Party leader in the French National Assembly.—Trans.]

is only a single monotonous fight, ended and begun at each moment, with no acquisition, no truces, no areas of abatement. Those periods of apparent relaxation in which the historian deludes himself into making up perspectives, into distributing both merit and blame, into passing from the bourgeois to the proletarian point of view and afterwards reconciling them in a larger view, are unreal for those who have seen the drama. If the proletariat does not advance, it retreats; if it is passive, it is because the bourgeoisie is active or rather because the bourgeoisie is the only class in the world and the proletariat has been fragmented, it is because the universe is bourgeois. Even then, in truth, there is only the tête-à-tête of contradictory positions, of the class which is and of the class which is not.

And even the struggle of the proletariat and its Party is nothing outside the signed and dated acts which stake it out; from bourgeois to bourgeois there is a solidarity of interests, but not from worker to worker. Their only common interest would be to not be workers. "I encounter in myself, in all men, in all groups and even in all classes, the presence of the Other, not only as a stranger to whom one is opposed in complicity, but as the objectifying power which penetrates us, divides us, and makes us possible traitors in the eyes of the other members of the group." [98] The workers' unity is always to be remade; they are no less tempted by their adversaries than by their fellows, they have not many more ties among themselves than with the bourgeoisie, and the problem is to erase by means of the class Other and through struggle the ineffaceable otherness of the individual Other. The bourgeoisie and the proletariat are struggling only because the bourgeoisie is compact, while the proletariat is opposed to itself; and this is to say that for the proletariat the struggle begins under almost desperate conditions. There can be a truth, a rationality of the bourgeoisie as a servicing of certain interests; there is in it a given sociality. The values of truth and reason are in complicity with it because it is in its interest to make people believe that man and the world are thinkable and therefore already made. The proletariat will be true if it itself acts; but for the moment it rises up in history only under the form of magical connections, and history shows in it its mystical essence. For it is not difficult, but also not convincing, to link consciousnesses through interests, that is to say, through things, through calculations and estima-

98. *RL*, p. 1615; *ET*, p. 282.

tions of probable results, or through customs, which are only the reflection of this quiet possession, the point of honor of interests. History—or metahistory—truly begins when men are linked through what they are not—through what they do; and that is communism.

Here all is to be constructed, and the oppositions are not arbitrated by things to be defended: the Party is at the heart of the proletariat as an other, and within communism each party is an other for its fraternal party. Precisely because it links each one to the others from the inside, because the stake for everyone is life itself, the relationship is one of rivalry, with that background of love that goes with rivalries, but also with their false relaxations, their false fraternity. It is a mixture of independence and submission, a "no" which ends up being "yes" and which waits only for a little violence to change into "yes"; it is always a provisional "yes," always to be re-examined after the surrender. Thus we find in Sartre terms which are not very Marxist: the class "surrenders itself" to an authority which, following Lefort, he is not afraid to call "military." [99] He says that the masses of 1919, which disavowed the old unionism and even their own representatives, *"would have condescended to submit themselves* only to an iron hand implacably fighting the constant unbalance of mass formations." [100] Like a woman they condescend, they condescend to surrender themselves, they wait to be forced, to be taken. Strange confidence. Confidence is distinct from vertigo and social eroticism only when it is confidence in an action, in a politics: but this sober confidence is impossible if the proletarian politics is without precise criteria, if the facts "say neither 'yes' nor 'no.'" This confidence will therefore be hollow and infinite: "the working class has coherence and power only in so far as it has confidence in the leaders: . . . the leader interprets the situation, illuminates it by his plans, at his own risk, and the working class, by observing the directives, *legitimizes* the authority of the leader." [101] ". . . lacking a minutely detailed knowledge of all events—possible only for the historian and in retrospect—it is confidence alone which will persuade a worker that he has not been fooled and that the sacrifices accepted were legitimate." [102] The proletariat thus really gives itself without con-

99. *RL*, p. 1621; ET, p. 288.
100. *CP*, p. 1788; ET, p. 197 (my emphasis).
101. *RL*, pp. 1606–7; ET, p. 272.
102. *CP*, p. 8; ET, p. 10.

dition or limit, and the leaders exercise a priesthood: no matter what they do, they are consecrated. "When a Communist makes known the interests or the feelings of the proletariat, rightly or wrongly, it is *in the name* of the proletariat that he speaks. But I am very much afraid that you, Lefort, speak only *about* the class." [103] "Rightly or wrongly" makes one reflect: for if it is wrongly, the damage is serious. Lefort makes inoffensive remarks about the class. The Communist makes the class itself speak incorrectly. At least, Sartre will answer, he makes it speak. And if one starts debating whether or not he makes it speak correctly, who will judge? The proletarians? They do not always take a correct view of things, and Marx and Lenin were the first to say so. However, no one knows better than the proletarians whether or not they should stick to the Party's politics, and the Party is judged according to whether or not it succeeds in carrying this weight along behind it. There is nothing like this in Sartre, there is no exchange between those who conceive the politics and those who execute it: the leader gives a meaning to the situation, the class carries out the orders. And what if the leader is wrong? "How can he be wrong?," replies Sartre. One can be wrong about the path to take when the path exists; but when it is entirely to be made, and when the proletarian condition does not define a strategy or a tactics, even the choice of a difficult line is not an error, since there is no true path and since what is essential is, not that the proletariat's existence be exactly translated by its politics, but rather that the proletariat exist and give life to the Party. The path chosen is the only one possible and is *a fortiori* the best. There is no conceivable adjustment between the principle of Communist politics and its line, the principle being of the order of duty, the line of the order of fact. One can therefore prove *a priori* that the Party's politics is, in general, the only one and the best one; this is not a question of experience.

> Even if he were more concerned with the apparatus than with his comrades, [the militant's] particular interest is the general interest; his personal ambitions, if he has any, can be achieved only by inspiring in the masses a confidence that is renewed daily; and he will inspire confidence in them only if he agrees to lead them where they are going. In a word, he must be *all of them* in order to be himself. [104]

103. *RL*, p. 1582; ET, p. 246.
104. *CP*, p. 1805; ET, pp. 216–17.

Let us make no mistake: *this daily renewed* confidence is not a judgment made on documents, which would demand deliberation and a probabilistic assent: we know that the masses never judge the Party when they say "no." Let us not believe either that Sartre is satisfied with the Maurassian reasoning which proved the king's utility by showing that his interest was the same as the nation's. Sartre knows very well that when it is a question of interests one can always discuss the best way to serve them. But here discussion is meaningless, and the leader *is* the proletariat *a priori* or by definition, because the proletariat is nothing at all and can be nothing except in its leaders and because the link between them is timeless and eternal. It can either hold or break, not slacken or tighten. Thus, when Sartre speaks of a daily renewal, it is a way of expressing that each day it could suddenly break, but it is not a question of control. Between the proletarian and the militants, between the militant and his leaders, then, there is literally an identification: they live in him and he lives in them. If there are only men and things, if each consciousness wishes the death of the other, how does one jump over the abyss to the other? This is accomplished before our eyes. It is the Party. The worker gives himself to his leader so that "in his person" the group exists; the leader thus has "charismatic power"; he lives in the group, as consciousness lives in the body, as an immediate presence which does not need to command to be obeyed. Who commands, since the leader is leader only through the militants' devotion? Who obeys, since the militant himself has made the leader's power? "If there is a leader, everyone is leader in the name of the leader," not only because he makes others obey him, but especially because, in obeying the leader, it is one's own better self that one obeys. Undoubtedly this principle brings back painful memories. But what is to be done? If the militant and the leaders are not linked by an action, by a political content, nothing remains except the encounter of absolute existences, sadomasochism, or, if one prefers, what Sartre once called magic or emotional action, that which throws itself directly toward its end or which awaits everything from the sorcerer. How can it be otherwise if there is neither degree nor path between the actual society and the revolutionary society? A *coup de force*, a methodical fetishism, are necessary. These analyses have the benefit of helping one understand how backward forms of sociability and the cult of the leader have re-emerged even in communism. When men wish to create things *ex nihilo*, then the supernatural reappears. Thus arise Sartre's religious formulas: the party and the class are ideally "pure linking, the relation which surges up wherever two workers are together." [105] But as a result, communism crosses over into the realm of the imaginary, it is the outer limit of the vertiginous encounter of persons, it is the imaginary become institution or myth. There is an encounter rather than a common action because, for Sartre, the social remains the relationship of "two individual consciousnesses" which look at each other. [106]

We are far from Marxism. The Bolsheviks knew that it is not easy to reconcile truth with struggle, that the Party's truth in battle is not absolute truth, and that in battle it yet has absolute value. "Our 'truth,' of course," wrote Trotsky,

> is not absolute. But *as in its name we are, at the present moment, shedding our blood,* we have neither cause nor possibility to carry on a literary discussion as to the relativity of truth with those who "criticize" us with the help of all forms of arms. Similarly, our problem is not to punish liars and to encourage just men amongst journalists of all shades of opinion, but to throttle the class lie of the bourgeoisie and to achieve the class truth of the proletariat, irrespective of the fact that in both camps there are fanatics and liars. [107]

History is action. The acts and the words of a party and a government cannot be judged according to the single criterion of what is true; rather one must consider the whole, form "truth" with force, impose a truth which, for the moment, is class truth and only later will be everyone's truth. *But it is already a class truth.* One cannot prove it by principles or by facts, by deduction or by induction; one can legitimize it by dialectic, that is to say, by

105. *CP*, p. 761; ET, pp. 129–30.
106. Here is the text: "What has been called 'charismatic power' proves well enough that the concrete unity of the group is *projective,* that is to say, that the unity is necessarily exterior to the group. The diffuse sovereignty assembles and is condensed in the person of the leader who subsequently reflects it to each one of the members; and each one, to the very extent that he obeys, finds himself, vis-à-vis others and outsiders, the repository of total sovereignty. If there is a leader, each one is leader in the name of the leader. Thus the 'collective consciousness' is necessarily incarnated: it is for each one the collective dimension which he grasps in the individual consciousness of the other" (*CP*, p. 1812, note; ET, p. 223, note).
107. *Terrorism and Communism: A Reply to Karl Kautsky* (Ann Arbor, 1961), p. 60. [Merleau-Ponty's italics.—Trans.]

having this truth recognized by the proletarians—by the "workers' democracy," Trotsky said; against the bureaucracy, Lenin said, at the end of his life. This guarantee is theoretically imprecise. Even the October, 1917, revolution and the proletarian uprising are proof only when seen through the lenses of Marxist thought, by the quality of the facts rather than by their number, provided one uses an appropriate reading, which does not impose itself as a statistic or as a crucial experiment. But if there is neither an objective proof of the revolution nor a sufficient speculative criterion, there is a test of the revolution and a very clear practical criterion: the proletariat must have access to political life and to management. At least in this, class truth certifies itself as truth, if not in the eyes of the others, at least in the eyes of the proletarians. History is not the unfolding of a ready-made truth; but from time to time it has a rendezvous with a truth which is made and is recognized in the fact that the revolutionary class, at least, functions as a whole and that in it social relationships are not opaque, as they are in a class society. The watchwords of the "democracy of the masses" or of "constant struggle against bureaucracy" have no precise meaning in Sartre's perspective. Party democracy is always "mass democracy," without a minority, without deliberation. In comparison to the menace which constantly threatens the proletariat, the revolution's manner of being—democratic or bureaucratic—is practically insignificant. But at the same time, the entire history of Bolshevism and of the revolution also becomes insignificant, and this is why Sartre speaks so little of it. The revolutionary choice is really a choice of "something or other."

IV

WE HAVE PERHAPS dwelt a little too long on the metamorphoses through which praxis, revolution, history, the proletariat, and the Party, taken in the sense Marx conceived them, are transformed into their Sartrean homonyms. If it were necessary to approach the philosophical and fundamental difference, one would say that, for Sartre, the relationships between classes, the relationships within the proletariat, and finally those of the whole of history are not articulated relationships, including tension and the easing of tension, but are the immediate or magical relationships of our gazes. The truth of a society is seen through the eyes of its least-favored member, not in his fate or in his role in production, and even less in his action; rather, it is seen in his gaze, the sole expression of a pure need, without means and without power. Relationships between persons stop being mediated by things; they are immediately readable in the accusation of a gaze. "Pure action" is Sartre's response to this gaze, which, like it, reaches its aim from a distance. We are in the magical or moral universe. The misery and exploitation of the least-favored are final arguments; and, as Péguy said, the city wherein a single man suffers injustice is an unjust city. But when revolution thus motivated ceases being a thought in order to become a deed, we will have to apply the same criterion to it, since there is no other, unless we wish to give up all points of reference and sink into the revolution as into a delirium. And if we look for the truth of the U.S.S.R. in the gaze of the least-favored—a political prisoner or simply the lowest-level unskilled worker—it is doubtful whether this gaze would be one of benediction. We will rightly refuse to judge on this basis, saying that it is necessary to situate the facts in their context, the present in the future which it prepares, the episode in the total action. And this is to speak politically. But it is also to consider suffering, misery, and death as elements of the whole, to make them the touchstones and revealers of the truth of that whole; it is to situate this truth elsewhere. And, since it would be a bit too much to look for the truth of the whole in the spirit of the leaders when one refuses to read it in that of the led, it is to grant an "objective" meaning to the enterprise and to come back to the problem of Marxist action as action in the realm of the probable—something that had been put aside a bit too quickly. The gaze of the least-favored thus has to be taken into account, but along with the geographical, historical, and political circumstances. This is an immoral attitude, but that is the way it is. The political man is someone who speaks about other people's deaths as statistical items. It is perhaps even still more immoral to ground a political revolution on morality. There is not in the present stage of our knowledge, and there may never be, a theoretical analysis that would give the absolute truth of a society, which would sort out societies as a teacher sorts the bluebooks written on the same subject, by students of the same age, in the same amount of time, and with the help of the same dictionaries and grammars. Since the original situations are not the same, since the "objective" possibilities are not computable, since one never exactly knows, for example, what Russia would have become without the revolution, political and historical judgment will perhaps never be objective; it will always be a bastard judgment. But precisely for this reason it escapes morality as well as pure science. It is of the category of action, which makes for continual oscillation between morality and science.

If this category does not appear in Sartre's analyses, it is because the social can enter his philosophy of the *cogito* only by way of the *alter ego:* if I am a thinking being, only another I can contest the thought that I have of myself. Inversely, the other can have the status of a self only by taking it away from me, and I can recover it only by reacting to the magic of the gaze with the countermagic of pure action. "Sociality" as a given fact is a scandal for the "I think." How could the "I think" take within itself the qualifications, opaque as things, which belong to it because of its insertion into a history? The scandal does not disappear but is at least stifled if one remakes history and the world, and such is the Party's function. Although the enlarged *cogito,* the philosophy of For-Others, does not confine itself to the perspective of self on self, it is inside this perspective that it must introduce what puts this position into question. The social never appears openly; it is sometimes a trap, sometimes a task, sometimes a menace, sometimes a promise, sometimes behind us as a self-reproach, sometimes in front of us as a project. In any case, it is never perceived or lived by man except as incompleteness [108] and oppression, or in the obscurity of action. It is the absolute of the subject who remakes himself when he incorporates the point of view of others, which he was dragging along behind him like a hardship, and he reappears after he has digested it, confirmed in himself, strengthened by the trial. With Sartre, as with the anarchists, the idea of oppression always dominates that of exploitation. If he is not an anarchist, it is because he suddenly passes from the poetry of the subject to the prose of the world at the same time as he passes from the for-self to the for-others. But the other is still a subject, and, to establish his rights, magical means are necessary. Behind the prose and discipline of the Party we have seen sorcery abound. One should not exactly say that the determinations attributed to me by the other's gaze are true; rather one should say that I am

108. [In the French: "décomplétude."—Trans.]

responsible for them, that I must, and that I can, modify them by acting in such a way as to put them in agreement with what I am in my own eyes.

It has not been sufficiently noted that at the very moment when he appeared to take up the Marxist idea of a social criterion of literature, Sartre did it in terms which are his alone and which give to his notion of historicity an absolutely new meaning. In *What Is Literature?* [109] the social is never cause or even motive, it is never behind the work, it does not weigh on it, it gives neither an explanation nor an excuse for it. Social reality is in front of the writer like the milieu or like a dimension of his line of sight. In choosing to write on this subject and in this form, he chooses to be the buffoon of the bourgeoisie or the writer of a potential and unlimited public. He therefore takes a position with respect to history; and since in any case he speaks of it, he will not know what he says, he will not be a writer, unless he speaks unmistakably about history. If not, he cheats, for he contributes to a drama which he agrees to see only in the dark mirror of literary anxieties. The task, in short, was to transform into meanings formed by myself what formerly passed for my historical determinants, to return to the *cogito* its truth by thinking my historical situation and making it one of my thoughts—and Sartre believed then that literature is capable of this conversion. If the *action* which he proposed was only one of *unveiling,* it was nonetheless irreplaceable. Literature seen as consciousness brought a revolutionary ferment, it changed the world in showing it, it had only to show the world to change it. Literature was, he said, the consciousness of a society in permanent revolution. This is why he approached the communist question only as a writer, to know whether it was possible for one to be a communist and remain a writer. Literature, if it was not revolution itself, was eminently revolution because it introduced into history a permanent element of imbalance and contestation by showing what can endure in obscurity but cannot support scrutiny. Today in Sartre's conception of the social the action of unveiling gives way to pure action. The writer in search of a potential public or of the universal is no longer the motor of the revolution. To be squared away with the social, it is no longer sufficient to unveil it and to make it

109. J.-P. Sartre, *Qu'est-ce que la littérature?* (Paris, 1948); English translation by Bernard Frechtman, *What Is Literature?* (New York, 1949).

an object of consciousness. One thought that in *What Is Literature?* Sartre was attempting to engage literature. He was attempting, at least as much, to disengage politics from the
dilemmas of the times. Today, on the contrary, it appears that he
holds these dilemmas to be insurmountable. The writer no longer
surpasses man. The writer wants to be "a man who writes." Sartre
no longer believes the demands of the action of unveiling to be
a priori the same as those of a valid or revolutionary society—
which was still a way of believing in salvation through literature. The truth of a society or of a history is no longer dependent
on a specialist of truth, the writer; it is in the gaze of the least-
favored, who is never the writer. Now it is no longer the writer
who appeals to the reader's freedom; it is the gaze of the oppressed which appeals to man's action. It is no longer literature
which animates a society in permanent revolution; it is the Party
which makes this society. But there is a constant in this development: whether it is the appeal of the writer to the potential public
and the response of the benevolent reader in the transparent
universe of literature, or the call of the proletarian to the writer,
who, as a man, recognizes in return pure action in the opaque
universe of history—whether white magic or black—the social
link remains immediate. Sartre's permanent revolution, whether
effected by the Party or by literature, is always a relationship of
consciousness to consciousness, and it always excludes that
minimum of relaxation that guarantees the Marxist claim to
truth and to historical politics. A Marxist does not expect literature to be the consciousness of the revolution, and this is exactly
why he will not admit in principle that it be made a means of
action. He respects the writer as the "specialist" which Sartre
despises, and he despises the writer where Sartre respects him:
when the writer thinks himself capable of thinking the present.
Writers are writers: they are men of speech and of experience;
one should not ask of them to think "objectively" the historical
totality. Trotsky said, and Lukács more or less agrees, that it is
enough for them to have their honor as writers, and whatever
they say, even what is tendentious, is recoverable for the revolution. Ultimately the writer's ideas are of little importance. Balzac's reactionary ideas make him feel and picture the world of
money, and Stendhal's progressist ideas do not give him any advantage as far as this is concerned. There is a center of history,
which is political action, and a periphery, which is culture.
There are infrastructures and superstructures. Things do not go

along everywhere at the same pace. A writer fulfills his role when
he presents typical situations and behavior, even if the political
commentary remains to be done, even if the work, as Engels said,
is without a thesis. For Sartre, on the contrary, since there is not
a single history behind us to which both our literature and our
politics belong, since their unity is to be made by us, since he
takes them at their common source, consciousness, then, if they
are to touch things, literature must deal with politics, and action
must stick to the event as in a novel, taking no distance. Marxist
action was a world; it went on at all levels, near and far from
everyday life, at both long and short terms. The vagueness that
reigned in the theory of superstructures allowed culture a certain
margin: sometimes culture was extended in the direction of
political orders, and sometimes the many imperishable texts condemning sectarianism were recalled. Marx and Lenin said that
in communist society there would no longer be painters or writers
but rather men who painted or who wrote. But this would be in
the communist society, after an immense historical work on man,
and not in the immediate future. For Sartre, it is now that literature and politics are the same struggle on the single plane of
events. In a word, for the Marxists consciousness can be mystified; for Sartre consciousness is in bad faith. For the Marxists
there are fools; for Sartre there are only scoundrels. Thus he ex-
hibits a generalized suspicion in which one again finds the tone
of the communist rather than Marx. How could it be otherwise?
History is waste, except for the history that is created by the
"potential public," now by "the gaze of the least-favored." In both
cases, how is it possible to wait without betrayal? How are we to
allow for these partitionings—politics, culture—between the subject and his world, partitionings which deaden the virulence of
the subject? Whether as a permanent spectacle or as a continued
creation, the social is in any case before consciousnesses and
is constituted by them. Yesterday literature was the consciousness
of the revolutionary society; today it is the Party which plays this
role. In both cases history, in regard to everything in it that is
living, is a history of projects. History is understood by that sight-
ing of the future which belongs only to consciousnesses and not,
as with Marx, by the point called revolution, where the past
grows hollow, is raised above itself, and is seized by the future.
    What continues to distinguish Sartre from Marxism, even in
recent times, is therefore his philosophy of the *cogito*. Men are
mentally attached to history. The *cogito* perseveres in its claim to

be everything that we are, taking as its own even our situation before others. This carries it far, as far as the obscurity of "pure action." There is a madness of the *cogito* which has sworn to recapture its image in others. But in the end it is the *cogito* itself which demands its own disavowal and puts itself in question, first by the clarity of thought and then by the obscurity of devotion. One finds several times in these articles of Sartre's a movement of thought which is the Cartesian movement. Show us, says Sartre to Lefort, this class or this history which you say are not made by the Party. Separate them from it so that we can touch them with our fingers. Produce the acts which would not have taken place without them. This challenge is not as conclusive as it seems to be. Sartre is too much of a philosopher to cherish illusions on the "method of differences." He well knows that no one can isolate the efficacy of a single element in a whole, separate what belongs to the class from what belongs to the Party, or, finally, examine history as a thing. He well knows that this causal or empiricist process is impossible. But from the fact that the social is a totality, it does not follow that it is a pure relationship of consciousnesses; and yet that is the very thing which, for Sartre, goes without saying. Since no historical reality is without contact with consciousnesses, history and revolution are nothing but a pact of thoughts or of wills. When consciousness intervenes, it does so as a sovereign legislator, because it is consciousness which gives meaning, because meaning is not more or less, because it is not divisible, because it is all or nothing. One recognizes the *cogito*. It is the *cogito* which gives to violence its Sartrean nuance.

THERE IS INDEED a Sartrean violence, and it is more highly strung and less durable than Marx's violence. The personal tone of the polemic with Lefort was surprising. Lefort, writes Sartre, "wants to anchor himself in the intellectual bourgeoisie." That kind of talk, if it is not a personal imputation, an allusion to the adversary's personal history, and, in short, aggression—but this cannot be the case, for clearly Sartre has no information about the man—then it is simply a manner of speaking. It is an allegorical way of saying that *if* Lefort had the same ideas as Sartre about the proletariat, the C.P., Marxism, history, subject and object, and freedom, and yet could decide against the C.P., this could only be for base reasons. One will easily agree to this. But is Lefort Sartre? Here is the question that Sartre forgets. Is what he thinks so true that any resistance would be impure? But he will say that Lefort is a Marxist and consequently a realist. Thus, if Lefort does not join the C.P., he renounces in practice working with and for the proletariat, and, using his language, I have the right to say that he prefers the other side. I neither attribute nor oppose my views to him, I place him in contradiction with himself. With himself? The whole question is there. It is certainly true if we are dealing with a pragmatic Marxism, realistic in the "bourgeois" sense, or with Marxism as seen by Sartre; but is this Lefort's Marxism, and, in the face of the immense Marxist literature, can Sartre presume that his own interpretation imposes itself on every man of good faith? We also believe, and have said in an earlier chapter, that the notion of a Marxist without a party is an untenable position in the long run and that it refutes the Marxist conception of history and even of philosophy. But one does not have to see this immediately. In the meantime, to rally to the Party in the dark is a pragmatic solution, but not a more Marxist one. For a reader of Marx who is not used to these *coups de force* it is natural to hold both ends of the chain and try to reweld them. To put him in contradiction with himself is then to smother a problem or to insinuate that there is none. The type of discussion which opposes, in Marx, the necessity of the whole to the contingency of historical details, which opposes in the spontaneists, the passivity to the activity of the class, and which opposes, in Lefort, Marxism to the critique of communism contributes and proves nothing when one is dealing with an author of any merit. Contradictions are the sign of a search, and it is this search that counts. To pin down the "contradictions" is to treat the adversary as an object; he is a Marxist, therefore he should think this or that. And what if he understands Marxism in another way? And what if his "contradiction" was already in Marx? And what if Lefort and Marx, like Sartre himself, are people who try to understand, who are Marxists when they can be and something else when there is no other way? And what if Lefort, instead of trying to anchor himself in the intellectual bourgeoisie (there are certainly less indirect means of doing it), was trying to understand the nature of revolution or truth in history? And what if one were to lend him a little of that freedom to be himself that Sartre does not begrudge himself? To place an adversary in contradiction *with himself* is fundamentally an arbitrary decision to express oneself only tacitly, by means of a Marxism that one rethinks but that one presents as

Marxism itself; it is to claim for oneself the right to be undecided or vague while refusing it to the adversary. You who are Marxist, says Sartre, you should join the C.P. But I, who teach you so well your Marxist duty without, fortunately, being a Marxist, I keep my freedom intact. The very difficulties that are called maneuvers in others are in Sartre only the proof of a free spirit. If Lefort asks himself questions about revolution and about truth, it is *so that he will not have to join the C.P.* If Sartre does not join the C.P., it is *because he is asking himself these questions or others.* This is unequal treatment; Sartre is plainly more conciliatory toward Sartre than toward Lefort.

Why all that, and is it not merely a question of temper? It is much more serious than that. What gives this strident tone to the discussion is Sartre's effort to annex history to his philosophy of freedom and of the other. Freedom as he conceives it is unstable and tends toward violence. Freedom is not at first an infinite power that we would notice in ourselves; it presents itself trapped and powerless: it is a quality which marks our entire life and which makes this life our charge. It is as if at each moment everything that has made us, everything from which we benefit, and everything which will result from our life were entered in our account. Sartre has even evoked the Kantian myth of choice and its intelligible nature in order to show that freedom first appears in the past as freedom to be found again, freedom lost. This is what he has so well expressed in saying that we are condemned to freedom. To say that we are free is a way of saying that we are not innocent, that we are responsible for everything before everyone as if we had done it with our own hands. Freedom, which Sartre, like Descartes, distinguishes absolutely from power, is almost identified with the simple existence around us of a charged field in which all our acts immediately take the aspect of merits and demerits. To live is to wake up bound like Gulliver at Lilliput, as if in a former life one had already disposed of oneself. It is to attempt to make up this perpetual delay, to transform into actual freedom the prenatal freedom which is there only to condemn us. Freedom is behind us, or perhaps in front of us; never are we able to coincide with it. Perhaps we can reverse the order of things: by living the future we put ourselves ahead of ourselves. We will never be on time. And this movement toward the future will be violence, as is our relationship to a world already there, and concerning which we have not been consulted. The other's gaze is nothing but another mark of this original delay, which comes from the fact that we are *born*. The image of me that the other evokes is once again an elsewhere that I will never be able to overtake and yet that I must overtake, since, as I acknowledge in shame, I am also over there in this gaze which I do not challenge. This accusation from outside takes up anew my grievance against myself. In private life and in literature there is some relaxation: I speak to others, I act with them, with them I move beyond my condition at birth and they, theirs, toward a common future or toward the world taken as spectacle. In action, or in the action of unveiling which is literature, there is a relationship of calling and response. This solution is more apparent than real, for the relationship with the other is never symmetrical; rather, it is always one of the two who proposes, the "common" life is his project, and even the effort he makes to associate the other to it is the product of his good will. The mutual project remains an individual one for the fundamental reason that the future lives only in consciousness, it never truly descends *between* us. The calling of one freedom to another through literature is even more illusory, since the call is always from the writer to the reader. What happens when one comes to the social bond, when it is a question of uniting the near and the far in a common enterprise in that social space in which everything becomes deadened and dissipated? Then the apparent liberalism which exists in common life and in literature is denounced. There is a liberalism for the internal use of the bourgeoisie because it manages its society like a private enterprise and forms its unity, as a couple does, through common "interests." But this community excludes others. And the others are not even united by the common exile: they suffer the same things at the same time, that is all. In the proletariat, insofar as it calls for a society which would be total or true, each life is condemned to the solitude and the surrender which defined consciousness in its first meeting with the other. So that, here too, a common future, a history, may efface the initial situation, it is necessary to make them out of nothing, it is necessary to set up pure wills—absolute commands, absolute obedience, indistinguishable because they are absolute—which will create history, since it was not given to us even in a relative sense, as was friendship or love. Everyone found himself by means of a common life, at least through things done together: he who loves, that is to say, who wants to be loved, found himself completed by these things (with the condition that he forget that the other's love is also nothing but the will to be loved and that the other also lives the enterprise as his alone; but in action this turning back upon oneself is suspended, and the two mirages confirm each other). In social life there are no things done together. They must be invented. One must here create from nothing the milieu of a common enterprise or history, and one must even create the subjects of this enterprise: the Party. There is no point in demanding here that each consciousness find itself through common action: it must transform itself and be converted into action. The "I think" was able to recover itself through the common life with the other; but where this common life does not exist, the "I think" must explode, it must first create the common life. Thus in Sartre what gives to the gaze of the least-favored its absolute authority and to the Party its historical monopoly, and consequently the duty of absolutely respecting communism, is the fact that the initial discord of the other with me and of me with myself lives again undisguisedly and imperiously in the discord between the bourgeoisie and the proletarians and that it demands a solution for which the elements this time are not given. It is Sartre's ontology that determines that history as a common future be sustained by the pure action of a few, which is identical to the obedience of the others. Choice, freedom, and effort become conquest and violence in order to become everyone's affair.

This violence thus does not come from temper; or rather temper, like all things, is, in a philosopher, philosophy. It is already there when freedom and impotence, the past and the future, the present and the distant, the I and the other, the gaze of the least-favored and the Party that claims it, are immediately united by the simple negation that separates them, are united one to another and all together in violence. When negativity descends into the world and takes possession of it by force, when it wants to become history immediately, everything that opposes it appears as negation and can be put pell-mell in the same bag. These mixtures, these short cuts, are the counterparts of the short circuit which goes directly from freedom to the Party. This is why Lefort is the philosopher of the young executives.[110] It is not so much due, as one sees, to Lefort and the young executives as it is to Sartre.

110. [The French is "jeunes patrons," which might be more fully translated as "young owner-directors of medium- to small-sized businesses." In France there is a semipolitical liberal group that goes under the name Jeunes Patrons.—Trans.]

Is violence Sartre's last word? Surely not, and for a fundamental reason, which is that pure violence does not exist. It is not
pure in the case of the Bolsheviks; it hides behind truth, and, as
we have seen, this is what makes it implacable. In reality ultrabolshevism throws off this cover: truth and reason are for
tomorrow, and today's action must be pure. But this is also to
say that ultrabolshevism is only adhering to the principles of
communism, to its desire to change the world. Pure action is
only the root of freedom; as soon as it is applied, it is in a world
of "probable" relations in a situation where it must find its way
and accept mediations. In truth, this is where politics begins.
The approbation in principle of the Party remains philosophical.
It concerns communism only as the negation of the bourgeoisie,
as thought or as conception, and not, except in certain of its
"aspects," as that which bears the name of communism over
there, in the sun or in the snow. It does not extend to the "probabilistic" consequences. The absolute choice, the choice of existence, beyond all the reasons, is violent only when it does not
present itself as a choice but takes itself for the law of the world.
It tacitly imposes its own categories on others under the pretext
that no one is supposed to ignore the world—the world such as
it has been chosen by the thinker. But as soon as the choice is
justified and declared, the discussion starts all over again. The
pure will to change the world is nothing but inner life so long as
we are not told how to do it. As long as this is not done, as long as
Sartre is not a communist, the judgment that "Lefort wants to
anchor himself in the intellectual bourgeoisie" means only that
Sartre wants to cut himself loose from his own anchorage [111] at
any cost. Lefort's "bad faith" is a projection of Sartre's own good
faith, which will be sorely tried when he has to move beyond principles. Sartre presents his polemic as a first phase, after which he
will say how the C.P. also does not express the proletariat. But if
he expresses it only *quatenus*, Sartre becomes a slippery customer
once more. Sartre's ontology, which was moving toward a C.P.
existing in ideas as its only possible issue, takes up a distinct existence and surveys the C.P. with a glance. Sartre's conclusion
is no longer pure action; it is pure action contemplated from a
distance—in other words, sympathy. On the concrete political
terrain Sartre may tomorrow reappear pacified, conciliatory, and
universalist, as he *also* is.

111. [In the French: "se désancrer."—Trans.]

V

Sartre's "reasons" are at the other extreme from those of Marxism, and it is because the dialectic has broken down that he defends communist politics. What conclusions now have to be drawn? For in showing Sartrean and Marxian motives to be parallel, we have not implied that Marx, rather the Sartre, was right; we were trying to restore the Marxist spirit only in order to show what is new in Sartre's analysis. To read Sartre with Marx's eyeglasses would be deliberately to ignore the real question that his studies raise—although he does not raise it himself—which is whether revolution in the Marxist sense is still the order of the day. It would also be to add to the confusions he creates, to obscure the debate ourselves, to conceal under Marx's authority a post-Marxian evaluation of history, which, on the contrary, must be made explicit. We have stressed that the return of dogmatism in its scientistic form to an offensive role, the isolation of the dialectic in being, and the end of philosophical Marxism signaled disillusion and difficulties in Marxist theory and practice. This was not done in order to now confront Sartre with this same philosophy, with this same ideology whose crisis is perfectly attested by his own analyses. As a description of existing communism, Sartre's antidialectic appears to us to be hardly questionable. We are only saying that it raises the question of the nature of communism, and we reproach him only for not having raised this question himself. Our problem would be his if only he had formulated it as a problem instead of acting as if the whole thing were a matter of "common sense." If in fact, as we believe, communism is what Sartre says it is, what attitude can and should one have toward it, and how can one evaluate Sartre's attitude?

Must we say that of course we can no longer expect either the accession of the proletariat to management, to politics, and to history or the homogeneous society—in short, what the dialectic promised—but that, anyway, that was only the final "optimistic twaddle" which experience has eliminated and that communism remains *on the right road*, that it is the proletariat's *only chance*, offering in the present a *progressive* regime and, for the future, a *revolutionary* perspective? Must we say that, beyond an official philosophy which is a collection of curiosities, beyond uncivil behavior toward intellectuals, beyond its undoubtedly super-

fluous violence, communism is still *preferable?* "The Stalinist
movement throughout the world," wrote F. Jeanson,[112]

> does not appear to us to be authentically revolutionary. Yet it is the
> only one which claims to be revolutionary, and, particularly in our
> country, it has organized the great majority of the proletariat. We
> are therefore at one and the same time against it, since we are
> critical of its methods, and for it, since we do not know whether the
> authentic revolution is not a chimera, whether the revolutionary
> enterprise does not first have to go along these paths before it is
> able to establish a more human social order, or whether the per-
> versions of this enterprise are not, given the actual context, pref-
> erable, all in all, to its pure and simple annihilation.[113]

An odd way of thinking. One has a certain idea of "authentic"
revolution; one verifies that the U.S.S.R. is not a revolution in this
sense; one then wonders whether authentic revolution is not a
dream; in the name of this doubt one keeps the label "revolutionary" for a regime which may perhaps mend its ways; but, as
this future is vague, one says only that it will be "a more human
social order." These lines give the entire essence of "progressism,"
its dreamy sweetness, its incurable bullheadedness, and its
padded violence. At the very bottom, there is always "authentic"
revolution. This is what is at the end of the journey and what
justifies it. And, certainly, the paths are indirect, but they are the
paths of revolution. Why not think rather about the goal and the
"more human social order"? In all this, how very little is asked
about what one *does* outside. How much one feels that it is only
a question of the relations of the self to itself. There is something
of this sort in certain of Sartre's lines, as, for example, when he
writes: "[The] 'Stalinists' would agree without hesitation that
neither the authoritarian Party nor the Soviet State can be envisaged as the definitive form of proletarian organization." [114] The
reference to the revolution or to "proletarian organization" at the
moment when one observes that the regime is far from it,
without any precision about the turning point which will bring it

112. [An important editor of *Les Temps modernes.*—Trans.]
113. *Les Temps modernes,* August, 1952, p. 378. Despite the "we,"
I have never agreed with this text. [For years Merleau-Ponty wrote
most of the political editorials for *Les Temps modernes,* was himself a
cofounder and editor, and largely decided on the political writings of
the review.—Trans.]
114. *RL,* p. 1616; ET, p. 283.

closer or about the forces which will impose this turning point, this oscillation from what one sees to what one dreams thus contaminating the real with the imaginary (without thereby achieving any true resemblance) and obscuring the harsh present under the haze of a fictitious future—these techniques recall the devices of physicists who encumber a theory with auxiliary hypotheses so as to avoid recognizing that it does not clarify what happens. If the Marxist revolution were a *general idea,* there would be nothing to say against this play of the imaginary and the real, of expediency and utopia. But the dialectical idea of revolution is no more an advance toward "some more human social order" than it is a "chimera" or a star in the farthest reaches of the future.[115] Revolution in its beginnings is rupture, because revolution is the seizure of power by the proletariat. The rupture is always to be renewed, for revolution is also self-suppression of the proletariat as a class. It is thus a process, but not an "advance" in the vague and "bourgeois" meaning of the word. It is an identifiable becoming because it always moves toward the development of the proletariat in consciousness and in power. Even in its beginnings, in its atypical forms, it is never a *perhaps.* When Lenin proposed the N.E.P., he was not content with vague allusions to the future; he explained and made the path accepted. Revolution as a "perhaps" is Marxist action disjointed between a utopia situated at infinity and a completely different present that it sanctifies. If one has to class the revolutionary dialectic as "optimistic twaddle," let us no longer speak of revolution.

The "perhaps," a formula of doubt as well as faith, aims at that which is absolutely beyond our grasp. How can the most categorical undertaking that exists be founded on a sigh? The communists are right to value the dialectic. Without it they are only progressists, and the progressist, left to himself, vegetates. In reading Sartre, one sometimes believes that he has set himself the task of proving that revolution is impossible. How could this proletariat which has lost its hold on history keep a historical mission? How could it propel an emancipated society if it is no longer skilled labor, know-how, and a capacity for management and for

115. The Marxist meaning of the word "progressism" or "progressist" is unequivocal: the progressist is he who in his field and without a full political consciousness thinks and acts in a way which helps the proletarian revolution. The idea of a "progressist party," that is to say, organized unconsciousness, is a humorous creation of the recent phase.

struggle but is only a "need" lacking political consciousness and power? Whatever the efforts of the C.P., how can one make a proletarian revolution with a neoproletariat? It will not be a proletarian revolution. But then what? Sartre's analysis presents communism as absolutely undetermined. He does not have in common with it a view of history, of its possibilities or its articulated causalities. He values communism because it has at its center the gaze of the least-favored. This is a great deal, because this argument can ground any kind of politics; and it is very little, because he defends it only in a formal manner and in terms of its internal principle. The reader gets the feeling that, for Sartre, communism is something holy but also something one talks about and looks at, something which remains remote and inaccessible. One has less respect and more passion for what one lives. For Sartre it is not a social fact that one examines as best one can, that one attempts to understand in its distinctive features, using the same criteria that are used for judging other societies. We lack information. I defy you, he says to Lefort, to prove according to the rules of historical criticism that the Russian working class disavows the regime.[116] A return to historical reality would be healthy if it were a question of refuting those who speak of opposition in Russia as a fact because it results from their principles. But it is not facts that Sartre reminds us of; it is our ignorance of facts. It would only be fair to observe that what is hidden is precisely that which renders the adversary's proof difficult. If Sartre readily resigns himself to this state of affairs, it is because he does not burden himself with the task of proving his position; for him it is enough that it cannot be disproved. And since it does not appear that we will be getting information for quite a while, communism becomes a negative being or even, like the moon and the sun, one of those "ultra things" that are seen only from afar. Or finally, torn from the world, floating equidistant between things and Sartre's gaze, it is like those tenacious appearances which no judgment can situate. Just as these appearances reside this side of articulated space, so, too, communism lies this side of proof.

If one must really get rid of all the optimistic twaddle that lies between the subject and the object—spontaneity, initiative of the masses, meaning of history—and leave the brute will of the leaders face to face with the opaque necessity of things, such ex-

116. *RL*, p. 1619; *ET*, p. 286.

treme realism cannot be distinguished from an extreme idealism. Men—proletarians and even leaders—are no more than beings of reason. What do you want the leader to do if not to lead the revolution, says Sartre. He is himself only in being everyone, he is nothing without the proletariat. This is to suppose that there are beings who are living definitions, whose existence is fully included in their essence. This is to forget that, from the day when the dialectic is only in the leaders' minds, from this very fact and without further inquiry it is no more than an accessory of power. The proletariat of which Sartre is speaking is not verifiable, debatable, or living. It is not a phenomenon but is rather a category delegated to represent humanity in Sartre's thought. Since the proletariat is nothing when it does not adhere to the Party, it never is the Party but is only a nameless mass which can be detached from it. It exists immediately through obedience, and it ceases to exist immediately through disobedience. It is not a historical reality with advances, peaks, declines, or variable historical weight. Like an idea, the proletariat exists in the instant; and if Sartre refuses it "spontaneity," this is only because the Party and history must appear by *spontaneous generation.* Sartre reproaches the Trotskyites with fabricating beyond observable facts a "real" proletariat which does the opposite of what the existing proletarians do. But this is the way Sartre himself operates, with the exception that, not being a Marxist, he does not bother to garb his proletariat in historical reality. "Spontaneity" passes to the side of the leaders and the militants because here, at least, we know what we are talking about, we are among men or among consciousnesses. But that is to say that the proletariat is an idea of the leaders. The proletariat is suspended above history, it is not caught in the fabric, it cannot be explained, it is cause of itself, as are all ideas. No conceivable method can reveal its historical presence, absence, or variations. The proletariat subsists through any disobedience, since, as soon as it disobeys, it is no longer it that disobeys. Obedience does not make it grow, because obedience is included in its definition. If some fact or symptom emerges to testify to its presence and its force, this is accepted only condescendingly; for when, on the contrary, such facts are lacking, nothing is changed as regards the proletariat's essence, which is always to obey the Party. The Party continues to "represent" it historically. The proletariat is untouchable because it exists only in the pure action of the Party, and this action exists only in Sartre's thought. All detectors and proofs are superfluous

when it is a question of capturing an essence, and this is undoubtedly why Sartre airily takes them or leaves them. When the
proletariat is not visible on the terrain of class struggle, he turns
to legislative elections and has no problem in showing that the
proletariat is still there, for it is electing Communist deputies. But
the same secret vote falsifies everything when the bourgeoisie
imposes it on the trade unions. It breaks the workers' unity of
action, destroys the proletariat as a class, and hides historical
reality; we are therefore invited to look for the proletariat in the
class struggle and in the democracy of the masses, a democracy
which is not obliged to prove itself through a bourgeois-style vote.
On June 2, 1952, the proletarians did not follow the Party. In his
articles Sartre comments that the proletariat was not involved.
By definition it was not involved since it is obedience to the Party.
Let us translate: it is a definition and exists only in Sartre's
mind. One might be tempted to see things differently. One could
note that the C.P. is sanctioned as a parliamentary party, that it
does not perform its functions on the street. One might remember,
then, that it gained votes from outside the working class, that for
a time it was part of the government, that perhaps its voters are
themselves "progressists" rather than revolutionaries, that the
essence of its action is no longer the strike, the insurrection, or
the revolution, which for the Party are now only means in the
parliamentary and diplomatic struggle. But this would be to make
the Party enter history, when it is supposed to make it; it would
be to subordinate the Party's authority to "probabilistic" discussions. It is better, if one wants certainty, to remain on the terrain
of pure action and of the proletariat as idea, which allows neither
exaltation nor discouragement, which is always absent and always present, which is the Party's thought—or rather Sartre's
thought. For the Party itself has the weakness (or the cleverness)
of providing proofs of its spontaneity: it makes itself responsible
for failures and exculpates the masses. This is a language for the
initiated, Sartre says to the Party, and I understand you at once—
it is not your role to put the blame on the masses, but the masses
do not judge the Party when they do not follow it. Sartre is un-
compromisingly rigid when the question concerns the duty of
the masses or even of the Party. Until now the only point on
which he has reproved the Party is the communiqué in which the
Party avowed its failure. Sartre, for his part, "note[s], like every-
body else, the discouragement of the masses," but he "still do[es]
not know whether the policy of the C.P. bears the responsibility

for it."[117] How, indeed, could the Party move away from the proletariat which it makes? Rather, it is the masses which renounce
being the proletariat. Yet here one feels that Sartre would like to
take a break. For if the C.P. is not wrong, if the masses as masses
can only fall back into dispersion, one does not see too well to
whom one should attribute the crisis. To the bourgeoisie, of
course—but one cannot ask it to change. To the noncommunist
Marxists, who encourage the masses in secession? Certainly. But
they are outside history. One is at dead center, there is really
nothing to do. Humanism based on need, which does not define
a strategy, calls us to an abstract duty, to respect for the C.P. in
its essence; but this sympathy, sometimes too demanding, since
it does not even accept the C.P.'s retraction, sometimes too docile,
since it always approves of the Party when it charges forward, is
not in any case a collaboration or an action. It is an operation in
Sartre's mind that in no way establishes a relation between him
and existing communism. Existing communism is in itself
Sartrean since it exercises unjustifiable choice. It is Sartrean as a
theme, as an object of analysis or of representation; but it can
neither live nor acknowledge itself as an unjustifiable choice, and,
in this sense, there is no Sartrean communism.

Sartre's attitude—assent in principle to pure action and agreement on particular points—leaves him free with regard to what
is essential to communism, that is to say, communist action, the
effort that translates pure action into applied action. And for this
very reason his attitude permits him only to oscillate between re-
bellion and forbearance. The agreement on the principle of pure
action is situated at the root of history, where the proletariat and
the Party are only names for the I, the Other, and freedom. In
short, it does not make the philosopher emerge from his own
thought. In truth, politics begins only afterwards, when it is a
question of knowing how pure action will be embodied. On this
plane the agreement on particular points or even on numerous
aspects of communism looks rather like reticence. For it means
that pure action does not necessarily lead to all the consequences
that communist politics derives from it and that when pure action
defines itself as a politics the problem remains completely un-
touched. Sartre stresses that whatever he said to lay the foundation of communism in principle leaves him entirely free to
evaluate the C.P. and communism in what they do. Lefort makes

117. CP, p. 762; ET, p. 131.

a value judgment on the C.P.; "I am not going to correct you," Sartre says.[118] To Lefort he opposes only the impossibility of making a judgment without endangering the existence of the Party and the proletariat. In the end he appears to accept this risk, since he admits that "the discussion is open" on the question of exploitation in the Soviet Union.[119] His sympathy for numerous aspects of the communist enterprise is a question of common sense and does not carry with it an evaluation of the whole. This he expressly reserves.[120] He even has an opinion about some decisions of pure action that the C.P. attempts to impose; for example, he judged the demonstration against Ridgway "inopportune." [121] We are not crushed between the Party's authority and the masses' discouragement. Undoubtedly one must get beyond their quarrel, understand the reasons for it, compare the Party's politics to the masses' attitude, and find in this analysis a way of joining them once more. This is what Sartre appears to be attempting in his third article, and its tone in some passages is fairly new. It is no longer a tone of urgency or ultimatum but rather one of history. We have seen that history is traversed by the mutually defiant gazes of the bourgeois and the proletarian; but the Party's decisions, by the single fact that they are introduced into the life of the class, are relativized. Already in his *Reply to Claude Lefort* Sartre spoke of a dialectic between the masses and the Party,[122] of a reaction of the masses organized around the apparatus,[123] and this would seem to be incompatible with pure action.[124] If the masses do not suppress themselves as

118. *RL*, p. 1622; ET, p. 289.
119. *RL*, p. 1619; ET, p. 286.
120. *RL*, p. 1615; ET, p. 282.
121. *CP*, p. 705; ET, p. 67.
122. *RL*, p. 1572; ET, p. 236.
123. *RL*, pp. 1600–1601; ET, p. 266.
124. Sartre indeed said that pure action is an ideal and that the real party and the labor movement are a mixture of action and passion: "I do not think that one can interpret the present situation except as an inextricable mixture of action and passion in which passion temporarily dominates" (*RL*, p. 1623; ET, p. 290). But how is one to understand this mixture of fire and water? How is one to add up action and passion, when Sartre says that communist action is either pure or nothing? To speak of a mixture amounts to admitting that in periods of stagnation the political and social facts belong to neither the order of things nor the order of meanings. The reader suddenly wonders whether both "pure" action and pure passion might not be precisely ideologies or phantasms of historical stagnation and

masses at the moment when they are organized into the Party, if they continue to live in it, if there they are something other than a permanent possibility of annihilation, then their resistance to the apparatus can be something other than a betrayal. This is undoubtedly why the interpretation of the unsuccessful strike of June 4 as a disavowal of the Party, at first categorically rejected, is in the end "not completely false." [125] Seen from the angle of pure action, pluralistic unionism was the ruin of the labor movement.[126] Considered from a historical perspective, that is to say, as effect as much as cause, it is "in a sense . . . legitimate." [127] The distinction between politics and economics, first treated as a bourgeois maneuver, receives an acceptable meaning in the second article; [128] and, using the double-objective strikes, the third article analyzes the expedient that the Party invented to reunite what history had thus separated. Like all alleged vices of the C.P., "bureaucracy" was taken in the first articles as one of those modalities of the proletarian movement which do not alter its essence and must be accepted in a realistic spirit. The Trotskyites' theses on bureaucratic society were not taken seriously. Indeed, a certain dosage of bureaucracy was necessary so that the proletariat, which is nothing, could be able to oppose *something* to the bourgeoisie's weighty apparatuses. In the third article, bureaucracy reappears as a trait common to all contemporary societies.[129] Is there, then, a history which the bourgeoisie and the proletariat share and which leaves its mark on both of them? And is one not giving up the struggle when one takes a view that incorporates both oppressor and oppressed? Can one thus without betrayal take a certain distance in order to evaluate the present forms of communist organization? Sartre has given up the point of view of immediacy. The emotion of 1952 recedes. The C.P. continues to exist, and so does its uneasiness. The problems cannot be posed, nor will they be resolved, in haste. There is time. The precept of not being the enemy of the C.P. is not sufficient. There must be an analysis of the present which can go far back

---

whether, to get out of this, it is not necessary to return, moving beyond the crisis which has disassociated them, to the proletariat's hold on history.

125. *RL*, p. 1623; ET, p. 290.
126. *CP*, p. 716; ET; p. 79.
127. *CP*, p. 1819; ET, p. 231.
128. *CP*, p. 709; ET, pp. 71–72.
129. *CP*, p. 1803; ET p. 213.

and an action that is not short-lived. It is not enough to know that without the C.P. the universe would be bourgeois. One cannot bring the masses back to obedience by this completely formal argument, reduce union pluralism to the bourgeois trick which it was in the immediate situation, conjure away "bureaucracy" and "spontaneity" as twin myths, or disregard the neoproletariat's impotence or compensate for it by an increase of authority. At last one speaks of politics, at last one has emerged from "certainty" and the inner life. But what remains of those massive certitudes with which we began, and how can they be reconciled with a positive politics? What is to be done if the C.P. refuses the concrete perspectives that we will propose to it? In his third article, Sartre insists on the fact of Malthusianism. It is a capitalistic fact, since the bourgeoisie manages our economy. Following the principle that holds a half-choice to be a choice of duplicity, the principle upon which his methodical mythology is based, Sartre presents even Malthusianism and the defense of small businessmen as a plot of the bourgeoisie. The remedy would thus be to destroy the bourgeoisie's power; but the world situation is such that, except in case of war, communism cannot soon take power in France. For the moment, the only efficacious struggle against Malthusianism is that of the neocapitalists. Should one therefore support them? But they may restore a semblance of health to dying capitalism. And, moreover, the defense of small business and trade is an article of communist action in parliament. The C.P. hesitates and the parliamentary group abstains when a government asks special powers to undertake this struggle. If pure action is paralyzed and deliberates, so much the more will this be the case for its sympathizer. In his third article, Sartre avoids the question by incorporating the analyses of Sauvy [130] and others in his indictment of the bourgeoisie. But the means compromise the end. For, in short, if the major crime of today's bourgeoisie is stagnation, and if only its most enlightened faction will, for the foreseeable future, be in a position to struggle against stagnation, is it not best to unite with it? What would the "least-favored" say if he had the right to gaze on these questions? And, since a gaze can grasp only the immediate present, where then is its immediate interest? When one leaves principles or intentions behind and

130. [The reference is to Alfred Sauvy, professor of social demography at the Collège de France. He wrote widely on population problems.—Trans.]

attempts to understand what is happening in France today, one meets the C.P., not as pure action, but as applied action, as action which is also attempting to understand what is happening in France today and to reconcile these local necessities with all the other necessities of communist action. On both these grounds the C.P. can be considered by Sartre only as one political factor among others, and one not meriting particular attention. If, on the contrary, one holds to the Party's prerogative in principle, it is useless and risky to enter into the discussion of concrete problems; the only thing to do is wait.

But just as it is distant, sympathy is so near that the sympathizer must be fooled when he is not fooling. He is not in the communist action and does not want communist power as such. He wants, one by one, the results which, for the communist, are stages of this action. He therefore accepts piecemeal what he refuses as a whole. It is sufficient to ask him the questions one at a time—and especially in a negative form: you are not in favor of atomic weapons? You are not, are you? Then you are going to sign this paper, which condemns them. You are not in favor of a few colonists' interests against those of colonial populations? You do not want the world to go up in flames because Laos is invaded? You will not, then, refuse to put your name on this petition against the internationalization of the war. The sympathizer realizes full well that elsewhere these protests have a positive aspect about which he is not consulted. But, as a sympathizer, he has agreed to decide what he does not want; he is only trying to achieve innocence. Questions are put to him the way he asks them himself, and he does have to agree with them. From time to time he find himself alone again: communism—which has a line of action, which does not proceed by single judgments, and which does not have to prove continuously that it is against capitalism—evacuates the positions that the sympathizer had sworn to uphold, leaving him there with his principles. The Viet-Minh's troops leave Laos; the C.P. proposes to the Socialist Party the very unity of action which Sartre said the communists should not be asked to initiate. The sympathizer then vaguely suspects that he and the communists are not altogether in the same world. But all the same, he is in order with himself, and, besides, some new protest will soon give him the occasion to link arms with men again. This is how serious politics forces the understanding into a corner. Or rather it is the understanding itself which sets the traps it will fall into, because it does not believe in the dialectic and reduces action to judgments the way Zeno reduced movement to positions, and because it has committed itself in advance to supply an action which is not its own with judgments which that action uses for other ends. Whether he judges for or against is of little importance; the sympathizer is outside action, if action is not a series of fulgurating judgments but the art of organizing the confluence of forces.

We do not mention these varying nuances and alternations of sympathy as signs of contradiction: speculatively speaking, it is not contradictory to respect the C.P. as the negation of bourgeois history and to judge it freely for what it is and for its daily action; the two things even complement each other very well, for they are not of the same order. One deals with a mental object, the C.P. insofar as it expresses the proletariat; the other deals with a historical being, the C.P. which perhaps does not express it. Without inconsistency the same man can maintain both representations, but he cannot follow their consequences in action, and his solution is to contemplate sympathetically. Sympathy is the action of those who are everywhere and nowhere: by their assent in principle they are morally in the Party, but they remain outside because they discuss it piecemeal. This is an external opposition, an imaginary action. Criticizing in all solidarity is a formula of action only in the case of a true opposition working within the Party and attempting to put its views forward. But the Party does not want opposition, which is why the opposition remains outside; and Sartre has explained to us that the Party is right. If he thus succeeds in respecting the Party while judging it, such a delicate balance is maintained only on the strict condition that he not take part in either its or any other action and that he remain at a speculative distance. When one judges the Party from outside and defers to it entirely, one dreams of a constructive opposition that in other respects one realizes is impossible. A dialectical Marxist communism has room for an opposition, but a Sartrean communism tolerates none, not even Sartre's, nor his own "reasons." The same reasons force him to respect the C.P. and force him not to join it.

There is thus no contradiction in Sartre's thought. Only it is a thought, not an action; and there is perhaps not much sense in dealing with communism, which is an action, by means of pure thought. Or, rather, let us say that there are two types of action: action of unveiling and action of governing. What is easy in one order is difficult in the other. The action of unveiling admits of reserves, nuances, omissions, and intermittencies, and it is incomparably easier to give a direction to a newspaper or a work of art than to a party or a government: the paper can endure anything, the readers fewer things, and the militants or the governed still fewer. The action of a party or a government cannot afford to lose contact even momentarily with the event: such action must remain the same and be immediately recognized throughout its different phases, it must comment practically on anything that happens, in each "yes" or "no" it must make the meaning of all the others appear (or, if it has variable principles, it must not change them too often). On the other hand, it is incomparably easier to navigate between communism and anticommunism (England and France did it at Geneva in 1954) than to reconcile in thought respect for and criticism of the Party. Neither a government nor the C.P. itself is obligated to have an opinion on the Soviet camps or, if they have one, to state it. The writer and the journalist must declare their position, for they *unveil,* their universe is a canvas upon which nothing exists unless it is represented, analyzed, and judged. The newspaper is the truth of the world; it acts by showing. As a result of this, there arise insoluble problems or illegitimate solutions which are not those of political action. The action of unveiling has its easy times and its torments, which are those of contemplation. They are mandarin problems and solutions. The mandarin myth unites the phantasm of total knowledge with that of pure action. The mandarin is thought to be present by means of his knowledge wherever there is a problem, and capable of acting immediately from a distance, anywhere, as pure efficient cause, as if *what he did* occurred in an inert milieu and was not at the same time theater, a manifestation, an object of scandal or of enthusiasm. The spectator consciousness is too busy seeing to see itself as a "particular" consciousness, and it dreams of an action which also would be ubiquitous. Such is the naïveté and the hoax of narcissism. Knowing everything, the spectator consciousness also knows that certain people want to change the world. Consciousness makes room for them in its universe, comprehends them like everything else, and justifies them in terms of the very thing that challenges it. But it can follow them only in thought; it cannot be one of them and remain itself. And there is nothing surprising if in the end it does not know what to do. The drama is not only that of the writer; it involves every man: it is the drama of a being who *sees* and *does*. Insofar as he sees, he transforms whatever he sees into

178 / ADVENTURES OF THE DIALECTIC

something seen; he is, one might say, a voyeur, he is everywhere present without distance; even among those who act, he insists on imposing his presence on them while knowing that they reject him. Yet, insofar as man acts, he cannot act without some perspective or refuse a minimum of explanation to those who follow the action. The worlds of vision and action are therefore different, and yet they act as cross-checks. This is why in the C.P., as in Sartre's work, the balance between the demands of seeing and those of doing is always difficult to obtain, and nothing *will remove* the difficulty. Marxism had conceived, not a solution, but a way of passing beyond the problem through the life of the Party, which was supposed to take each person where he was situated and offer him a view of the whole, rectifying its perspectives by means of its action and its action by its perspectives. These illusions have been dispelled, and we still have two distinct ways of going to the universal: one, the more direct, consists in putting everything into words, the other consists in entering the game, with its obscurity, and creating there a little bit of truth by sheer audacity. One cannot therefore reproach the writer with a professional defect when he tries to see everything and restricts himself to imaginary action: by doing so he maintains one of the two components of man. But he would be quite mistaken if he thought he could thus glue together the two components and move to political action because he looks at it.

The compromise of being an external communist, of imposing on communism a gaze which comes from outside and which is not hostile, might be said to be the only possible attitude in a time when communism expels those who wish to see. While possible in the noncommunist world, it is not possible in the communist world. For here one must reason in the opposite sense: *since* communism has expelled its opposition, one therefore cannot be halfway into communism—one can only be in it completely or not at all. The weakness of Sartre's position is that it is a solution for someone who lives in the capitalist world, not for someone who lives in the communist world, although this is what is at issue here. He decrees coexistence between communism and the external opposition, but this has yet to be acknowledgd by the C.P. At the very moment when Sartre attaches the greatest importance to the Other, since he wants to see the noncommunist world through the eyes of the least-favored, it is still in terms of himself that things are ordered. At the very moment when he affirms only a sympathy of principle for communism, he places himself in the noncommunist world, and he is still not speaking of communism.

External opposition, all right; but he situates himself in such a way that one fears he may give up unveiling without being able to act. Internal opposition is impossible; therefore I carry it outside. But if it is not possible from the inside, it is even less possible from the outside. From the outside it is rivalry, threat. The oppositionist pays for his criticism, and this is why his criticism is an action. The external oppositionist never completely proves that he is faithful from a distance. He will not use the right of criticism that he reserves for himself for fear of abusing it. Because his relationships with the Party are of a mental order only, they are broad and intermittent: regardless of what the Party does, one can support it when one does not belong; and whatever one says in its favor is, like all things that have been said, to be said again tomorrow. True commitment would be practically the inverse: agreement not on principles but in an action that one is called upon to elaborate; agreement not on particular points but on a line which connects them; relationships, then, simultaneously differentiated and continual. Always present, always absent, the "slippery customer" is the spectator consciousness, and we have to ask ourselves whether commitment as understood by Sartre does not transform the relationships of action into relationships of contemplation: one dreams of touching the things themselves through action; to better get outside oneself, one agrees that it is only a question of preferring one or another of existing things or even that it is only a matter of *choosing* one without there being a preference of man as a whole. But this is actually how one proves that it is only a question of spectacle and of relationships of thought: since communism, for a communist, and in reality, is not just one of the existing things in the world, the U.S.S.R. over there, planning God knows what; and this masked giant is not something we can take or leave—we have to know and to say what we like and what we dislike and why, what we want and do not want from life. Direct contact with the thing itself is a dream. Except in certain instances, in the case of the executioner who chops off a head or the leader who decides on a war or an insurrection, all contacts with history are indirect, all actions are symbolic. The writer would act more surely by accepting this kind of action, which is eminently his, by reporting his preferences, his internal debates with communism, than by bringing to others the austere news of the choice he has made, out of duty, between existing things.

One will still say: all right, it is not a question of choosing the U.S.S.R. but rather of remaining faithful to what you think of capitalism and pursuing the consequences of this position. If capitalism overturns personal relationships by subjugating one class to another, if it even succeeds in depriving the oppressed class of any hold on history, dispersing it through the democratic game, which allows for all opinions but not for the enterprise of recreating humanity and beginning history anew, and if you do not want to become the enemy of the proletariat and of mankind by opposing this enterprise—if, additionally, you hold with Sartre that the dialectic, aside from a few privileged moments, never was anything but a cover for violent action, that the solutions for the communism of hope and for Western Marxism have remained on paper—then what is there to do except to open a credit account (which cannot be precisely measured in advance) to the only party that claims kinship with the proletariat, all the while reserving only your right to inspect the account? In a history which is without reason, in the name of what would you proclaim that the communist enterprise is impossible? This reasoning takes into account only intentions, not what one prefers or chooses; it tells us on what condition we will be irreproachable before the proletariat, at least in the short run, but it does not tell us how our action will liberate the proletariat. Yet it is the liberation of the worker that you are pretending to pursue. If the facts "say neither yes nor no," if the regime the proletariat desires is equivocal, and if, being aware of that and knowing the liabilities of the system, you help the proletariat establish such a regime, it is because you are thinking less of the proletariat than of yourself.

But whether there is a Marxist critique of capitalism which is still valid and which is not a moral judgment—this remains to be seen. The Marxist anaylsis of capital is indeed presented as "scientific," not as an always subjective perspective on history, and still less as a moral judgment. But because it *gives itself* the perspective of socialist production as the alternative to capitalism, there is thus scarcely any choice to be made, since the socialist future is hypothetically free of shackles, advance deductions, and the contradictions which make capitalism's existence a deferred bankruptcy. Yet now we know well, from the example of Soviet society, that other advance deductions, other shackles, and other contradictions may appear, once those of capitalism are suppressed; consequently, socialist production in Marx's sense once again becomes overtly what it always was: a *constructum* in the economist's mind. The choice is only among several types of social stratification, among several forms of the State. The disgraces of capitalism remain disgraces; they are certainly not erased by the eventual defects of the other system: but the disgraces of both systems are entered on a complex and "probabilistic" balance sheet, and a critique of one of the systems cannot by itself ground one's choice of the other. There is quite a difference between a critique of capitalism which believes it sees in it the last obstacle to the homogeneous society, the last bond before the liberation of true production, and a critique which perceives behind capitalism still other states, other armies, other elites, other police forces—all this constructed, as in capitalism itself, with institutions, myths, social symbols, human initiatives, and compensated errors, with no "natural" preordination. In the first case the critique is almost sufficient, because it is only the inverse of a positive truth. In the second case, it is conclusive only if one resolutely makes up one's mind on the basis of what one refuses and knows, without trying to know what one accepts in exchange. In other words, far from supplying a properly rational basis for the choice, this absolute critique is already the choice of noncapitalism, *whatever it may be*.

The fact is that the "objective" critique of capital hardly enters into Sartre's study. Inside an immediate or moral relationship of persons, he deliberately focuses on those that capitalism ruins, on those of whom we are starkly reminded by the gaze of the least-favored. His idea therefore seems to be that, even undetermined and destined to unforeseeable results, the communist enterprise deserves a favorable prejudice because the least-favored demand it and because we are not to be the judges of their best interests. But can one say that they demand it? Sartre himself explains that the least-favored are hardly militant and do not support communist action or any other action. It is he who interprets the curse hurled by the proletariat at bourgeois power; it is he who decides that it is aimed only at bourgeois power and that the suppression of this power, even if it makes way for another oppression, is in any case preferable. To prefer anything to what exists now simply because the proletariat condemns it would be to give oneself a good conscience under the pretext of giving the proletariat its historical chance. This can be very costly to the proletariat and is, moreover, an illusion, for one yields less to the will of the proletariat than to the will one attributes to it. The same reasons which made the proletariat lose its hold on history also make us, for better or for worse, judges of its interests. As soon as we leave the domain of good intentions, we cannot do without an analysis of communism, we cannot rest with negations, we must become acquainted with what we prefer, or in any case choose, *for* the proletariat.

Now if one stops projecting on the U.S.S.R. the light of the classless society and of socialist production in Marx's sense, what one sees is not sufficient to prove that the proletarians' interests lie in this system. One sees industrialization and a higher standard of living, but one also sees the differences in salaries and positions, the personalities of people like Kravchenko,[131] the authoritarian Party customs, the uniforms, the decorations, the self-accusation of the leaders, soon expressly contradicted by the power itself, the zigzags of power in the people's democracies, and the alternately opportunistic and suicidal politics of the fraternal parties in the noncommunist world. All of this, which is not open to debate, and which is public knowledge, says as clearly as possible that there is a State apparatus in the U.S.S.R., that it makes concessions on everything except State property and planning, which do not constitute socialism since they are made to support the cost of a managerial group and the lost opportunities caused by rigid leadership. All this does not make the U.S.S.R. an evil, or even an evil for Russia; but it does raise the question whether this is the concern of proletarians of all countries. Sartre says that one must "liquidate merit" and move toward a humanism based on need, the only one which is appropriate for the least-favored. As far as one can judge, it is rather the humanism of work which is the order of the day in the U.S.S.R., and the Soviet people seem to have set themselves the task of forming that working elite for which Sartre shows very little sympathy. Should one say that this is not definitive? But if there is change, it will be because the privileged of the regime will have judged it appropriate to share their privileges, which is good,

131. [V. A. Kravchenko, author of the book *I Chose Freedom*, which revealed the existence of Soviet labor camps to the French left. The trial for defamation against the communist paper *Les Lettres françaises* was one of the more sensational issues in that period.— Trans.]

but not very different from the concessions of a healthy capitalism. Sartre said that, since there is no dialectic, one can maintain the *aura* of revolution for communism such as it is. We would say that, if there is no dialectic, communism must be secularized. Capitalism may indeed be the exploitation of the working class. But if, despite what is professed by the communists, the social is inert in itself, an unpolarized chaos; if there is no historical moment, and even less a durable regime, in which all problems converge toward the power of a class which will suppress itself as a class; if there is only the leaders' authority, the manipulation of the masses, the rigging of congresses, the liquidation of minorities, the masquerading of majorities as unanimity: then how can we prefer this system, of which we know only one thing—that it is not what it pretends to be—and which probably does not know itself? If there is no logic of history, then communism is to be judged piecemeal; and favorable judgments, even on numerous "aspects" of the system, cannot give adherence to the whole as long as the whole is hidden. To secularize communism is to deprive it of the favorable prejudice to which it would be entitled if there were a philosophy of history and, moreover, to give it an even fairer examination, since one does not expect it to bring an end to history. There would undoubtedly be some features to touch up in the outline that we gave earlier, and they will be gladly rectified as the relevant information comes to our attention. It is essential for peace that communism stop being this ghost floating somewhere between transcendental freedom and everyday prose, which attracts both fervent sentiments and warlike dispositions.

If one decides to change the world and to overcome adversities, not together with the proletariat, but by giving it "orders," not by realizing a truth which comes to be in the course of things, but by manufacturing it out of nothing, in short, if one upsets the game in order to begin history again at zero, no one can say exactly what he is doing. The only thing which is sure is that the basis, the pure relationships of persons, will not be found again in things and that yet another State will be manufactured. It may be good, mediocre, or bad; that remains to be seen. But we will see only by placing the "revolutionary" country in common history; we will see nothing if we place ourselves in the perspective of the latest intentions of its leaders. For from then on there is nothing left to *learn*. Leaders change, Stalin's successors repudiate some of his acts. The sympathizer does not consider

184 / ADVENTURES OF THE DIALECTIC

himself defeated. There was Stalin's action and perspective,
there are Malenkov's and his colleagues'. The U.S.S.R., both
obscure and too full of meaning, still says neither "yes" nor "no."
On the other hand, the sympathizer always says "yes"—to Malenkov as before to Stalin. He is the friend of everyone because he
does nothing. One must not tell him that under Stalin history
was choked, that there were latent questions and a dynamic of the
system which were not given expression. Those are beings of
reason. There are men and things; things are mute, and meaning
is only found in men. Thus history merges into official history.
Those who have lived in the U.S.S.R. know that this is not the case
and that Malenkov's or Stalin's action, and even planning itself,
are episodes or aspects of an actual functioning of the U.S.S.R.
which includes official decisions but also the unofficial cycles of
production and of exchange, the makeshift measures of leaders
behind schedule on the plan, the unwritten distribution of powers,
the questions unformulated but present in opposition, "sabotage,"
and "espionage." Only God knows this true history, and one cannot judge the U.S.S.R. on the unknowable. But it would be a little
bit less unknowable if the proletariat had a political life in the
U.S.S.R. Then one could say that, whatever its defects for an
absolute observer, the system is everything that a revolutionary
dictatorship can humanly be. Without this guarantee, it cannot
be judged. One cannot at the same time play both the game of
truth and that of "pure" morality. If communism is true, it does
not need so much respect; and if it is only respectable, this is because it is chiefly intention. To say, as Sartre does, that it *will* be
true is to bet on our power of forgetfulness, on the dizziness of
freedom and of the future, and, at the same time, to cover the bet
with a veil of reason. But it was already objected to Pascal that an
eternity of imaginary happiness could not possibly be the equivalent of a moment of life.

It seems to us, therefore, that one can draw only an agnostic
conclusion from his analyses. To adhere in principle to a "pure
action" which cannot be translated into facts without equivocation is to throw probabilities overboard in a domain where there
is only the probable. Anyone who either closely or remotely associates himself with the communist enterprise for reasons like
Sartre's thereby becomes impervious to experience. Agnosticism,
on the contrary, is first of all the promise to examine, without
fervor and without disparagement, all that one can know about
the U.S.S.R. This is an easy promise if one does not keep com-

munism within oneself as a remorse or resource, if one has exorcised the "optimistic twaddle" and can consider communism relatively. Agnosticism, despite the word, is here a positive behavior, a task—as, on the contrary, sympathy is here an abstention. It still remains to be clarified what politics can be deduced from this position. Let us say here only that a-communism (and it alone) obliges us to have a positive politics, to pose and resolve concrete problems instead of living with one eye fixed on the U.S.S.R. and the other on the United States. As to the benefits that communist action can reap from this frank politics, the rule is to face the stratagem of things and to thwart that of men. If the right to strike, political liberties, and the fulfillment of our promises to the colonies risks bringing communism, the risk should be run; for those who want to protect themselves from it have only to organize repression everywhere. On the contrary, men's stratagem—which presents as a politics of peace a politics which would give the U.S.S.R. victory without war, which breaks down the political problem into small problems of conscience and stakes out the path of communist actions with democratic protestations—this stratagem must be rejected, and all the more so if one is for a noncommunist left. The noncommunist left is not a left which fails to speak publicly about communism or one which, together with it, fights its enemies. To deserve its name, it must arrange a ground of coexistence between communism and the rest of the world. Now, this is in fact possible only if it does not adhere to the principle of communism: it is difficult to see why the communist world would grant the noncommunist one the concessions that are necessary from both sides to ground coexistence if those who negotiate with the U.S.S.R. declare in advance that it is in the right. One fears that a sympathetic attitude would prevent precisely those who want peace from working for it. When Sartre writes that "the U.S.S.R. wants peace," one feels uneasy in the same way as when someone gives his conclusions without giving his premises. Sartre surely knows that neither the U.S.S.R. nor the United States, nor any State with a long tradition, has ever chosen between peace and war. Only pacifist leagues and fascist States deal in these abstractions. The U.S.S.R. wants other things as well as peace, and for some time it has not appeared ready to sacrifice any of them for peace. It wanted peace but did not prevent North Korea from invading South Korea. Was this not an internal problem? Those who truly want peace and coexistence cannot dismiss as "internal problems" the communist movements that may go beyond the borders of the communist world. This does not mean that repression is called for. To hold or to surrender is a military alternative; the politics of coexistence is to act in such a way that this alternative does not arise. The noncommunist left is not practicing such a politics when it simply tells us that the U.S.S.R. wants peace. If it "understands" in communism, as the inevitable consequence of the proletarians' situation, what it cannot accept, when, then, can it say "no"? And if it says "no" only on details, by what right does it call itself noncommunist? Because it does not share the communist philosophy? But then the only freedom it retains for itself is the freedom to justify communism with different motives; it again becomes a pretext and a smoke screen. Shall one say that there are more things in communism than in all its philosophy, that there is a radical will to make be those who are nothing, a will which is not bound up with the letter of communism? This is quite certain. But for coexistence on this basis to be something other than a thought the noncommunist left has, it would at least be necessary that communism accept being right in terms of wider principles than its own, admit therefore that there are also reasons for not being communist—and this it has never done. If one wishes it to do so, one must not start by simply telling it that it is right. That is to tempt it on its weak point, which is to believe that it is alone in the world. One must, on the contrary, say that one is not a communist, and why. Coexistence is threatened when one of the partners understands the other without the other understanding him; and any agreement is illusory when one of the parties denies in thought the other's existence.

It happens that the U.S.S.R. seems to have understood all of this. It imposed an armistice in Korea, and it negotiated in Indochina when the Viet-Minh was near victory. It no longer seems to hold as impossible those buffer zones that Stalinism had suppressed. After all, it is a question of negotiating with America, not with sympathizers. The change probably goes further than one thinks. When Tito is rehabilitated and—who knows—tomorrow perhaps Slansky,[132] *objectively* one abandons the Stalinist principle according to which opposition is treason. Perhaps this

132. [Rudolf Slansky, Czech politician, member of the communist guerilla resistance during World War II, later vice-premier of Czechoslovakia. Executed for treason in 1951 and "rehabilitated" in 1963.—Trans.]

is the end of ultrabolshevism.[133] In any case, to stay with the question of peace—and if really the problem is one of the relationship between *the communists and peace*—a noncommunist left should, in matters which depend on it, push communism in the direction indicated instead of proposing a spare-tire philosophy that justifies communism as it is and that, moreover, it cannot want.

Perhaps in the end this is what Sartre will do. This would be a completely new type of sympathizer, not one who acts out of the weakness of thought which prevents one from joining or breaking when one agrees or disagrees on what is essential and which prefers to refuse tacitly what in fact it accepts, or to accept tacitly what in truth it refuses. On the contrary, sympathizing boldly because he understands situations other than his own while remaining irreducibly himself, Sartre certainly does not stand before communism like an unhappy conscience before God; he visits but does not inhabit it, he remains in the universal, and it is rather communism that he transmutes into Sartre. Tomorrow he might invent a real ground of coexistence between noncommunism and communism. This will be true if he exposes himself more, and if he puts into a politics the freedom that he so jealously keeps for himself. A philosopher's temptation is to believe that he has really joined others and has attained the concrete universal when he has given them a meaning in his universe, because for him his universe is being itself. The true universal demands that the others understand the meaning that we give them, and until now the communists have never accepted as true the image that noncommunists have formed of them. But perhaps it is Sartre's idea that they are on the brink of doing it. He writes:

> It has happened over and over again, since the Congress of Tours, that "left-wing" men or groups proclaim their *de facto* agreement with the C.P. while at the same time stressing their differences of

133. The changes that have recently taken place in the Soviet government do not exclude this hypothesis. While they may put an end to the politics of *détente* which followed Stalin's death, they cannot restore the equivocal character of ultrabolshevism, of which Stalin was more than the emblem: he was its historical bearer. As we have said, ultrabolshevism exists only as dialectic in disguise. It could thus come apart either through the "liberalization" of the regime, which stressed pragmatism in the Stalinist period, or by evolving toward a "hard" regime without Marxist principles.

principle. And if their collaboration seems desirable to the Party, it accepted this alliance *in spite of* those differences. It seems to me today that the situation has changed, both for the Party and for us, in such a way that the Party must desire such alliances in part *because of* the differences.[134]

Sartre does not mean, of course, that it is useful to the communists to rally noncommunists to serve as a smoke screen for them: this would not create the new situation of which he is speaking. No, this time the communists should seek an agreement with the noncommunists because there really is a politics common to them which not only tolerates differences of principle but demands them. This perhaps announces a reciprocal recognition between communists and noncommunists beyond the equivocations that we have emphasized—and which therefore needed to be emphasized.

ONE SEES THAT what separates us from Sartre is not the description he gives of communism but rather the conclusions he draws from it. It is true that the divergence is all the more profound because it does not come from the facts but from the way they are taken, from the answer given to them, from the relationships that one establishes between the internal and the external. It is as personal and as general as possible; it is philosophical. When Sartre passed from a philosophy that ignored the problem of the other, because it freed consciousness from any individual inherence,[135] to a philosophy which, on the contrary, makes consciousnesses rivals, because each one is a world for itself and claims to be the only one—or when he passed from conflict between rival freedoms to a relationship of call and response between them—each time his previous views were at the same time preserved and destroyed by a new intuition that they put into contrast: the other was this impossibility that, nonetheless, the "I think" could not challenge; it was this enemy that, nonetheless, freedom fed with its own substance and from which it expected response and confirmation. In going from personal history or literature to history, Sartre does not for the time being believe that he is meeting a new phenomenon which demands

134. *CP*, p. 706; *ET*, p. 68.
135. This philosophy was expressed in the article "La Transcendance de l'Ego," *Recherches philosophiques*, VI (1936–37), 85–123.

new categories. Undoubtedly he thinks that history, like language in his view, does not pose metaphysical questions which are not already present in the problem of the other: it is only a particular case to be thought through by the same means that serve to treat the other. The class "other" is so established a phenomenon that the individual other is always in competition with it. The proletarian class exists only by the pure will of a few, as language exists only as carried by a consciousness which constitutes it. Consciousness manages to make prose a transparent glass, whereas it never reads unambiguously in historical action. What is certainly new in history is that the resolution to bring into being at any cost a society which excludes no one entails a whole mythology, whereas, in prose, consciousness immediately shows itself to be universal. But this particularity of history and politics does not make them another type of being: it is only men's freedom, this time grappling with *things* that thwart it and passing beyond them. Politics and action stand out over and against everything, like appendages or extensions of personal life, and this at the very moment when it is proved that they are something else. We wonder whether action does not have both servitudes and virtues that are of an entirely different order and whether philosophy should not explore them instead of substituting itself for them. We see proof of this in the fact that Sartre does not end up with a theory of action, that he is obliged to divide the roles between a sympathy limited to pure principles and to certain aspects of action, and an action which itself is completely in the in-between. Sympathy has meaning only if others move to action. Is it not their action which is an experiment of history—their action or another, if decidedly one cannot be communist—but assuredly not the relationship of sympathy, which is at times too close, at times too remote, to be political? Is not action made up of relations, supported by categories, and carried on through a relationship with the world that the philosophy of the I and the Other does not express?

In truth, the question arose as soon as Sartre presented his conception of commitment, and it has accompanied his entire development of this idea. For, regardless of appearances, it is indeed a development at issue here, and Sartre in his present-day positions is not at all unfaithful to himself. Commitment was at first the determination to show oneself outside as one is inside, to confront behavior with its principle and each behavior with all the others, thus to say everything and to weigh everything anew, to invent a total behavior in response to the whole of the world. *Les Temps modernes* demanded of its founders that they belong to no party or church, because one cannot rethink the whole if one is already bound by a conception of the whole. Commitment was the promise to succeed where the parties had failed; it therefore placed itself outside parties, and a preference or choice in favor of one of them made no sense at a moment when it was a question of recreating principles in contact with facts. Yet something already rendered this program null and void and announced the avatars of commitment: it was the manner in which Sartre understood the relation between action and freedom. Already at that moment he was writing that one is free to commit oneself and that *one commits oneself in order to be free.* The power of acting or not acting must be exercised if it is to be more than just a word, but it remains, in the choice or after the choice, exactly what it was before; and indeed there was choice only in order to attest a power of choosing or not choosing, which, without it, would have remained potential. We never choose something for what it is, but simply to have done it, to construct for ourselves a definable past. We never choose to become or to be this or that, but to have been this or that. We are faced with a situation, we think we examine it and deliberate, but we have already taken a stand, we have acted, we suddenly find ourselves stewards of a certain past. How it becomes ours is what no one understands; it is the fact of freedom. Freedom is thus in every action and in none, never compromised, never lost, never saved, always similar. And certainly the presence of the other strongly obliges us to distinguish between behaviors which liberate others and those which enslave others, to reject the second, to prefer the first, to propagate freedom around us, to embody it. But this second freedom proceeds entirely from the first, the order is irreversible, and the preferences it leads to are always in the end pure choice. All that can be known about history and men, this encyclopedia of situations, this universal inventory that *Les Temps modernes* undertook, could not diminish by an inch the distance between radical and savage freedom and its embodiments in the world, could not establish any measure between it and a given civilization, a given action, or a given historical enterprise. For one commits oneself only to get rid of the world. Freedom is not at *work* there, it makes continual, but only momentary, appearances; and except in fascism, which fights it on all levels, it always recognizes itself in some aspect of a political system, be it on the level of intentions or on that of daily actions, and does not identify itself with any one system, for it has no means of summing up the total or the balance of an enterprise, a good not being able to redeem an evil or join with it in a comprehensive appraisal. One could thus denounce facts of oppression and speak of Blacks, Jews, Soviet camps, Moscow trials, women, and homosexuals; one could live all these situations in one's mind, make oneself personally responsible for them, and show how, in each one, freedom is flouted; but one would not find a political line for freedom, because it is embodied as much, or as little, in the diverse political actions which compete for the world, as much, or as little, in Soviet society as in American society. One can recognize in the principle of communism the most radical affirmation of freedom, for it is the decision to change the world; and one can also find unlimited good will in the heart of the American liberal, even though Puritan wickedness is never far away. This is why *Les Temps modernes* did not refuse the United States world leadership [136] at the very moment when it was attacking segregation and why, at the very moment when it was speaking of Soviet camps, it was preparing to make the U.S.S.R. the proletariat's only hope. One can confront freedom with individual acts or facts but not with regimes or large formations, for it always appears in them at some moments without ever being found in all of them. If "each person is responsible for everything before all others," that is to say, if one must take as one's own, in themselves and as if they were their own ends, each phase of an action, each detail of a regime, then actions and regimes are all alike and are worth nothing, for all of them have shameful secrets.

Commitment organizes for us a confrontation with situations the farthest removed from one another and from ourselves. This is exactly why it is so different from historical and political action, which does move within situations and facts, sacrifices this to obtain that, excuses the details in the name of the whole. As far as regimes and actions are concerned, commitment can only be indifference. If it attempts to become a politics, to invent its own solutions on the terrain of action, to impose its ubiquity, its immediate universal, on political life, it will only disguise as a double "yes" its double "no," proposing to correct democracy by

136. No. 11–12, p. 244. [The word leadership is in English in the original text.—Trans.]

revolution and revolution by democracy. It is then democracy and revolution which refuse to allow themselves to be united. What is to be done then? Should one continue the work of humanist criticism? It is good, indeed indispensable, that along with professional politicians there should be writers who, without mincing words, expose some of the scandals politics always hides, because it wraps them inside a whole. But as the situation becomes more tense and charged, commitment, even if it continues to be exercised according to its principles, becomes something else. Even though *Les Temps modernes* continued to distribute its criticism equitably, circumstances underlined some remarks, conjured away others, and gave the review an involuntary line. The study it published on the Prague trials was ignored, while what it said about the Indochinese war hit home every time. Sartre's essay on *The Communists and Peace* attests to this factual situation: since concrete freedom was not able to invent the solutions put forward there, or since these were not listened to, since circumstances have transformed his independent criticism into a political line and carried humanist commitment onto the terrain of action, Sartre accepts responsibility for a state of things which he neither wanted nor organized. When today he states a preference in principle for the U.S.S.R. and an agreement with the communists on particular points, he seems far from his initial conception of commitment; but it is not so much he that has changed as it is the world, and there is absolutely no inconsistency on his part. It remains true that freedom does not see its own image in any existing regime or political action. From communism it accepts only the internal principle of "changing the world," which is its own formula; and from communist action it accepts only some "aspects" or "particular points." No more today than yesterday is freedom made flesh, nor does it become historical action. Between freedom and what it does, the distance remains the same. Commitment is still the same brief contact with the world, it still does not take charge of it; it renders judgments only about very general principles or about facts and particular aspects of action. Quite simply, one today consents to make, if not a real balance sheet, at least an algebraic sum of these very general or very particular judgments, and one declares that it is more favorable to the U.S.S.R. Sympathy for communism and unity of action with it on certain particular points represent the maximum possible action in a conception of freedom that allows only for sudden interventions into the world,

for camera shots and flash bulbs. Today, as yesterday, commitment is action at a distance, politics by proxy, a way of putting
ourselves right with the world rather than entering it; and, rather
than an art of intervention, it is an art of circumscribing, of pre-
venting, intervention. There is thus no change in Sartre in relation to himself, and today, in a different world, he draws new
consequences from the same philosophical intuition. For Sartre,
as for Descartes, the principle of changing oneself rather than the
order of things is an intelligent way of remaining oneself over and
against everything. The preference for communism without adherence to it, like yesterday's nonpartisan critique, is an attitude,
not an action. Freedom projects its essential negation into communism and is linked to a few of its aspects; but it exempts from
scrutiny, neither approving nor blaming communist action taken
as a whole, the work which for thirty-five years has been eliciting
concrete determinations from its principles. The paradox is only
that he makes a contemplative attitude work for the benefit of
communist action. We wonder whether, rather than ending up
with this semblance of action in order to remain faithful to
principles, this would not be, on the contrary, the time to recon-
sider them; whether, instead of reducing action to the propor-
tions imposed by commitment, it would not be better to re-
examine commitment as Sartre understands it; and whether, by
so doing, we would not with a single stroke cure action of its
paralysis and remove from philosophy its gag.

As first-rate philosophical experience, the development of
Sartre's ideas, like any experience, needs to be interpreted. Sartre
thinks that the difficulties of his position today come from the
course that things have taken and leave his philosophical premises intact. We wonder whether these difficulties are not the uneasiness of a philosophy confronted with a type of relationship to
the world—history, action—that it does not want to recognize.
For commitment in Sartre's sense is the negation of the link between us and the world that it seems to assert; or rather Sartre
tries to make a link out of a negation. When I awake to life, I
find I am responsible for a variety of things I did not do but for
which I take responsibility by living. In Sartre this *de facto* commitment is always for the worse; the existing world and history
never call for anything but my indignation, and commitment in
the active sense, which is my response to the original trap, consists then in building myself, in choosing myself, in erasing my
congenital compromises, in redeeming them through what I de-

vise as their issue, in beginning myself again, and in again beginning history as well. The very way in which Sartre boorishly
approaches communism, not through the history of the undertaking, but by taking it in the present, in this instant, according
to the promises or menaces it offers to a consciousness that wants
to redeem itself through the future, shows clearly enough that it
is not so much a question of knowing where communist action is
going, so as either to associate oneself with it or not, as it is of
finding a meaning for this action in the Sartrean project. Of
course we know that no history contains its entire meaning in
itself; it is obscure and too full of meaning as long as I have not
put it in perspective. But there are perspectives which take into
account all preceding perspectives (particularly those of the
actors of the drama), which take them seriously, which attempt
to understand them even if it means putting them in their proper
place and establishing a hierarchy among them, which owe to
this contact with the perspectives of others—with their divergences, with their struggle, and with the sanction that events
have brought to these struggles—if not a demonstrative value, at
least a certain weight of experience. History itself does not give
its meaning to the historian, but it does exclude certain readings
into which the reader has obviously put too much of himself and
which do not stick closely enough to the text; and it accredits
others as probable. For Sartre this probability is the same as
nothing. But in rejecting the probable, it is theoretical and practical contact with history that he rejects; he decides to look to
history only for the illumination of a drama whose characters—
the I and the Other—are defined a priori by means of reflection.
By taking as his own the gaze that the least-favored casts on our
society, by his willingness to see himself through these eyes, by
extending an open credit of principle to the party and the regime
that claim kinship with the least-favored, Sartre seems to have
the greatest concern for the Other. But Sartre hides his reasons
from the Other; it is not Sartre that is given to him, it is almost
an official personage. The homage rendered to the principle of
communism is not only accompanied by all sorts of reservations
about the existing regime but is indeed itself a measure of opposition, since what Sartre honors in communism is "pure action," which it cannot be every day. Thus, despite appearances,
the Other is less accepted than neutralized by a general concession. The cogito empties like a container through the gap opened
by the Other's gaze; but since there is no meaning visible in

history, Sartre finds himself caught in no perspective other than his own, a perspective in which he would have to confront himself. For him, to be committed is not to interpret and criticize oneself in contact with history; rather it is to recreate one's own relationship with history as if one were in a position to remake oneself from top to bottom, it is to decide to hold as absolute the meaning one invents for one's personal history and for public history, it is to place oneself deliberately in the imaginary. The operation has no other principle than my independence of consciousness, no other result than its confirmation: for others and for history it substitutes the role I decide to let them play; it justifies in principle, but it also limits and terminates, their intervention in my life. It limits impingements, circumscribes evil, transforms the ravenous outside demands into a pact, concludes with history an accord of unity of action which is actually an accord of nonintervention. From the single fact that it is a question of committing *oneself*, that the prisoner is also his own jailer, it is clear that one will never have other bonds than those one currently gives oneself and that one never *will* be committed. Descartes said that one could not at the same time do and not do something, and this is undoubtedly how Sartre understands commitment: as the minimum of coherence and of perseverance, without which one would have had only an intention, one would have tried nothing, one would have learned nothing about the direction to follow. But in reality Descartes's formula states an endless task: when one begins to act, when will one be able to say that one has finished the endeavor? If it fails, it immediately leads us to another action; and the major proof that Sartre's thesis is not a thesis of action is that it is not susceptible of flat contradiction: the esteem in principle for pure action remains intact no matter what existing communism is like. Commitment is so strictly measured out that one cannot conceive of any circumstance that could validly undo it: it can cease only through weariness. Action is another commitment, both more demanding and more fragile: it obliges one always to bear more than what is promised or owed, and at the same time it is susceptible to failure because it addresses itself to others as they are, to the history we are making and they are making, and because it does not relate to principles and particular points but to an enterprise which we put ourselves into entirely, refusing it nothing, not even our criticism, which is part of the action and which is the proof of our commitment. In order for that kind of commitment to be possible, I must not define my relationships with the outside by contract; I must stop considering my thoughts and the meaning I give to my life as the absolute authority, my criteria and my decisions must be relativized and committed to a trial which, as we have said, can never verify them in a crucial way but which can weaken them. This praxis is just the opposite of pragmatism, for it submits its principles to a continuous critique and tries, if not to be *true*, at least *not* to be *false*. Precisely because it agrees to commit itself to more than what it knows of a party and of history, it allows more to be learned, and its motto could be *Clarum per obscurius*. Choosing according to principles or incontestable details, but without ever seeing where his reticent action leads him, Sartre on the contrary practices *Obscurius per clarum*.

Behind these two commitments there are two meanings of freedom. One is the pure power of doing or not doing, of which Descartes speaks. Remaining the same over the entire course of an action, this power fragments freedom into so many instants, making it a continued creation and reducing it to an indefinite series of acts of positing which holds it at arm's length from annihilation. This type of freedom never becomes what it does. It is never a *doing*—one cannot even see what this word might mean for it. Its action is a magical fiat; and this fiat would not even know what it is applied to if what was to be done were not simultaneously represented as *end*. This freedom that never becomes flesh, never secures anything, and never compromises itself with power is in reality the freedom to judge, which even slaves in chains have. Its equally impalpable "yes" and "no" relate only to things seen. For the power of not doing the things that are done is null at the moment one is doing them, not only, as Descartes believed, because one thereby enters into the external domain where a gesture, a movement, or a word has to either be or not be, but also because this alternative is in force even in ourselves, because what we do occupies our field and renders us, perhaps not incapable of, but unconcerned with, the rest. The pure power of doing or not doing indeed exists, but it is the power of interrupting; and from the fact that defection is always possible, it does not follow that our life needs first to obliterate this "possible" or that it interposes between me who lives and what I live a distance that all actions would arbitrarily have to overcome. With this casing of nothingness, which is simultaneously the separation and the joining of freedom and its acts, both the fiat and the representation of an *end* disappear. Life and history are there for me, in their own mode, neither *ponens* nor *tollens:* they continue and are continued even when they are transformed. My thoughts and the sense I give to my life are always caught in a swarm of meanings which have already established me in a certain position with regard to others and to events at the moment when I attempt to see clearly. And, of course, these infrastructures are not destiny; my life will transform them. But if I have a chance to go beyond them and become something other than this bundle of accidents, it is not by deciding to give my life this or that meaning; rather, it is by attempting simply to live what is offered me, without playing tricks with the logic of the enterprise, without enclosing it beforehand inside the limits of a premeditated meaning. The word "choice" here barely has a meaning, not because our acts are written in our initial situation, but because freedom does not *descend* from a power of choice to specifications which would be only an exercise, because it is not a pure source of projects which open up time toward the future, and because throughout my present, deciphered and understood as well as it can be as it starts becoming what I will be, freedom is diffused. The meaning of my future does not arise by decree; it is the truth of my experience, and I cannot communicate it other than by recounting the history that made me become this truth. How then shall I date my choices? They have innumerable precedents in my life, unless they are hollow decisions; but in that case they are compensations, and therefore they still have roots. The *end* is the imaginary object that I choose. The end is the dialectical unity of the means, Sartre said somewhere; and this would have happily corrected his abuse elsewhere of this notion, if he had not deprived himself, by rejecting dialectical thought, of the right of recourse to an open consciousness.[137] When did a communist start being a communist, and when did a renegade stop being one? Choice, like judgment, is much less a principle than a consequence, a balance sheet, a formulation which intervenes at certain moments of the internal monologue and of ac-

137. It is a misunderstanding to believe that for Sartre transcendence opens up consciousness. One might say that, for him, consciousness is nothing but an opening, since there is no opacity in it to hold it at a distance from things and since it meets them perfectly where they are, outside. But this is exactly why it does not open *onto* the world, which goes beyond its capacity of meaning; it is exactly coextensive with the world.

tion but whose meaning is formed day by day. Whether it is a question of action or even of thought, the fruitful modes of consciousness are those in which the object does not need to be posited, because consciousness inhabits it and is at work in it, because each response the outside gives to the initiatives of consciousness is immediately meaningful for it and gives rise to a new intervention on its part, and because it is in fact what it does, not only in the eyes of others but for itself. When Marx said, "I am not a Marxist," and Kierkegaard more or less said, "I am not a Christian," they meant that action is too present to the person acting to admit the ostentation of a declared choice. The declared choice is nearly the proof that there has been no choice. One certainly finds in Sartre something similar when he writes that freedom is not in the decision, that one's choices are dominated by a fundamental choice which is dateless and which is symbolized by the myth of the intelligible character. But everything takes place as if these thoughts do not intervene when it is a question for Sartre of taking a position in the present: then he returns to the ideology of choice and to "futurism."

Ultimately it is perhaps the notion of consciousness as a pure power of signifying, as a centrifugal movement without opacity or inertia, which casts history and the social outside, into the signified, reducing them to a series of instantaneous views, subordinating doing to seeing, and finally reducing action to "demonstration" or "sympathy"—reducing doing to showing or seeing done.[138] The surest way of finding action is to find it already present in seeing, which is very far from being the simple positing of something meant. A meaning, if it is posited by a consciousness whose whole essence is to know what it does, is necessarily closed. Consciousness leaves no corner of it unexplored. And if, on the contrary, one definitely admits of open, incomplete meanings, the subject must not be pure presence to itself and to the object. But neither at the level of the perceived, nor even at the level of the ideal, are we dealing with closed meanings. A perceived thing is rather a certain *variation* in relation to a norm or to a spatial, temporal, or colored level, it is a certain distortion, a certain "coherent deformation" of the permanent links which unite us to sensorial fields and to a world. And in the same way an idea is a certain excess in our view in regard to the

138. [In the French: "le faire au faire-voir ou au voir-faire."—Trans.]

available and closed meanings whose depository is language and their reordination around a virtual focus toward which they point but which they do not circumscribe. If this is so, the thought of thoughts, the *cogito*, the pure appearance of something to someone—and first of all of myself to myself—cannot be taken literally and as the testimony of a being whose whole essence is to know itself, that is to say, of a consciousness. It is always through the thickness of a field of existence that my presentation to myself takes place. The mind is always thinking, not because it is always in the process of constituting ideas but because it is always directly or indirectly tuned in on the world and in cycle with history. Like perceived things, my tasks are presented to me, not as objects or ends, but as reliefs and configurations, that is to say, in the landscape of praxis. And just as, when I bring an object closer or move it further away, when I turn it in my hands, I do not need to relate its appearances to a single scale to understand what I observe, in the same way action inhabits its field so fully that anything that appears there is immediately meaningful for it, without analysis or transposition, and calls for its response. If one takes into account a consciousness thus engaged, which is joined again with itself only across its historical and worldly field, which does not touch itself or coincide with itself but rather is divined and glimpsed in the present experience, of which it is the invisible steward, the relationships between consciousnesses take on a completely new aspect. For if the subject is not the sun from which the world radiates or the demiurge of my pure objects, if its signifying activity is rather the perception of a *difference* between two or several meanings—inconceivable, then, without the dimensions, levels, and perspectives which the world and history establish around me—then its action and all actions are possible only as they follow the course of the world, just as I can change the spectacle of the perceived world only by taking as my observation post one of the places revealed to me by perception. There is perception only because I am part of this world through my body, and I give a meaning to history only because I occupy a certain vantage point in it, because other possible vantage points have already been indicated to me by the historical landscape, and because all these perspectives already depend on a truth in which they would be integrated. At the very heart of my perspective, I realize that my private world is already being used, that there is "behavior" that concerns it, and that the other's place in it is already prepared, because I find other historical situations to be occupiable by me. A consciousness that is truly engaged in a world and a history on which it has a hold but which go beyond it is not insular. Already in the thickness of the sensible and historical fabric it feels other presences moving, just as the group of men who dig a tunnel hear the work of another group coming toward them. Unlike the Sartrean consciousness, it is not visible only for the other: consciousness can see him, at least out of the corner of its eye. Between its perspective and that of the other there is a link and an established way of crossing over, and this for the single reason that each perspective claims to envelop the others. Neither in private nor in public history is the formula of these relationships "either him or me," the alternative of solipsism or pure abnegation, because these relationships are no longer the encounter of two For-Itselfs but are the meshing of two experiences which, without ever coinciding, belong to a single world.

The question is to know whether, as Sartre says, there are only *men* and *things* or whether there is also the interworld, which we call history, symbolism, truth-to-be-made. If one sticks to the dichotomy, men, as the place where all meaning arises, are condemned to an incredible tension. Each man, in literature as well as in politics, must assume all that happens instant by instant to all others; he must be immediately universal. If, on the contrary, one acknowledges a mediation of personal relationships through the world of human symbols, it is true that one renounces being instantly justified in the eyes of everyone and holding oneself responsible for all that is done at each moment. But since consciousness cannot in practice maintain its pretension of being God, since it is inevitably led to delegate responsibility— it is one abdication for another, and we prefer the one which leaves consciousness the means of knowing what it is doing. To feel responsible for everything in the eyes of everyone and present to all situations—if this leads to approving an action which, like any action, refuses to acknowledge these principles, then one must confess that one is imprisoned in words. If, on the contrary, one agrees that no action assumes as its own all that happens, that it does not reach the event itself, that all actions, even war, are always symbolic actions and count as much upon the effect they will have as a meaningful gesture and as the mark of an intention as upon the direct results of the event—if one thus renounces "pure action," which is a myth (and a myth of the spectator consciousness), perhaps it is then that one has the best chance of changing the world. We do not say that this margin we give ourselves serves only our personal comfort, by endowing knowledge and literature with a good conscience that pure action refuses them. If truly all action is symbolic, then books are in their fashion actions and deserve to be written in accordance with the standards of the craft, without neglecting in any way the duty of unveiling. If politics is not immediate and total responsibility, if it consists in tracing a line in the obscurity of historical symbolism, then it too is a craft and has its technique. Politics and culture are reunited, not because they are completely congruent or because they both adhere to the event, but because the symbols of each order have echoes, correspondences, and effects of induction in the other. To recognize literature and politics as distinct activities is perhaps finally the only way to be as faithful to action as to literature; and, on the contrary, to propose unity of action to a party when one is a writer is perhaps to testify that one remains in the writer's world: for unity of action has a meaning between parties, each one bringing its own weight and thus maintaining the balance of the common action. But between him who handles signs and him who handles the masses there is no contact that is a political act—there is only a delegation of power from the former to the latter. In order to think otherwise, one must live in a universe where all is meaning, politics as well as literature: one must be a writer. Literature and politics are linked with each other and with the event, but in a different way, like two layers of a single symbolic life or history. And if the conditions of the times are such that this symbolic life is torn apart and one cannot at the same time be both a free writer and a communist, or a communist and an oppositionist, the Marxist dialectic which united these opposites will not be replaced by an exhausting oscillation between them; they will not be reconciled by force. One must then go back, attack obliquely what could not be changed frontally, and look for an action other than communist action.

Epilogue

On that day, everything was possible . . . the future was present . . . that is to say, time was no more a lightning flash of eternity.

Michelet, *Histoire de la Révolution française*, IV, 1

The question today is less of revolutionizing than of establishing the revolutionary government.

Correspondence of the Committee of Public Safety.

DIALECTIC IS NOT THE IDEA of a reciprocal action, nor that of the solidarity of opposites and of their sublation. Dialectic is not a development which starts itself again, nor the cross-growth of a quality that establishes as a new order a change which until then had been quantitative—these are consequences or aspects of the dialectic. But taken in themselves or as properties of being, these relationships are marvels, curiosities, or paradoxes. They enlighten only when one grasps them in our experience, at the junction of a subject, of being, and of other subjects: between *those* opposites, in *that* reciprocal action, in *that* relationship between an inside and an outside, between the elements of *that* constellation, in *that* becoming, which not only becomes but becomes for itself, there is room, without contradiction and without magic, for relationships with double meanings,

[203]

for reversals, for opposite and inseparable truths, for sublations, for a perpetual genesis, for a plurality of levels or orders. There is dialectic only in that type of being in which a junction of subjects occurs, being which is not only a spectacle that each subject presents to itself for its own benefit but which is rather their common residence, the place of their exchange and of their reciprocal interpretation. The dialectic does not, as Sartre claims, provide finality, that is to say, the presence of the whole in that which, by its nature, exists in separate parts; rather it provides the global and primordial cohesion of a field of experience wherein each element opens onto the others. It is always conceived as the expression or truth of an experience in which the commerce of subjects with one another and with being was previously instituted. It is a thought which does not constitute the whole but which is situated in it. It has a past and a future which are not its own simple negation; it is incomplete so long as it does not pass into other perspectives and into the perspectives of others. Nothing is more foreign to it than the Kantian conception of an ideality of the world which is the same in everyone, just as the number two or the triangle is the same in every mind, outside of meetings or exchanges: the natural and human world is unique, not because it is parallelly constituted in everyone or because the "I think" is indiscernible in myself and in the other, but because our difference opens onto that world, because we are imitatable and participatable through each other in this relationship with it.

The adventures of the dialectic, the most recent of which we have retraced here, are errors through which it must pass, since it is in principle a thought with several centers and several points of entry, and because it needs time to explore them all. With the name "culture," Max Weber identified the primary coherence of all histories. Lukács believes it possible to enclose them all in a cycle which is closed when all meanings are found in a present reality, the proletariat. But this historical fact salvages universal history only because it was first "prepared" by philosophical consciousness and because it is the emblem of negativity. Thence comes the reproach of idealism that is made against Lukács; and the proletariat and revolutionary society as he conceives them are indeed ideas without historical equivalents. But what remains of the dialectic if one must give up reading history and deciphering in it the becoming-true of society? Nothing of it is left in Sartre. He holds as utopian this continued intuition which was to be confirmed every day by the development of action and of revolutionary society and even by a true knowledge of past history. To dialectical philosophy, to the truth that is glimpsed behind irreconcilable choices, he opposes the demand of an intuitive philosophy which wants to see all meanings immediately and simultaneously. There is no longer any ordered passage from one perspective to another, no completion of others in me and of me in others, for this is possible only in time, and an intuitive philosophy poses everything in the instant: the Other thus can be present to the I only as its pure negation. And certainly one gives the Other his due, one even gives him the absolute right to affirm his perspective, the I consents to this in advance. But it only consents: how *could it accompany* the Other in his existence? In Sartre there is a plurality of subjects but no intersubjectivity. Looked at closely, the absolute right that the I accords to the other is rather a duty. They are not joined in action, in the relative and the probable, but only in principles and on condition that the other stick rigorously to them, that he does credit to his name and to the absolute negation that it promises. The world and history are no longer a system with several points of entry but a sheaf of irreconcilable perspectives which never coexist and which are held together only by the hopeless heroism of the I.

Is it then the conclusion of these adventures that the dialectic was a myth? The illusion was only to precipitate into a historical fact—the proletariat's birth and growth—history's total meaning, to believe that history itself organized its own recovery, that the proletariat's power would be its own suppression, the negation of the negation. It was to believe that the proletariat was in itself the dialectic and that the attempt to put the proletariat in power, temporarily exempted from any dialectical judgment, could put the dialectic in power. It was to play the double game of truth and authoritarian practice in which the will ultimately loses consciousness of its revolutionary task and truth ceases to control its realization. Today, as a hundred years ago and as thirty-eight years ago, it remains true that no one by himself is subject nor is he free, that freedoms interfere with and require one another, that history is the history of their dispute, which is inscribed and visible in institutions, in civilizations, and in the wake of important historical actions, and that there is a way to understand and situate them, if not in a system with an exact and definitive hierarchy and in the perspective of a *true*, homogeneous, ultimate society, at least as different episodes of a single life, where each one is an experience of that life and can pass into those who follow. What then is obsolete is not the dialectic but the pretension of terminating it in an end of history, in a permanent revolution, or in a regime which, being the contestation of itself, would no longer need to be contested from the outside and, in fact, would no longer have anything outside it.

We have already said something about the concept of the end of history, which is not so much Marxist as Hegelian and—even if one construes it with A. Kojève [1] as the end of humanity and the return to the cyclical life of nature—is an idealization of death and could not possibly convey Hegel's core thought. If one completely eliminates the concept of the end of history, then the concept of revolution is relativized; such is the meaning of "permanent revolution." It means that there is no definitive regime, that revolution is the regime of creative imbalance,[2] that there will always be other oppositions to sublate, that there must therefore always be an opposition within revolution. But how can one be sure that an internal opposition is not an opposition to revolution? We thus see the birth of a very singular institution: official criticism, a caricature of permanent revolution. One would be wrong to think that it is only a ruse, a mask, or an application of Machiavelli's famous prescription which teaches that one rules better through persuasion than through force and that the summit of tyranny is seduction. It is probable that true demands and true changes pass through this door. But it is also certain that they only serve to make the apparatus' grip stronger and that, when it has become an element of power, criticism must stop at the moment at which it becomes interesting, when it would evaluate, judge, and virtually contest the power in its totality. In principle, then, this power is unaware of its truth—the picture

    1. [Alexander Kojève, the author of several noted philosophical works, including the *Introduction à la lecture de Hegel* (Paris, 1947). Selections from this work have been translated into English by James Nichols in *Introduction to the Reading of Hegel* (New York, 1969). Merleau-Ponty and Sartre were influenced by his lectures at the Ecole des Hautes Etudes during the latter part of the 1930s.—Trans.]
    2. "For an indefinitely long time and in constant internal struggle, all social relations undergo transformation. Society keeps on changing its skin. . . . Revolutions in economy, technique, sciences, the family, morals, and everyday life develop in complex reciprocal action and do not allow society to achieve equilibrium" (Leon Trotsky, *The Permanent Revolution and Results and Prospects*, trans. J. Wright and B. Pearce [New York, 1969], p. 132).

that those who do not exercise the power have of it. The truth that it claims is only that of its intentions, and thus its truth becomes a general license for coercion, while the regime's practical necessities become an adequate basis for affirmation. Truth and action destroy each other, while dialectic asks that they sustain each other. As we said, this is a caricature of permanent revolution; and one may perhaps propose a return to the original. But the question is to know whether there is an original, other than in the realm of the imaginary; whether the revolutionary enterprise, a violent enterprise directed toward putting a class in power and spilling blood to do so, is not obliged, as Trotsky said, to consider itself absolute; whether it can make room in itself for a power of contestation and thereby relativize itself; whether something of the belief in the end of history does not always remain in it; whether the permanent revolution, a refined form of that belief, does not strip itself, once in power, of its dialectical-philosophical meaning; and finally, whether the revolution does not by definition bring about the opposite of what it wants by establishing a new elite, albeit in the name of permanent revolution. If one concentrates all the negativity and all the meaning of history in an existing historical formation, the working class, then one has to give a free hand to those who represent it in power, since *all that is other is an enemy*. Then there no longer is an opposition, no longer a manifest dialectic. Truth and action will never communicate if there are not, along with those who act, those who observe them, who confront them with the truth of their action, and who can aspire to replace them in power. There is no dialectic without opposition or freedom, and in a revolution opposition and freedom do not last for long. It is no accident that all known revolutions have degenerated: it is because as established regimes they can never be what they were as movements; precisely because it succeeded and ended up as an institution, the historical movement is no longer itself: it "betrays" and "disfigures" itself in accomplishing itself. Revolutions are true as movements and false as regimes. Thus the question arises whether there is not more of a future in a regime that does not intend to remake history from the ground up but only to change it and whether this is not the regime that one must look for, instead of once again entering the circle of revolution.

Inside revolutionary thought we find not dialectic but equivocalness. Let us try to lay bare its driving force while it is still in a state of purity. It always grants a double historical perspective. On the one hand, revolution is the "fruit" of history, it brings to light forces which existed before it; the course of things carries this apparent rupture in the course of things, and revolution is a particular case of historical development (Trotsky even said: an "incidental expense" [3] of historical development)—revolution puts the development back on tracks which are the tracks of history. Considered in such a way, revolution can happen only at a certain date when certain external conditions are united. It thus ripens in history, it is prepared in what precedes it through the constitution of a class which will eliminate the old ruling class and take its place; it is a fact or an effect, it imposes itself even on those who do not want to recognize it. This is what the Marxist term "objective conditions" so well expresses: for the objective conditions of revolution are the revolution insofar as it is in things and incontestable (if not for those who are not at all revolutionary, at least for theoreticians who are not immediately revolutionary); the "objective" conditions are, ultimately, the revolution seen from outside and by others. The elimination of a class by the one it oppressed or exploited is an advance that history itself accomplishes. Such is the foundation of revolutionary optimism. But it would not be revolutionary if it contented itself with recording an objective development. The objective conditions can indeed weigh heavily on the consciousness forming in the rising class, but in the end it is men who make their history. The historical advent of a class is not an effect or a result of the past; it is a struggle, and the consciousness that it gains of its strength on the occasion of its first victories itself modifies the "objective" relationship of the forces—victory calls for victory. There is an "internal mechanism" which makes the revolution exalt itself and, in meaning and power, go beyond the strict framework of the average objective conditions, the given historical surroundings. A little while ago revolution was a wave of history. Now, on the contrary, history reveals its revolutionary sub-

3. "We do not want to negate or underrate revolutionary cruelties and horrors; . . . they are inseparable from the whole historical development. . . . These tragic hazards enter into the inevitable incidental expenses of a revolution *which is itself an incidental expense in the historical development*" (italics added) (Leon Trotsky, *Histoire de la Révolution russe*, III, 177, 63 [*History of the Russian Revolution*, trans. Max Eastman (London, 1932–33)]. Cited by Daniel Guérin, *La Lutte des classes sous la Ire République* (Paris, 1946), II, 50.

stance: it is continual revolution, and it is the phases of stagnation that are to be interpreted as particular cases and temporary modalities of an essential imbalance resident in all of history. In this new light, revolution as an objective fact, as the substitution of one ruling class for another, is far from being a completion. The establishment in power of a class, which was previously seen as progress, also appears as regression or reaction. Precisely because it rules, the new ruling class tends to make itself autonomous. The essence of revolution is to be found in that instant in which the fallen class no longer rules and the rising class does not yet rule. This is where one catches a glimpse, as Michelet put it, of "a revolution under the revolution." [4] He goes on to say: "The French Revolution in its rapid appearance, in which it accomplished so little, saw, in the glimmers of lightning, unknown depths, abysses of the future." [5] To establish a class in power is, rather than revolution itself, to be robbed of the revolution; the open depths close themselves, the new ruling class turns against those who had helped it to triumph and who were already moving beyond it, reinstating over them its positive power, which is already being challenged. Revolution is progress when one compares it to the past, but it is deception and abortion when one compares it to the future that it allowed a glimpse of and smothered. Marxist thought attempts to unite and hold together these two concepts of revolution, revolution as an incidental expense of historical development and history as permanent revolution. Its equivocal character lies in the fact that it does not succeed in doing so. The synthesis is sought at that point of history's maturity in which historical and objective development will lend such support to the internal mechanism of history that the permanent revolution can establish itself in power. History as maturation and history as continued rupture would coincide: it would be the course of things which would produce as its most perfect fruit the negation of all historical inertia. In other words, history will secrete a class that will put an end to the mystifications of unsuccessful revolutions

4. Jules Michelet, *Histoire de la Revolution française* (Paris, 1939), p. 19; English translation by Charles Cocks, *History of the French Revolution* (Chicago, 1967). [The reference is to the 1868 second preface, which is not found in the English edition. Michelet (1798–1874) was known for his liberal views and exactitude in historical study.—Trans.]
5. *Ibid.*, p. 21; ET, p. 13 [translation modified].

because it will not be a new positive power which, after dispossessing the fallen classes, would in turn assert its own particularity; rather, it will be the last of all classes, the suppression of all classes and of itself as a class. If one focuses history on this future, if one calls it the proletariat and the proletarian revolution, it becomes legitimate to attribute the equivocations of preceding revolutions to the "bourgeoisie": they were at once progress and failure, nothing in them was pure, nothing exemplary; they were contradictory because they put into power a class which was not universal. But *there is* a class which *is* universal and which therefore will accomplish what all the others have vainly begun. And in this certitude of an already present future, Marxism believes it has found the synthesis of its optimism and its pessimism. The whole Trotskyite analysis of permanent revolution, which allowed us to deeply penetrate revolution as the sublation of given conditions, as an interhuman drama, as a struggle and a transtemporal creation, suddenly turns into the simple description of a state of historical maturity in which the subjective and objective conditions concur. Philosophical naturalism and realism, which remain the framework of Marxist thought at the very moment it plunges into the analysis of struggle and intersubjectivity, allow Trotsky, under the guise of an ineluctable future, to situate in the development of things, and to attribute to a class which objectively exists, this crossing of time and this permanent negativity and, finally, to give this philosophical investiture to proletarian power. But of course, once "naturalized," the revolutionary process is hardly recognizable; and, once raised to the dignity of truth in action, proletarian power is autonomized, remaining revolution only for itself. It becomes extreme subjectivism, or, what amounts to the same thing, extreme objectivism, and cannot, in any case, bear the gaze of an opposition. The question is to know whether one can attribute to the *bourgeoisie* alone and can explain as the particularities of that same class (which would make them a surmountable historical fact) the equivocations, the betrayal, and the ebb of past revolutions; whether the proletarian revolution, as a revolution without equivocation, and the proletariat as the final class are something other than an arbitrary way of closing history or prehistory, an ingenuous meta-history into which we project all our disgust, taking the risk of assuring a new victory to the mystifications of history, which would be all the more serious since so much is expected.

These reflections arise when one reads the very beautiful book that Daniel Guérin has written on the French revolution.[6] The double game of Marxist thought and the *coup de force* by which it finally escapes its equivocations are presented here in a light that is all the more convincing since, by virtue of knowledge, of revolutionary sympathy and honesty, the author has assembled rich historical material which contests his Marxist categories without his desiring or knowing it. In appearance everything is clear: the Mountain,[7] the revolutionary government, Robespierre's action, and indeed the French Revolution are progressive when one compares them to the past, regressive when one compares them to the Revolution of the Bras Nus.[8] Guérin shows very convincingly that we are witnessing the advent of the bourgeoisie, that it uses the support of the Bras Nus against the old ruling classes but then turns against them when they want to push on to direct democracy. When one speaks of the links between the Mountain and the bourgeoisie, it is not a matter of conjecture: the maneuver is conscious and clearly appears in the writings, action, speeches, and official correspondence of the members of the Committee of Public Safety,[9] particularly of the "specialists." Cambon [10] is a representative of the new bourgeoisie, not "objectively" and in spite of his intentions, but very deliberately, as his profitable operations on behalf of the national wealth show. And the evolution from the Gironde [11] to

6. Guérin, *La Lutte des classes*.

7. [The Mountain or Montagne: A group in the Convention which occupied the highest benches, from which comes their name. They voted the most violent measures in the Convention. Danton, also one of the founders of the Committee of Public Safety, was one of its members. He was executed by Robespierre in 1794.—Trans.]

8. [Guérin takes the term from Michelet's *History of the French Revolution*, where it originally referred to the workers doing difficult physical labor. Guérin uses it to distinguish, insofar as was possible at the time, the workers from the petty bourgeoisie.—Trans.]

9. [The Committee of Public Safety, consisting of twelve members and headed by Robespierre, was organized in 1793 to concentrate the executive powers of the Convention. Robespierre was its leading member until he was overthrown on the ninth of Thermidor, Year II (July 27, 1794).—Trans.]

10. [Joseph Cambon, member of the Convention, who in 1793 drew up the *Grand Livre* of the public debt.—Trans.]

11. [The Gironde: A group of revolutionary delegates whose original leaders came from the department of the Gironde. They sat on the right side of the Convention and were opposed to the "Mountain"

the Mountain takes place through the conversion of a part of the bourgeoisie, which until then had occupied itself with trade and shipping, to new forms of exploitation. No one can question, therefore, the equivocal character of the French Revolution or that it was the installation in power of a class which intended to stop the revolution the moment its own privileges were secured. There is no dispute about the fact, but there is reason to discuss its meaning. Can one be content with Guérin's analysis and say with him that the French Revolution and the revolutionary government's dictatorship are progress *and* reaction? Can one dissociate these two aspects or relations of the event? For Guérin stresses that the objective conditions of a total revolution were not present. At that time in France there was not a sufficient mass of conscious proletarians to pass beyond the bourgeoisie's interests and go on to the proletarian revolution. Thus, within the given conditions, only a bourgeois revolution was possible, and the revolution had to stop there. Yet, as Guérin says, borrowing a phrase from Vergniaud,[12] to stop is to recede. Thus the dictatorship of the revolutionary government had to be supplanted by Thermidor and Bonaparte. But with the same stroke, the whole is found to be justified and historically founded, true in relation to the circumstances of the time, and all the more reason to justify Robespierre's thought as an effort to reunite the two truths of the time, to stabilize the revolution. The Enragés and the Hébertists,[13] who were polemizing against the revolutionary government and demanding application of the 1793 constitution, "forgot that the men of the Mountain were still a minority in the country and that new elections risked giving birth to an assembly even more reactionary than the Convention." [14] They "lost sight of the necessity of a dictatorship to subdue the counterrevolution." [15] "The persecutions of which the avant-garde had been the

---

group, seated on the left. The Girondists were ousted by the men of the Mountain in 1793, and many of its members were guillotined, among them Brissot.—Trans.]

12. [Pierre-Victurnien Vergniaud, member of the Convention.—Trans.]

13. [Jacques René Hébert, editor of the *Père Duchesne,* one of the violent revolutionary newspapers, which approved the September massacres. Arrested by Robespierre, he was executed together with a large number of his followers, who were called Hébertists or Enragés.—Trans.]

14. Guérin, *La Lutte des classes,* II, 60.

15. *Ibid.,* II, 332, footnote.

victim made it lose sight of the *relatively progressive* character
of the revolutionary government, despite its reactionary aspects.
With its thoughtless diatribes it played the game of counterrevolution." [16] If the proletarian revolution is not ripe, Robespierre is
relatively progressive and the leftism of the Bras Nus relatively
counterrevolutionary. Given the conditions of the time, the revolutionary government and Robespierre represent success. They
were the ones who had a chance to make history advance, they
are the ones who exist, if not humanly, at least politically and
historically. Ultimately it was not the forced rate of the *assignats*,[17] the demonetization of money, the total taxation, the unlimited powers of the representatives in the field to suspend the
laws, raise taxes, sentence to death, and contest the local powers
or the agents of the central power; nor was it the subjection of
hoarders to search without warrants or the expeditions of the
"revolutionary armies" among the peasants which moved in the
direction of the history of the moment. Rather, as was said in the
correspondence of the Committee of Public Safety, ultrarevolution was counterrevolution; and Guérin cannot think differently,
for he admits that at that date it could not pass into fact. "The
question today is not so much to revolutionize as to organize the
revolutionary government," [18] wrote the Committee of Public
Safety, and this means that the Bras Nus's action at the time in
question was incompatible with any government. While imprisoned by the revolutionary government, Varlet [19] was to
write that, "For any reasoning being, government and revolution
are incompatible." [20] This means that the government was counterrevolutionary but also that the revolution made government
impossible and that, in a time when the direct democracy of the
Bras Nus could not lean upon a sufficiently numerous and solid
avant-garde to replace the government, Robespierre was right in
his struggle against them. The Bras Nus were impulse; together
with the bourgeoisie, the revolutionary government was technique. Confronting each other here through the existing classes

16. *Ibid.*, p. 351.
17. [*Assignats* was the name for French paper money from 1789
to 1797.—Trans.]
18. Guérin, *La Lutte des classes*, II, 7.
19. [Jean Varlet, a young postal clerk, who became famous in
1791. A champion of the industrial workers, he was referred to as an
Enragé and was a member of the Hébertist party.—Trans.]
20. Guérin, *La Lutte des classes*, II, 59.

were revolution as immediate will and instituted revolution, revolution as a fact of intersubjectivity and revolution as a historical fact.

> The substitution of bourgeois technique for popular ardor is one of the essential phenomena of the last phase of the Revolution. We have already seen this take place in the domain of waging war. The mass movement that had conferred on the Revolution an irresistible impulse and had allowed it to face external danger and to crush the internal enemy found itself little by little driven back. The regime lost its dynamism. But this inconvenience also had corresponding advantages: the establishment of a strong power, administrative centralization, and the rational and methodical organization of requisitions, war manufacturing, and military operations gave it a strength which no other European power possessed at that time. This skeleton of a totalitarian state, as one says today, assured it victory.[21]

Guérin adds that it was "a victory of the bourgeoisie, not of the people." But at that time no other victory was possible but the bourgeoisie's, and the choice was between that victory and the Restoration. Consequently, it is paradoxical to look to the Bras Nus for *what really happened* and to recount the entire history of the French Revolution as merely an internal quarrel of the bourgeoisie, as if the nuances of the bourgeoisie did not at that time in history represent the gauge of human possibilities. When he wants to find the 1793 proletariat, Guérin is, of course, obliged to put aside the Gironde, but also the Mountain and, naturally, the "specialists" and Robespierre and the Hébertists and even the "plebeians," who came from the side of the Bras Nus but who were also thinking of holding office. In short, all the professional revolutionaries have to be listed on the side of the bourgeoisie, and only those who had no part in the official powers represent the proletariat. One cannot say of Robespierre that he was a conscious bourgeois; unlike most of his colleagues, he did not take advantage of the Revolution to get rich. But he was a "petty bourgeois," that is to say, as Marx teaches, a living contradiction —capable of understanding the Bras Nus but still a man of order and of government. But if this was the contradiction of the age, Robespierre, in his hour, was historical man; and one must say the same of his colleagues, even the corrupt ones and the bankers who "financed the Revolution" or advised keeping the gold stand-

21. *Ibid.*, II, 22.

ard because the Republic could not win the war without buying abroad. Focusing the whole Revolution on the action of the Bras Nus which, one admits, could not succeed, leads us to underestimate the struggles between the Gironde and the Mountain, between Danton and Robespierre, between Robespierre and the Thermidorians, when indeed this is the history of the French Revolution, and to hold as true history a history which did not occur: that of the proletarian revolution, which emerged along with the action of the Bras Nus but which could not be a political fact. The history which was is replaced by the history which could have occurred in another time, and the French Revolution then completely disappears into a future that it hatched and smothered, the proletarian revolution. If we want to understand history—that which at a given moment was present and on which the contemporaries staked their lives—one must, on the contrary, admit that what exists historically is not the heroism of the Bras Nus, which could not, as we are told, inscribe itself in a politics and mark history, but rather it is what the others contrived to do in the juncture, according to the inspiration of the revolutionary spirit, but also keeping in mind the "ebb" and thus their prejudices, their idiosyncrasies, their manias, and also, on occasion, their role as "men of order." All this, summarily imputed to the "bourgeoisie," belongs to the history of the Revolution—a bourgeois revolution, but at that time there was no other, and the "bourgeoisie" was history itself. The two historical perspectives that Marxist thought would like to assemble come apart: if history is maturation, objective development, then it is Robespierre who is right, and the Bras Nus are right only later on, which is to say that they are wrong for the moment. And if history is permanent revolution, time does not exist, there is no past, all of history is only the eve of a tomorrow which is always deferred, the privation of a being which will never be, it awaits a pure revolution in which it would sublate itself.

Guérin would undoubtedly say: *in which it will sublate itself* —and that is the whole question. For if we admit that in a given moment—let us say the French Revolution—it is impossible to distinguish between what is progressive and what is reactionary or to accept one as "proletarian" and to refuse the other as "bourgeois," if both must be accepted or refused together in the absolute of the moment as the objective aspect and the subjective aspect, the "outside" and the "inside" of the Revolution, the question arises of knowing whether at every moment of every revolution the same kind of ambiguity will not be found again, whether revolution will not always have to take account of an inert "outside" in which it must nevertheless inscribe itself if it wants to pass into history and uncontested fact. Of course, stages will have been crossed, the proletariat will be more numerous and perhaps more homogeneous than it was in 1793, the constituted bourgeoisie will perhaps no longer be there to dispute the power. We do not at all want to say that history repeats itself and that everything amounts to the same thing; but the same typical situation will be reproduced, in the sense that we will always have to deal with something only "relatively progressive," that revolution, precisely if one calls it permanent, will always have to take inertia into account, that it will never break through history, that we will never see it face to face, that it will always be possible to treat the Robespierre of the epoch as a "petty bourgeois" and to condemn him in the perspective of the Bras Nus, as it will also always be possible to place in evidence the historical role of "specialists" and "technicians" at the expense of "popular ardor." For it to be otherwise, it would be necessary for the revolution to stop being a government, for the revolution itself to replace government. As Babeuf [22] said, "Those who govern make revolution only to continue governing. We want to make one to assure the people of an everlasting happiness through a true democracy." [23] This is exactly the question: is revolution an extreme case of government or the end of government? It is conceived in the second sense and practiced in the first. If it is the end of government, it is utopia; if it is a type of government, it always exists only in the relative and the probable, and nothing allows us to treat as the fact of a particular class and to group pell-mell under the designation of "bourgeoisie" the contradictions which break out between the exigencies of the government and those of the revolution, and even less to give ourselves, under the name of "proletarian power," a ready-made solution to this antinomy. Guérin wrote that, "If the sans-culottes [24] of this epoch had been able to elevate themselves to the notion of the dictatorship of the proletariat, they would have demanded *both* dictatorship against the enemies of the people and complete democracy for the people

22. [François-Emile Babeuf, French revolutionary who espoused a sort of communism.—Trans.]
23. Guérin, *La Lutte des classes*, II, 347.
24. [The name given by the aristocrats to the revolutionaries, who wore long pants rather than knee breeches.—Trans.]

themselves." [25] This democracy for the people and dictatorship against the enemies of the people is not in the facts; it is in Guérin's mind. We recognize in it the classical notion of a proletarian power, and it is only by conceiving everything under this category that the emergence of the true revolution is divined in the action of the Bras Nus. But how can a power which is a dictatorship against the enemies of the people be completely democratic for the people themselves? Are the limits between the "inside" and the "outside" so clear? The people cannot be seduced by the bourgeoisie, and they do not have enemies among themselves? On the other hand, cannot some bourgeois, the "specialists," at least apparently rally to the people's cause? How is one to know when a sans-culotte speaks as a sans-culotte and when he speaks as a dupe of the bourgeoisie? How is one to know when a specialist speaks as a specialist and when he speaks as a bourgeois in disguise? Thus in the end the dialectical line that Guérin draws from the Bras Nus to the future is only the projection of a wish, the wish for a power that would be action, or violence *and* truth. Yet, he will say, there were months when the Terror was that of the Bras Nus, when the dictatorship was "popular, democratic, decentralized, propelled from the bottom up." [26] "Danton proposed something completely different; he asked for a dictatorship from *above.* He proposed that the local administrators become agents of the central power, named by it and closely subordinated to it." [27] When the sans-culottes demanded the Terror, they were asking for their own terror but were given another one, that of the revolutionary government, that is, one of them wrote, "the baleful spirit of vengeance and particular hatreds." *Another* terror? Is that certain? Is it not the same terror mediated, no longer only exercised but undergone, that is to say, become governmental, and consequently striking not only the counterrevolution, but also the ultrarevolution, which "plays its game"? Trotsky did indeed distinguish between them, but Guérin reproaches him for having believed "that in the end the two dictatorships merged, once the Convention got rid of the Girondins." [28] Guérin concedes that "It is true that immediately after May 31 the two tendencies appeared for an instant to mingle, but, as was proved by the following events, this merger was only ephemeral." Alas, Trotsky

25. Guérin, *La Lutte des classes,* II, 332.
26. *Ibid.,* II, 4–5.
27. *Ibid.,* II, 9.
28. *Ibid.,* II, 6, footnote.

had governed, and one fears that he is right. Guérin proves very well that the revolutionary government turned against the immediate demands of the Bras Nus. But this does not prove that there were two opposing politics, and this is where the question lies. Guérin says that when Chaumette, the syndic prosecutor of the Paris Commune, had to take the title of national agent, he stopped being "the sans-culottes' attorney" to become "the central power's domestic." [29] But Guérin also admits that this power is "the first since the beginning of the Revolution whose statute gives it the means of executing its will." [30] If the same man, as soon as he becomes "national agent," stops serving the true Revolution, it is because the bourgeois spirit has spread well beyond the bourgeoisie, it is because it is then synonymous with official power, and because the proletarian spirit can arouse only an opposition. "Direct democracy," "dictatorship propelled from the bottom up,"—Guérin's *true solution*, as different from government terror as from bourgeois democracy—is a pompous political concept with which one clothes the Apocalypse. It is a dream of an "end of politics" out of which one wants to make a politics. Like "proletarian power," it is a problem that presents itself as a solution, a question which is given as an answer, the sublation of history in ideas.

It is true, one will say, that the Bras Nus's action in 1793 was not a political fact. But Guérin consciously takes an overview of the French Revolution. As he says, the proletarian revolution then was premature, and he himself introduces this idea in order to marshal the facts. But a more recent history would counterbalance ideas with experience. It is in relation to 1848, 1871, and 1917 that he is focusing. No one in 1793 could draw the future dialectical line, but we can see it retrospectively and throw light on 1793 by what followed. Yet could we ever, even in 1917, find realized, except episodically, a "dictatorship against the enemies of the people" which would be "completely democratic for the people themselves"? And if the episode did not last, if a truly soviet system is scarcely to be found in the history of the Russian Revolution, if it was especially before October 17 that it worked, it is perhaps because a revolution is proletarian only before it succeeds, in the movement which precedes the taking of power, in its "ardor," not in its technique. The fact is that today's soviet power

29. *Ibid.*, II, 12.
30. Sainte-Claire Deville, cited by Guérin, *ibid.*

reminds us more of the Committee of the Public Safety than of the Bras Nus. And if one still wanted to attribute the "dictatorship from the top" to the bourgeoisie, to the "remnants" of the bourgeoisie in the Soviet Union or to the bourgeoisie pressing at its borders, this would be to admit that one does not want to look at the facts, that one masks as a historical process the idea of proletarian power as the resorption of the "outside" by the "inside," of the "objective" by the "internal mechanism," and that one is guided by the phantasm of a kind of final conflagration in which, at last, desire would immediately be reality. Guérin, a historian and a Marxist, knows better than we that the "dictatorship of the proletariat" was never more than the index of a problem, and he knows how difficult it is to find a path between social democracy and the dictatorship of the party. The idea of the dictatorship of the proletariat expresses in particular our desire to find ready made in history a resolution of history's horrors, to think of history as an Odyssey, to return to a solution already given in things, or at least to base our will on a movement of things. If one takes away this ideology, what remains? Only revolutionary movements which indeed avoid the alternatives of personal dictatorship and democratic consultation because they are a resistance, because they are not a recognized power, but which have no other reason for existing than to create one, which therefore do something other than what they want to do. The abortion of the French Revolution, and of all the others, is thus not an accident which breaks a logical development, which is to be attributed to the particularities of the rising class, and which will not take place when the rising class is the proletariat: the failure of the revolution is the revolution itself. Revolution and its failure are one and the same thing.

Guérin asks himself, incidentally, why the right wing of today's bourgeoisie hates the French Revolution, which put it in power. And he gives the profound reply that it considers the French Revolution "from the viewpoint of permanent revolution" and hates in it "revolution *itself*." [31] These words bring a third dimension of the revolutionary dialectic out of the shadows: there is not only an objective development from the past which was to the present which is, and not only a subjective reconstruction of this development, starting with our present wills, but in addition there are, between the past and the present, vague links, con-

31. *Ibid.*, II, 368.

taminations, identifications, which cross the given or voluntary relationships of filiation, a kind of obliteration or deadening of the real past. Today's bourgeois is no longer the one who made the French Revolution or the one who was born from it. The bourgeoisie was, as the rising class, the revolution of the epoch, it was, for the epoch, revolution *itself;* and although it served particular interests, it was neither subjectively nor objectively reducible to these interests, its historical function was to precipitate and transform into institution, into acquisition, a new idea of social relations—and this is why, incidentally, it could sometimes rally the Bras Nus. But there is no definitive acquisition from which history can rise without losing an inch of the height it has attained: the bourgeoisie which was the revolution became the *ancien régime,* and, when reflecting on the French Revolution, it identifies itself with the old ruling class. At the same time that there is historical progress, there is, therefore, a consolidation, a destruction, a trampling of history; and at the same time as a permanent revolution, there is a permanent decadence which overtakes the ruling class in proportion as it rules and endures, for by ruling it abdicates what had made it "progressive," [32] loses its rallying power, and is reduced to the protection of private interests. Throughout history, revolutions meet one another and institutions resemble one another; every revolution is the first revolution, and every institution, even a revolutionary institution, is *tempted* by historical precedents. This does not mean that everything is in vain and that nothing can be done: each time the struggle is different, the minimum of demandable justice rises, and, besides, according to these very principles, conservatism is utopian. But this means that the revolution which would recreate history is infinitely distant, that there is a similarity among ruling classes insofar as they are ruling and among ruled classes insofar as they are ruled, and that, for this reason, historical advances cannot be added like steps in a staircase. The Marxists know this very well when they say that the dictatorship of the proletariat turns *the weapons of the bourgeoisie* against the bourgeoisie. But then a proletarian philosophy of history holds to the miracle that the dictatorship may use the bourgeoisie's weapons without becoming something like a bourgeoisie; that a class may rule without becoming decadent when in point of fact any class which rules the whole proves to be particular by

32. *Ibid.*

that very action; that a historical formation, the proletariat, may be established as a ruling class without taking upon itself the liabilities of the historical role; that it may accumulate and keep intact in itself all the energy of all past revolution and unfailingly give life to its institutional apparatus and progressively annul its degeneration. It is to act as if everything that historically exists were not *at the same time* movement and inertia, it is to place in history, as *contents*, on the one hand the principle of resistance (called the bourgeoisie) and on the other the principle of movement (called the proletariat), when these are the very *structure* of history as a passage to generality and to the institution of relationships among persons. The Committee of Public Safety was progressive relative to 1793, that is to say, absolutely progressive in its time, regardless of the fact that it was a mixed historical reality and that one can already discern in it bourgeois interests becoming autonomous. In the same way, the dictatorship of the proletariat, even if one supposes its mission to be the implanting in history of the relationships among men as the proletariat discovers them, will accomplish this work only in ambiguity and with the loss of energy which is inseparable from power and social generality. To assume that the proletariat will be able to defend its dictatorship against entanglement is to assume in history itself a substantial and given principle which would drive ambiguity from it, sum it up, totalize it, and close it (even if only by opening to history a future of pure movement); whoever assumes this principle and attempts to put it in power thereby gives investiture to an impure power. If revolution is permanent in the sense that its "final" form is already anticipated in its initial outlines, it also must be permanent in the sense that it is never completed, always relative, and that in it victory and failure are one. For it is difficult to see how this excess of "internal mechanism" over "objective conditions" which makes for historical anticipations will be annulled when a stronger and more conscious proletariat is constituted: it is the excess of "ardor" over "technique," of immediate will over institutions, of the rising class over the class in power, of civil society over the State; and to say that these differences do not exist in a proletarian power is to give a nominal definition which teaches us nothing about things. To believe in proletarian revolution is to arbitrarily assert that history's sliding back on itself and the resurrection of past ghosts are bad dreams, that history carries within itself its own cure and will surprise us with it—and, precisely because one yields to this belief, a power is established which is all the more autonomous because it is thought to be founded on objective history. If one then wants to take back one's bet, if one protests that the proletarian society is, on the contrary, a society in permanent crisis, it is because one renounces revolution: for who would undertake to make a revolution without the conviction of creating another society, not only because it will contest itself and be able to correct itself, but also because it *is the good*? One does not kill for relative progress. The very nature of revolution is to believe itself absolute and to not be absolute precisely because it believes itself to be so. If it knows itself to be relative, if it admits that it is at each moment doing something merely "relatively progressive," then it is very close to admitting that revolution and nonrevolution make a single history. On this basis a person can have sympathy for revolutions, judge them inevitable at certain times, ascertain their progress, and even associate himself with them: he still does not believe in them as they believe in themselves, he does not *make* them, he is not a revolutionary. There are undoubtedly many men of this sort in all revolutions: they work in the enterprise, they render it services, they do not put it in question, but precisely for this reason they are not revolutionaries. Revolutions allow for this astonishing division of roles: those who *are* the most revolutionary often go over to the opposition, and those who *make* the revolution are not always revolutionaries. Some few exceptional men top it all and succeed in governing while keeping their revolutionary consciousness; but whether they do so because they make the revolution or because their consciousness is satisfied with bird's-eye views, one cannot say. These men thus give the illusion of having achieved the synthesis, but the antinomy continues in them.

These remarks relatively justify communism in what it is doing: it has renounced being a society of permanent crisis and continual imbalance, replacing government by revolution and making up for the objective conditions by their "internal mechanism." There would be something healthy in this disillusionment if it were lucid; but if it were lucid and acknowledged its condition, the U.S.S.R. would cease to be the fatherland of the revolution. The fiction of proletarian power, of direct democracy, and of the withering-away of the State must therefore be all the more energetically maintained as the reality becomes more and more distant, either because for some this fraud is consciously accepted as the heritage of a project which they do not want to be-

tray or because, in the decadence of Marxist culture which results from it, the fraud ceases to be perceptible and is all the less
conscious the more it is constantly lived. Perhaps no one is closer
to the ideas we are defending here than an informed Soviet
citizen: no one is more convinced that all revolution is relative
and that there are only *progresses*. Today's communism verges
on *progressism*. If one sees more and more men who have never
shared the "illusions" of Marxism gravitating around it, it is no
accident; it is because communism has indeed renounced these
"illusions." But if it presented itself as the progressism that it is,
it would lack the conviction, the vigilance, the authority, and the
moral right to demand every sacrifice. This is why, as we have
said, the progressist is never alone, he lives only in symbiosis: behind him he must have a solid communist who works, who believes, or makes others believe, that the proletariat is in power. In
itself the Soviet regime is a progressism, but it is important that in
relation to capitalism it remains the absolute other. This is what
remains in it of the revolutionary point of honor (the phrase, of
course, being taken in the Marxist sense, for in other respects,
from all the evidence, the regime transforms the countries it
governs). It therefore amplifies, generalizes, makes irrevocable,
and extends over the entire future the equivocalness essential to
any revolutionary government, indeed to any institution. It eludes
understanding in such a way that one cannot judge it. Of course,
just as did the Committee of Public Safety, the U.S.S.R. works
in the realm of the objective, makes history, wins wars. But one
could more or less see what the Committee of Public Safety cost
and what it yielded. When, on the contrary, the apparatus becomes so dense that there is no longer an "interior" of the revolution, no one can say what history it is making or at what price.
It could be justifiable only relatively, and it refuses precisely this
justification by presenting itself as absolute. The Marxist synthesis of the subjective and the objective comes apart, leaving two
terminal formations: on the one hand, an extreme objectivism
which no longer allows us to discern the system's meaning; on
the other hand, a theory of permanent revolution which, on the
contrary, overestimates the intersubjective factors but which
ultimately challenges all instituted revolutions and therefore the
very idea of revolution.

    The revolutionary politics which, in the perspective of 1917,
was historically to take the place of "liberal" politics—occupied
with difficult organizational problems, with defense, and with im-

provements—has become more and more a politics for new countries, the means for semicolonial economies (or for civilizations long since paralyzed) to change to modern modes of production. The immense apparatus that it constructed, with its disciplines and its privileges, at the moment when it shows itself to be efficacious for building an industry or for putting a new proletariat to work, evacuates the terrain of the proletariat as ruling class and forfeits the mystery of civilization which, according to Marx, the Western proletariat carried. In the end, have the French, German, and Italian proletariats more to expect from a communist-directed regime than from the one they now live under? Is the Czech proletariat happier today than before the war? The fact that the question is asked is enough to show that the great historical politics, which had for its motto the power of the workers of all countries, is itself in crisis. We will not speculate here about the "egoism" of the advanced proletariats. What we wonder is whether, even in the future and even deducting the sacrifices which the system will ask of them in order to help the backward proletariats, they can receive from it what the communists expect. The so-called proletarian regimes frame their proletariat in an aggregate of powers whose output and social cost, and, finally, whose historical meaning, are as poorly known as the system of precapitalist societies and whose sociology is entirely left to be done. Thus, where there is a choice between famine and the communist apparatus, the decision goes without saying; but, on the contrary, wherever modern modes of production exist and, with them, certain ways of doing things, the question is to know whether, for the proletariat, communism is worth what it costs; then the enormous problem of its nature and of its real contours —a problem displaced elsewhere by the threat of death—again becomes primordial. Two rival and symmetrical maneuvers prevent us from considering communism as an unknown to be understood: on the one side, the maneuver that presents it as the heir to Marxism, on the other, the maneuver that attempts to cover up the "free world's" problems under the pretext of anticommunist defense; on the one side, the attempts to have communism accepted under Marx's shadow, on the other, the attempt to eliminate Marx's problems in favor of the anticommunist defense. Communism's nostalgia and the neurosis of anticommunism join forces to promote the equivocation we mentioned earlier between the revolutionary ideology and the "progressist" reality of the U.S.S.R. and to forbid any direct and frank view of it even with our limited information. This situation can end only with the birth of a noncommunist left. The first article of this new left should be that the rivalry between the United States and the U.S.S.R. is not between "free enterprise" and Marxism. Under the cover of philosophies that date back a century or two, the established politics are building something entirely different. In the vices as in the virtues of the two systems there are so many geographical, historical, or political conditions which intervene that the philosophies they claim are clearly mere ornaments. If we want to abandon our daydreams, we must look at the *other thing* these ornaments are hiding and put ourselves in a state of methodical doubt in regard to them. We should give them the attention without reverence that is appropriate for large, confused undertakings whose analysis and balance sheet have not yet been made—and whose collision would be the greatest of catastrophes, since those who would die would not even know why they were dying. A noncommunist left therefore sets itself the constant task of evading the antagonists' hostility, of springing the traps that the one prepares for the other, of thwarting the complicity of their pessimisms. We are not dealing here with any opportunism of the golden mean or of pacifism. A-communism is a necessary condition for knowledge of the U.S.S.R. because it confronts what we know of communist reality with communist ideology; and it is, at the same time and without paradox, the condition of a modern critique of capitalism because it alone poses Marx's problems again in modern terms. It alone is capable of a perpetual confrontation and comparison of the two systems. One glimpses a generalized economy of which they are particular cases. This awareness, and with it the action that it commands, is the task of a noncommunist left, which thus will not be a compromise between the given ideologies.

We see now in what sense one must speak of a new liberalism: it is not a question of returning to an optimistic and superficial philosophy which reduces the history of a society to speculative conflicts of opinion, political struggle to exchanges of views on clearly posed problems, and the coexistence of men to relationships of fellow citizens in the political empyrean. This kind of liberalism is no longer practiced anywhere. There is a class struggle and there must be one, since there are, and as long as there will be, classes. There is and there must be a means of exceptional action for the proletarian class, the strike, since its fate is also exceptional and since by definition it is in a minority.

Moreover, this class has the right to be represented, if it so desires, by a party which refuses the rules of the democratic game, since this game places it at a disadvantage. The Communist Party is and must be legal. In addition: there have been and there will be revolutionary movements, and they are justified by their own existence, since they are proof that the society in which they arise does not allow the workers to live. If we speak of liberalism, it is in the sense that Communist action and other revolutionary movements are accepted only as a useful menace, as a continual call to order, that we do not believe in the solution of the social problem through the power of the proletarian class or its representatives, that we expect progress only from a conscious action which will confront itself with the judgment of an opposition. Like Weber's heroic liberalism, it lets even what contests it enter its universe, and it is justified in its own eyes only when it understands its opposition. For us a noncommunist left is this double position, posing social problems in terms of struggle and refusing the dictatorship of the proletariat. Someone will say: but since this struggle is the struggle for power, either you condemn a noncommunist left to exercise power only in a parliamentary or bourgeois sense, which is the socialist dream, or for it this power is only a transition on the way to dictatorship, and then your left is cryptocommunist. A noncommunist left exercises such a freedom of criticism in regard to the dictatorship of the proletariat that its action in itself distinguishes it from communist action. To remove any equivocation, it is sufficient that the noncommunist left pose the problem of the nature of the Soviet State, which is not only to admit, with Sartre, that "the discussion is open," but to open it oneself or, in any case, to take part in it. As for the limitations of parliamentary and democratic action, there are those which result from the institution, and they should be accepted, for Parliament is the only known institution that guarantees a minimum of opposition and of truth. There are other limitations which are the result of parliamentary usage and maneuvers; these deserve no respect at all, but they can be denounced in Parliament itself. Parliamentary mystification consists in not posing the true problems or in posing them only obliquely and too late. A noncommunist left could do much against these practices. We have somewhat lost the habit of parliamentary action, and the Communist Party has played its role in this decline of the system: committed to a strategy of defending the U.S.S.R. on a world-wide scale, it oscillates between agitation and opportunism. It foregoes a harassing action, which thus falls to the noncommunist left.

This is not "a solution," and we know it full well; what we are saying is that the social realm is only beginning to be known, and, besides, a system of *conscious lives* will never admit of a solution the way a crossword puzzle does or an elementary problem of arithmetic. Our approach involves instead the resolution to keep a hand on both ends of the chain, on the social problem and on freedom. The only postulate of this attitude is that political freedom is not only, and not necessarily, a defense of capitalism. We said that there is no dialectic without freedom. But is there one with freedom? There is one if capitalism is no longer a rigid apparatus with *its* politics, *its* ideologies, and *its* imperious laws of functioning and if, under the cover of its contradictions, another politics than *its own* can pass. A noncommunist left is no more linked to free enterprise than to the dictatorship of the proletariat. It does not believe that capitalist institutions are the only mechanisms of exploitation, but it also does not judge them to be any more natural or sacred than the polished stone hatchet or the bicycle. Like our language, our tools, our customs, our clothes, they are instruments, invented for a definite purpose, which found themselves little by little burdened with an entirely different function. A complete analysis of this change in meanings has to be made, going beyond the famous analysis of surplus value, and a program of action established consequent upon it. What is sure is that nothing like this will take place without a system which proceeds, not only by plans, but also by balance sheets. Today revolutionary action is secret, unverifiable, and, just because it wants to recreate history, encumbered by burdens which have never been measured. At the same time, it has given up the philosophical guarantees of the dictatorship of the proletariat. This is why it appears to us to be less practicable now than ever before; but by this we in no way imply acceptance of the eternal laws of the capitalist order or any *respect* for this order. We are calling for an effort of enlightenment which appears to us impossible for reasons of principle under a communist regime and possible in the noncommunist world. If we overestimate the freedom of this world, the "barometer of revolution" will say so.

IT IS ALWAYS unbecoming to cite or to comment on oneself. But, on the other hand, anyone who has published his opinions on vital problems is obliged, if he changes them, to say so and to say why. In such matters, one cannot give an author the right to produce his ideas as a locomotive produces its smoke: he must relate what he thought yesterday to what he thinks to-day. Just as he would be wrong to look to his former writings for all the ideas he holds today—this would be to admit that he has not lived, that he has learned nothing in the interim—so he must explain the change. This is his main reason for being. That he thought one thing and now thinks another interests no one. But his path, his reasons, the way in which he himself understood what happened: this is what he owes to the reader, this is what he can say without any difficulty, if he has remained himself. One should not therefore be surprised that, in conclusion, we should like to connect these pages to a previous essay.[33]

Just after the war we tried to formulate a Marxist wait-and-see attitude. It seemed to us that the Soviet society was then very far from the revolutionary criteria defined by Lenin, that the very idea of a criterion of valid compromises had been abandoned, and that, consequently, the dialectic threatened to become once more the simple identity of opposites, that is to say, skepticism. A completely voluntaristic communism became evident, based entirely on the consciousness of the leaders—a renewal of the Hegelian State and not the withering-away of the State. But however "grand" Soviet "politics" may have been, we observed that the struggle of communist parties is in other countries the struggle of the proletariat as well, and it did not seem impossible that Soviet politics might thereby be brought back to the ways of Marxist politics. We said that the U.S.S.R. is not the power of the proletariat, but the Marxist dialectic continues to play its role throughout the world. It jammed when the revolution was limited to an underdeveloped country, but one feels its presence in the French and Italian labor movements. Even if the Marxist dialectic did not take possession of our history, even if we have nowhere seen the advent of the proletariat as ruling class, the dialectic continues to gnaw at capitalist society, it retains its full value as negation; it remains true, it will always be true, that a history in which the proletariat is nothing is not a human history. Since adherence to communism was, we thought, impossible, it was all the more necessary to have a sympathetic attitude which

33. Merleau-Ponty, *Humanisme et Terreur* (Paris, 1947); English translation by John O'Neill, *Humanism and Terror* (Boston, 1969).

would protect the chances of a new revolutionary flow. We said that we do not have to choose between communism as it is and its adversary. Communism is strategically on the defensive. Let us take advantage of this pause, let us watch for the signs of a renewal of proletarian politics, and let us do what we can to help it. "If it happens tomorrow that the U.S.S.R. threatens to invade Europe and to set up in every country a government of its choice, a different question would arise and would have to be examined. That question does not arise at the moment." [34]

The U.S.S.R. did not invade Europe, but the Korean War raised this "different question," which was not posed in 1947; and it is with this question that we are now dealing. We know everything that one can say concerning the South Korean regime, and we do not claim that the U.S.S.R. wanted or set off the Korean War. But since it ended it, it undoubtedly could have prevented it; and since it did not prevent it, and military action took place, our attitude of sympathy was obsolete, because its meaning was changed. In a situation of force it became an adherence in disguise. For it was very clear that any movement of the U.S.S.R. beyond its borders would be based on the struggle of local proletariats; and, if one decided to see in each affair only an episode of the class struggle, one brought to its politics precisely the kind of support it wanted. Marxist wait and see became communist action. It remained itself only insofar as there was a margin between communism and noncommunism, and this margin was reduced by the state of war. The Korean War has ended, and the Soviet government seems to have become aware of the conditions for a true coexistence. But it remains the case that the United States has rearmed and evolved toward fanaticism, that a politics of peace between it and the Soviet Union has, because of this, become incomparably more difficult. In this situation of force, any initiative from other countries is equivalent to overthrowing alliances, and one must ask oneself whether this would not bring the U.S.S.R. back to a "hard" politics. In short, since the Korean War, all questions have been considered on the level of relationships of force and traditional diplomacy. The formula "Sympathy without adherence" had to be re-examined in a new situation. The Korean War obliged us neither to desire the conquest of the whole country by one of the two armies nor to set the communist and noncommunist worlds face to face like

34. *Ibid.*, p. 202; ET, pp. 184–85.

two blocs between which it was necessary to choose, reducing the entire political problem to this choice; we thought, and we still think, that communism is ambiguous and anticommunism even more so. We thought, and we still think, that a politics founded on anticommunism is in the long run a politics of war and in the short run a politics of regression, that there are many ways of not being communist, and that the problem has barely been taken up when one has said that one is not a communist. But the critique of anticommunism in a situation of force is distinct from adherence to communism only if it places itself unequivocally outside communism. The choice was never between "being communist" and "being anticommunist," but, *on the other hand, it was necessary to know whether one was communist or not.* The polemic against anticommunism remained independent only if it also attacked cryptocommunism. The struggle against these opposites, which live off each other, was a single struggle. Wait-and-see Marxism had been a position just after the war because it had objective conditions: those neutral zones throughout the world, in Czechoslovakia, in Korea, where the two actions had a pact. Since these zones were disappearing, wait-and-see Marxism was for us nothing more than a dream, and a dubious dream. It was necessary to emphasize that independence in itself situated us outside communism. One could no longer be satisfied with not choosing: in the perspective of war, to put it clearly, the refusal to choose becomes the choice of a double refusal. Such are, it seems to us, the obligations of commitment.

But was it only a concession to practical realities? Could we keep on the level of thought the same favorable prejudice toward a Marxist philosophy of history? Or did the episode have the value of an experience, from which, even on the theoretical level, one must draw the consequences? Could we continue thinking that, after all reservations had been made with respect to the Soviet solutions, the Marxist dialectic remained negatively valid and that history should be focused, if not on the proletariat's power, at least on its lack of it? We do not want to present as a syllogism what gradually became clear to us in contact with events. But the event was the occasion of a growing awareness and not at all one of those accidents that upsets without enlightening. The Korean War and its consequences confronted us with a condition of history from which the postwar years had only apparently freed us. It recalled to us the identity of practice and theory; it made us remember that even the refusal to choose must, to be considered a political position, become a thesis and form its own platform, and that the double truth ceases to be duplicity and complicity only when it is avowed and formulated unequivocally, even in its practical consequences. To say, as we did, that Marxism remains true as a critique or negation without being true as an action or positively was to place ourselves outside history, and particularly outside Marxism, was to justify it for reasons which are not its own, and, finally, was to organize equivocalness. In history, Marxist critique and Marxist action are a single movement. Not that the critique of the present derives as a corollary from perspectives of the future—Marxism is not a utopia—but because, on the contrary, communist action is in principle only the critique continued, carried to its final consequences, and because, finally, revolution is the critique in power. If one verifies that it does not keep the promises of the critique, one cannot conclude from that: let us keep the critique and forget the action. There must be something in the critique itself that germinates the defects in the action. We found this ferment in the Marxist idea of a critique historically embodied, of a class which is the *suppression of itself*, which, in its representatives, results in the conviction of being the universal in action, in the right to assert oneself without restriction, and in unverifiable violence. It is the certitude of judging history in the name of history, of saying nothing that history itself does not say, of passing on the present a judgment which is inscribed in it, of expressing in words and ideas pre-existing relationships such as they are in things; in short, it is materialism that, in the guise of modesty, makes the Marxist critique a dogma and prevents it from being self-criticism. It is therefore quite impossible to cut communism in two, to say that it is right in what it negates and wrong in what it asserts: for its way of asserting is already concretely present in its way of negating; in its critique of capitalism there is already, as we have said, not a utopian representation of the future, but at least the absolute of a negation, or negation realized, the *classless* society called for by history. However things may appear from this perspective, the defects of capitalism remain defects; but the critique which denounces them must be freed from any compromise with an absolute of the negation which, in the long run, is germinating new oppressions. The Marxist critique must therefore be taken up again, re-exposed completely, and generalized, and we were speaking abstractly when we said that Marxism "remains true as a negation." We said that perhaps no proletariat would come to play the role of ruling class that Marxism assigns it but that it is true that no other class can replace it in that role and that, in this sense, the failure of Marxism would be the failure of philosophy of history. This in itself shows well enough that we were not on the terrain of history (and of Marxism) but on that of the *a priori* and of morality. We meant to say that all societies which tolerate the existence of a proletariat are unjustifiable. This does not mean that they are all of equal worth and worth nothing or that there is no meaning in the history which produces them one after the other. This Marxism which remains true whatever it does, which does without proofs and verifications, is not a philosophy of history—it is Kant in disguise, and it is Kant again that we ultimately find in the concept of revolution as absolute action. The events which obliged us to consider from outside, "objectively," our wait-and-see Marxism estranged us in the end only from a Marxism of internal life.

"AND SO YOU RENOUNCE being a revolutionary, you accept the social distance which transforms into venial sins exploitation, poverty, famine. . . ."

"I accept it neither more nor less than you do. Yesterday a communist wrote: 'There will be no more October 17s.' Today Sartre says that the dialectic is twaddle. One of my Marxist friends says that Bolshevism has already ruined the revolution and that it must be replaced with the masses' unpredictable ingenuity. To be revolutionary today is to accept a State of which one knows very little or to rely upon a historical grace of which one knows even less; and even that would not be without misery and tears. Is it then cheating to ask to inspect the dice?"

"*Objectively* you accept poverty and exploitation, since you do not join with those who reject it unconditionally."

"They say they reject it, they believe they reject it. But do they reject it *objectively*? And if they reply that the object is unknowable or formless, that truth is what the most miserable want, we must reply that no one has gotten rid of poverty by hailing the revolution. It does not require only our good will and our choice but our knowledge, our labor, our criticism, our preference, and our complete presence. Revolution today does not want any of this."

"Here it is, this terrible maturity which made Man, Mussolini, and so many others move from 'verbal international socialism' to 'lived national socialism.'"

"Those people wanted to rule, and, as is appropriate in that case, they appealed to darker passions. Nothing like this threatens us, and we would be happy if we could inspire a few—or many —to bear their freedom, not to exchange it at a loss; for it is not only their own thing, their secret, their pleasure, their salvation —it involves everyone else."

July, 1953
April–December, 1954

Index